Tolley's Tax Investigations

Second Edition

by

Peter Howarth AIIT,
formerly one of HM Inspectors of Taxes

Peter.J.Howarth@btinternet.com

Tolley
LexisNexis

Members of the LexisNexis Group worldwide

United Kingdom	Butterworths Tolley, a Division of Reed Elsevier (UK) Ltd, Halsbury House, 35 Chancery Lane, LONDON, WC2A 1EL, and 4 Hill Street, EDINBURGH EH2 3JZ
Argentina	Abeledo Perrot, Jurisprudencia Argentina and Depalma, BUENOS AIRES
Australia	Butterworths, a Division of Reed International Books Australia Pty Ltd, CHATSWOOD, New South Wales
Austria	ARD Betriebsdienst and Verlag Orac, VIENNA
Canada	Butterworths Canada Ltd, MARKHAM, Ontario
Chile	Publitecsa and Conosur Ltda, SANTIAGO DE CHILE
Czech Republic	Orac sro, PRAGUE
France	Editions du Juris-Classeur SA, PARIS
Hong Kong	Butterworths Asia (Hong Kong), HONG KONG
Hungary	Hvg Orac, BUDAPEST
India	Butterworths India, NEW DELHI
Ireland	Butterworths (Ireland) Ltd, DUBLIN
Italy	Giuffré, MILAN
Malaysia	Malayan Law Journal Sdn Bhd, KUALA LUMPUR
New Zealand	Butterworths of New Zealand, WELLINGTON
Poland	Wydawnictwa Prawnicze PWN, WARSAW
Singapore	Butterworths Asia, SINGAPORE
South Africa	Butterworths Publishers (Pty) Ltd, DURBAN
Switzerland	Stämpfli Verlag AG, BERNE
USA	LexisNexis, DAYTON, Ohio

A CIP Catalogue record for this book is available from the British Library.

First published in 2000

ISBN 0 75451 212 6

Typeset by Phoenix Photosetting, Chatham, Kent
Printed and bound in Great Britain by the Cromwell Press, Trowbridge, Wiltshire

Visit Butterworths LexisNexis *direct* at www.butterworths.com

Preface

I am flattered to have been asked to produce a second edition of this work but also relieved. It has been difficult trying to judge the level of the required content, but it seems we are about right.

This edition introduces new material on:

- The prevention of investigations
- Provision of information following the European Union Savings Directive
- Finance Act 2001
- Human Rights
- Case law relating to third party information powers and legal privilege
- Common profit margins

It has expanded and improved the material on:

- Meetings with the Revenue
- Disclosure of tax irregularities
- Revenue powers
- Client relationships
- Money laundering
- Statements of assets
- PAYE and NIC

The coming year will bring further changes, probably not so much from legislation but from Revenue practice and tribunal decisions on self assessment issues; my appetite for a third edition is already whetted.

The theme of this book remains as one for the non-specialist general practitioner who has no desire to be an investigation expert but whose daily life inevitably brings him into contact with the Revenue and whose clients first look to for guidance at a stressful time. This book helps such a practitioner cope with conflict situations; it equips him to deal with most matters himself, with confidence, and helps him decide when to call in specialist help; it helps him retain his clients confidence and so protects his business.

I have retained the theme of assuming little or no knowledge of any subject by the reader. Hopefully this will not cause offence, especially as this book is also for the non-accountant tax specialist who may also come across tax investigation work in his day-to-day life.

Preface

I have tried to write a simple, understandable and readable work on tax investigations. This book is not for the tax investigation expert, who should be familiar with its contents. The aim is to have a practical guide that helps you decide the best course of action to take for your client. I have tried to avoid the mere repetition of the statutes but it is sometimes unavoidable when looking at a piece of legislation. I hope you will use it as a quick guide. The contents really come from my view of what you need. Such views having been formed from the many questions put to me at seminars and at the many informal meetings I have with general practitioners during the 30 years, or so, I have now been involved in tax investigation work. In that time I have been involved in countless investigations on both sides of the investigation fence, and now share some of that experience with you. I am sure you will continue to let me know your views, send them to me at Peter.J.Howarth@btinternet.com

It should be noted that the word 'enquiry' is used in the legislation, not 'investigation'. This appears to be an attempt to use less emotive language; however, my thesaurus suggests the word investigation as an alternative to enquiry. It should perhaps be remembered that the Inland Revenue have previously referred to investigations as enquiries. Inspectors of Taxes from the 1970s and earlier will recall the term 'Back Duty Settlement' to describe the conclusion of an investigation, and having to record the fact that they had commenced an investigation in the Back Duty Enquiry Note Book. Let us also not forget that the Revenue's serious fraud office, now called the Special Compliance Office, was once referred to as Enquiry Branch.

I have referred to 'enquiries' as investigations in this book.

The legislation governing investigations used to refer to Inspectors of Taxes, indeed it still does, but new legislation changes him to an 'officer of the Board'. I have found this phrase tedious and so have continued to use the word 'Inspector' whenever I refer to the man, or lady, from the tax office.

On the subject of gender, I did set out by writing 'his or her' every time. This was irksome so I have stuck with the masculine: I hope female readers will not be offended.

I must, of course, thank all those who have made it possible for me to complete this second edition. First mention must go to my family; especially my wife Bernadette for her continued encouragement. I must acknowledge my former colleague, Andrew Stephenson, for his assistance with the VAT content of the Appendix. My thanks also to all those who commented on the first edition, both positive and negative, it has all been welcome and useful. Finally my gratitude to the Tolley team assigned to this task for their advice and support.

Peter Howarth
September 2001

Contents

Table of Statutes

Table of Statutory Instruments

Table of Cases

Chapter 1

Introduction

1.1 Tax investigations are a serious business. The Inland Revenue are committed to applying more of their resources to what they term 'compliance'. They have considerable powers at their disposal to assist in their investigations of accounts and tax returns and they do not shirk from exploring the boundaries of these powers. They constantly ask Parliament for new or extended powers and these are usually granted. The Inland Revenue investigator is well trained and will stick to the task of the investigation with some determination. He is not easily shaken off.

At present clients are potentially faced with two investigations, one by the Inland Revenue concerning direct taxation matters and another by H M Customs & Excise with respect to VAT matters or other indirect duties such as landfill tax or betting duty for example. Agreeing figures with one of the Revenue authorities does not guarantee acceptance of the same figures by the other. This book does not look at income tax and corporation tax in isolation; it considers how investigations interact with other taxes (Chapter 11).

Self-assessment both for individuals and companies has brought with it new problems for the practitioner, and indeed for the Inland Revenue, and it will take a few years for this system to bed down and for the new legislation to become familiar. Self-assessment has also brought with it new information-gathering powers and some procedural changes that can confuse those of us who have been involved in tax investigation work for many years; this includes experienced inspectors of taxes.

A self-assessment 'enquiry' can be one of two types. It may be what is referred to as an 'aspect' enquiry. This will deal with just one or two points that the Revenue may want to check. A typical example may be for the Revenue to ask for evidence of pension contributions paid or for a copy of the capital gains tax computation. Employees are most likely to experience one of these, probably on a random basis. These are not what I would call an investigation but 'full' enquiries are. Full enquiries will call for the accounts of a business and its underlying books and records; these are the cases dealt with in this book. The self-employed and company directors are the ones most likely to fall victim to these. It is of course possible for an 'aspect' case to be upgraded to a 'full' case if the Revenue become concerned during its course.

The other investigation likely to be faced by a business is the PAYE one. These are a real danger area. There are close to 1,000 different rules relating to the operation of PAYE and National Insurance and so it is easy to get something wrong. Not only will this cost a client money in itself but it is likely to lead to the Revenue starting a full investigation into the accounts of the business. Chapter 14 takes a long hard look at PAYE/NIC problems.

Companies and partnerships are more complex than sole traders and there are technical differences in the way investigations are commenced into these. Company investigations in particular give rise to different liability issues such as who is liable? Is it the company or the directors? Chapter 12 deals with this subject.

All of these issues are examined and fully debated in the course of the book.

1.2 This book will take you through the field of investigation work starting with a look at why certain cases are targeted and selected for investigation in the first place, right through an investigation itself to the negotiation of a settlement. A detailed look is taken at the powers that an inspector of taxes has and what your defences to the use of these powers may be (Chapter 7).

We start by considering the criteria from which an inspector decides to commence an investigation. The author reveals where the Revenue's information comes from together with how it is processed and presents his top ten reasons why your clients are investigated (Chapter 2). He also gives an insight into who the inspector is and how he is trained.

The vexed subject of meetings, or interviews, with the Revenue is examined in Chapter 5 with a thorough guide to the thought process that should be gone through when deciding to attend one or not. And, importantly, how you and your client should conduct yourselves in the meeting should you decide to agree to one.

Chapter 6 provides useful and practical guidance on mounting a challenge against the inspector's proposals for additional profits and discusses the standard of evidence needed. Looking at penalty negotiations in Chapter 15 follows this up.

With an aggressive prosecution policy in place care must be taken if you have a client who wants to disclose problems to the Revenue; advice can be found in Chapter 10.

Handling a tax investigation

1.3 The skills that are needed to handle tax investigation work effectively should not be underestimated. It has been said that tax investigation work has little to do with tax. There is an element of truth in this, but good tax knowledge is essential as will be demonstrated throughout this book. So what skills are needed?

Tax expert. Obviously it is necessary to be able to apply the tax code to the eventual figure to be taxed, but the need for technical proficiency is much more serious than that. If you are about to argue that a deposit in a bank account was a gift, have you stopped to consider if it is still taxable on the recipient? Will the VAT consequences be detrimental to your client? Are you agreeing the correct taxation principles in any event?

Accountant. The profits to be taxed are those arrived at using commercial accountancy principles. It is therefore necessary to know what those principles are and to apply them. Tax investigation work also involves looking at books and records and using information from them. It involves carrying out cash flow tests as well as, in some cases, actually preparing a set of accounts.

Lawyer. A basic knowledge of contract law will prove most useful during many an investigation, not least to enable you to explain what the letter of offer in settlement really means to your client. Property deals will be encountered frequently as will unlawful and illegal transactions. It is vital to understand the standards of evidence needed in a tax appeal.

Team leader. A modern-day tax investigation will often call for the needs of professionals with different skills. The need for the accountant and tax adviser is obvious but others may also be needed:

- A solicitor may be required to advise on a legal point e.g. is a trust deed valid?
- A barrister may be needed for an opinion on a technical point of law.
- A valuer may be wanted to give a view on the value of an asset.

The list of possibilities is endless but you will need to know whom to call in, and when. You will need to co-ordinate their activities. You require the skills needed to lead a team.

Negotiator. Very few tax investigations are black and white. If a client has omitted some bank interest then the figure to be taxed is fixed and there will be little, if any, scope for negotiation with the inspector of taxes. In most cases you will be faced with establishing a best estimate of omitted income. The inspector will have his views, the client will have his own view, but you will need to form your own view and negotiate its acceptance by the inspector. After that you will need to negotiate the settlement. That may include the level of the penalty loading, mitigation of interest, the number of 'back years' to be included and the time over which the settlement can be paid. Do not forget that the usual rules of negotiation do not always apply. Unlike in the commercial world, where both sides must be able to profit from a negotiation and, once one party sees that there is no profit for him the deal will fail, the client in a tax investigation does not have a real option of withdrawing (other than deciding to flee the country and even that may not work). The inspector gains little from the case personally: he will still get paid the same salary next month whether he agrees with you or not. He will be under some pressure to meet his targets, but unless he is getting to desperation stage with those, it will make no difference to his world.

Mediator. A tax investigation is a stressful time for a client. It will go on for quite some time and it is likely to end up with him having to pay something to the Revenue. The client will feel that his honesty is being challenged and will want things settled. Inspectors are doing their everyday job and often have no, or little, idea of the real impact an investigation is causing. They will overcome refusals to co-operate. Threats of complaints will only make them more determined to carry on and find something to justify their actions. You need to ensure that the inspector continues to respect you as a professional, but at the same time you need to ensure your client maintains his confidence in you. It is all too easy, at times, to seem as if you may be on the inspector's side against the client. Equally, you may be tempted to try and present your client's case a little too favourably and destroy the trust the inspector has in you.

Advocate. You cannot possibly agree with the inspector of taxes all of the time and there will be times when your powers of persuasion have no effect on him. On these occasions you could end up in front of an appeal tribunal. You will need to be aware of the rules of evidence, the rules of procedure and how to behave in the hearing. You will need to present evidence, examine and cross-examine witnesses and argue how the law should be applied to the facts.

The inspector

1.4 Many clients, and indeed accountants, often regard the inspector as a bureaucrat with little or no ambition, a person who has no appreciation of business life. To have such an attitude is a mistake that could cost your client dearly. An inspector of taxes is a professional who is well trained and intelligent; he should not be underestimated. Francis Bacon (1561–1626) said 'for knowledge itself is power'; it is therefore useful to have some knowledge of the person you are dealing with. Some may say the 'enemy', but again this may be the wrong attitude. The least stressful investigations, and the best results usually obtained, are those in which there is a spirit of working with the inspector to find the correct answer, as opposed to conflict for the sake of it.

Inspectors are recruited directly from university but it is possible to be promoted from the clerical ranks.

The graduate entrant is fast tracked to become what we would commonly refer to as a senior inspector. His intelligence and academic qualities are obvious from the fact that he is a graduate; there are also a number of Oxford and Cambridge graduates amongst these. The Revenue have consistently recruited good quality graduates who are attracted by the complex and challenging job, perhaps encouraged by Einstein who thought tax was more difficult than physics, because in physics everything behaves to set rules that never change!

He receives intensive training over a number of years from a structured course with examinations at various stages requiring a very high pass mark. This is accompanied by desk training in the office under the watchful eye of experienced and qualified inspectors.

This training covers taxation law, the interpretation of this by the courts and Revenue practice. There is training on investigation techniques, interviewing and conducting appeal hearings. The Revenue refer to this as 'professional training'.

These inspectors will usually become officers in charge of an office (frequently referred to as the district inspector) and could become specialists in a head office division. You may come across him in smaller investigations whilst he is undergoing his training programme and later during the course of investigations into larger companies.

Those selected from the clerical grades would typically have been in that grade for a few years and displayed the skills needed to complete the course and do the job of an inspector. They would, in the main, be selected for a shorter inspector training course with the emphasis on accounts investigation. They are not trained in the full range of tax law in the same way as the fully-trained inspector on the professional course. These are the inspectors you are likely to encounter in most investigations, especially non-company ones, and they will be of varying technical ability. You should therefore consider any technical argument they put forward critically, as they may not have a deep knowledge of the subject.

Chapter 2

The Causes of an Investigation and Preventative Measures

Summary of chapter

2.1 This chapter looks at some of the common reasons why investigations commence and preventative measures:

- the sources of information available to an inspector, i.e. banks, property transactions, H M Customs and Excise, informers, and the returns of other businesses;
- the use of business ratios used by the Revenue in planning their investigation programme, i.e. gross profit margins, profitability, stock ratios, debtors and creditors, liquidity, return on capital, wages;
- the work of the Revenue's intelligence officers;
- the data used to consider if drawings are adequate;
- why PAYE compliance is so important to avoid being investigated;
- the role of technical accountancy and tax matters as triggers for investigations;
- how the choice of agent can cause problems;
- how an investigation may be a random selection;
- what agents can do to help prevent an investigation.

The top ten causes of investigations

2.2 A client can now be selected for investigation on a purely random basis but the Revenue's experience is that random selections do not produce good results and so the majority of cases taken up will be the result of some form of targeting. There is little, in fact nothing, you can do to prevent a client from being selected at random but there is much that can be done to reduce the risk of him being selected on a review of his tax return or accounts.

2.3 To make their targeting effective the Revenue has developed a programme that scans some 500 differing factors for each business and allocates a weighted score to each one. The result is an overall risk assessment score and, rather obviously, the higher the risk score the greater the chance of investigation. The factors are clearly many and varied and includes the more obvious high and low gross margins, absence of a balance sheet and drawings. It monitors ratios and contains data covering three years so variations from year to year can be spotted as well as deviations from the norm for the industry sector.

2.4 The accountant's role in defending his client from an attack by the tax authorities begins well before any tax returns or accounts are ever delivered. It starts with educating clients in the keeping of accurate records. It continues by reviewing the results the accounts show, not just the net profit but also other factors such as business ratios. Doing this will alert you to possible bookkeeping errors, or mis-postings and accounting errors and so give an opportunity to ensure accounts are correct before any information is ever given to the Revenue. It may of course be that your client is deliberately omitting transactions from his records. If you alert him to the fact that this is being indicated by his accounts it may persuade him to stop; many clients do believe that getting their books past their accountant is sufficient to prevent an investigation.

2.5 Providing extra information when submitting the self-assessment return can help to prevent a client being selected for investigation. If a particular risk arises from an exceptional item alerting the Inspector to this could make him decide to pass on to the next case and leave yours alone. The Revenue prefer their enquiries to result in extra tax becoming payable and so Inspectors are looking for 'winners'. If he has a choice of two cases to investigate and one gives possible explanations for a high score and the other does not then he may decide not to gamble on yours!

2.6 It is therefore important to ensure that when submitting a return sufficient information is given to permit the Inspector to decide if he is to make an enquiry or accept the return.

If a ratio has changed significantly and you are aware of a valid reason why this should be then making a note of this on the return could help your client. If drawings are low but there has been another source of funds then alert the Inspector.

It is not desirable for reams of paper and explanations to be supplied with returns in the hope that the Inspector cannot be bothered to search through it all. The Revenue has in fact warned against this. In a Press Release of 31 May 1996 they say:

> 'Taxpayers and agents should be aware that the submission of accounts and computations or other documents may not provide protection . . . there may be so much material that the Revenue officer "could not have been reasonably expected, on the basis of the information made available to him" . . . be aware . . . Where voluminous information beyond the accounts and

computations is sent in with the return, therefore, it is recommended that there should be a brief indication of the relevance of the material.'

Information to go with a return is discussed in more detail in Chapter 3.

Some knowledge of the main causes of investigations is necessary to give your clients this service: so what does attract the attention of the inspector of taxes? What makes him select a case for investigation? The causes can be many and varied. My top ten are as follows.

1. Information held

2.7 In the good old days, when inspectors of taxes had to say why they had opened an investigation, a letter from an inspector of taxes would often read something like 'information in my possession suggests that your client's tax returns may be incomplete'. Information flows to the inspector of taxes from various sources but common ones could be as follows:

Banks

2.8 A bank, or any other payer of interest, has to provide the Revenue with details of interest paid when required to do so by an inspector of taxes. [*TMA 1970, ss 17, 18*]. The workings of *TMA 1970, ss 17, 18* will rarely, if ever, trouble a general practitioner and so are not examined here in any greater detail. In practice the Revenue usually ask for interest details annually but provide the banks with a *de minimis* limit under which no return needs to be made.

The details provided by the banks are collated and distributed to tax offices throughout the country to be checked against tax returns that have been submitted. An omission of interest frequently brings to light deposit accounts that have been hidden from the Revenue because they contain previously undisclosed taxable income and so a full investigation commences.

2.9 The Inland Revenue cannot require an offshore bank to provide details of interest on their customers' accounts and so the attractions of an offshore deposit account for those wanting to hide a pot of money from the UK Revenue authorities becomes obvious. The European Union Savings Directive starts to change this however. Following suggestions from the UK the EU has proposed that from 2003 all EU member states must have legislation that requires their financial institutions to disclose details of interest paid to a non-resident individual. That information will then be exchanged. Each country will be able to choose if it will have a withholding tax or exchange details, but within seven years must introduce disclosure rules (at present it seems that Austria, Belgium, Luxembourg, Greece and Portugal will stick with a withholding tax). There is plenty of time for things to be changed but it is already happening.

This is not confined to the EU. Some countries already provide such details and pressure is on others to join in, especially the offshore Islands [Channel Islands and the Isle of Man] and we can expect others to join the list soon.

The UK has already introduced disclosure rules effective from 6 April 2001 (FA 2000) and expects to receive details from:

EU Countries

Denmark

Finland

France

Italy

Spain

Sweden

Non-EU Countries

Australia

Canada

Japan

South Korea

New Zealand

Norway

USA

Others will be added to the list as they introduce legislation or make reciprocal arrangements.

It is likely to be a couple of years before you see many investigations arising out of interest information from on offshore account.

2.10 It would be rare indeed for the investigating inspector to disclose his hand by revealing the fact that he knows of an account, but if he does go that far it is highly unlikely he would reveal the identity of the bank he is aware of. All inspectors of taxes, and many practitioners, will have their own individual tales to tell concerning investigations arising from a return of interest by a bank. In one case in which the author was involved, a client revealed 15 different accounts when challenged by the Inland Revenue, with £10,000 in each one.

Assuming that at some point the inspector does at least reveal that he has information relating to a suspected undisclosed bank account, it should not be assumed that the information being held is absolutely correct, although the author has only ever come across incorrect information given by a bank twice in nearly 30 years.

2.11 This source of information is common to all investigations, be they individuals, partnerships or companies. They can be triggered by the accountant netting off interest received against interest paid and so the inspector jumps to the conclusion that an account is omitted. This provides a good example of the problems that can now be caused by inspectors not having to give reasons for their investigation. If he said it was because he believed an account was omitted an explanation could be given immediately and the case closed. It also illustrates how the accountant can unwittingly be the cause of his clients' problem.

Property transactions

2.12 Virtually every property transaction that takes place within the United Kingdom incurs stamp duty and so has particulars of the transaction delivered to the Land Registry. It should be noted that the Inland Revenue administers stamp duty and so becomes aware of virtually all property transactions that take place within the United Kingdom. Such information can find its way to the inspector of taxes' desk and can reveal a great deal of information. He will become aware of the amount of the transaction, details of the vendor and the purchaser and the identity of their respective solicitors.

Such information has sometimes led the Revenue to uncover undisclosed assets that existed in previous investigations but were not revealed at the time. It may also give rise to intelligence relating to omissions of capital gains and would probably give rise to suspicions that resources for a purchase came from a source that a client may not wish the inspector to discover. It also leads inspectors to check where the proceeds of a sale may have been invested because he may think it odd that a substantial sum of money has been received for the disposal of a property yet sees no investment income on the following year's tax return. If there has been a property disposal and no subsequent investment income it may be worth putting a note of why this is so on the next tax return. Needless to say, it may also reveal a previous failure to disclose rental income that has been received.

It was once the case that the tax office network would receive such details automatically in all cases where particulars were delivered to the Stamp Office, but the author has received conflicting stories from current serving inspectors of taxes. Some say that these details are no longer provided to them, others say that they do see them on occasions. Whatever the case, information is clearly going into the vaults of the Inland Revenue department and it would be surprising if they did not use that information in some way.

You can help your client by thinking intelligently about information on returns. If there has been rental income on a return in previous years and it suddenly ends, or is reduced, do you know why?

2. H M Customs & Excise

2.13 It seems a bit odd to many people that there are two revenue-collecting agencies and indeed there has been talk about the possible merger of the Inland Revenue and H M Customs & Excise, in particular in relation to value added tax (VAT) matters, at some point in the future. H M Customs & Excise has a programme of checking VAT returns and visiting traders on a regular basis. Their computers are also programmed to spot anomalies in VAT returns and report them to the local VAT office network for checking.

In the course of his day-to-day activities the VAT man does therefore come across information that is of interest to the Inland Revenue, and indeed vice versa. Legislation [*FA 1972, s 127*] permits both departments to exchange information with each other and although the extent of this exchange does appear to vary from region to region there is no doubt that it does happen. See also Revenue Investigation Handbook, IH 1280–1283.

In some areas of the country it is known that inspectors of taxes and VAT officers have regular meetings to swap notes and indeed in some towns the joint working of a case has been known. In practice, such joint working has been welcomed by practitioners and their clients because it does save time and costs and avoids the situation in which one department has negotiated a settlement but the other refuses to agree on the same basis and so a fresh investigation commences. In the author's experience it is usually the Revenue who refuse to accept the figures agreed with Customs & Excise; Customs frequently accept figures agreed with an inspector of taxes.

You should assume that details of an investigation by one department would be given to the other.

3. Informers

2.14 To some this is a rather strange distasteful area. It is however one that is on the increase and most certainly the Revenue do appear to be willing to act upon informers' information far more readily that was historically the case.

Very often an informant's information is useless to an investigating inspector. An anonymous letter that simply identifies a person as 'fiddling' will at best lead the inspector to pick up that person's file and he may notice something that gives him cause to start an enquiry. Other than that it gives absolutely no detail whatsoever and no opportunity for the inspector to go back to the informant for further and better particulars.

The better informers give specific information about what was done, when, where and how much was involved. If they can direct the inspector to where information can be found, especially from a third party, then so much the better. If the informant identifies himself it allows the inspector to explore the accuracy of the information given.

Inspectors are alert to the fact that informers are usually motivated by some desire for revenge. Their information may therefore be mischievous, exaggerated or even misguided. For example, simply because sums were paid in cash does not necessarily mean the cash has been omitted from the business records. The Revenue's policy on informers is set out in their Investigation Handbook at IH 1295.

2.15 The modern enquiry system does not require an inspector to give a reason for his investigation. It is therefore far more likely that the Revenue will act upon an informant's information. However, in the author's opinion, the Revenue should take great care because any enquiry from the Revenue causes stress and professional costs are incurred. It is therefore easy for someone to be mischievous and cause a high degree of distress to someone they have a desire to upset.

Good informants are frequently those who have once been close to the client. Cheated wives, jilted lovers, disgruntled and ex-employees are frequent whistle-blowers. They are often able to give much important detail to an Inspector so enabling him to pinpoint precisely where he needs to look to check the information and also where he may find evidence to prove his case.

If faced with an enquiry for which there is no obvious or apparent reason but in the recent past, say the last one or two years, there has been an upset with someone, then knowing what that person may be able to tell the inspector could give the practitioner vital clues as to the angle the inspector is working from.

2.16 The Revenue will protect the identity of an informer but inspectors are told not to guarantee this. They may be forced by a tribunal to disclose documents, or the identity could be inferred from the information given. The Revenue can pay rewards to informants [*Inland Revenue Information Act 1890, s 32*], but will not commit itself to one. It is apparently *ultra vires* for the Revenue to enter into an agreement to pay a reward because the legislation only gives the Revenue a discretionary power to do so. (*Riach v Lord Advocate 1931 18 TC 18*).

4. Third party information

2.17 In the course of their day-to-day activities tax offices come into possession of a considerable amount of information. It is reported that the Revenue information distribution office (TIDO) is holding 120 million pieces of information! Some of this is deliberately gathered in, other information is the result of enquiries made elsewhere. The Revenue has information-gathering powers to collect details of those who have received income from various sources. The common ones are as follows.

From those who have income belonging to others

2.18 Those in receipt of income that belongs to some other person can be required to provide details by an inspector of taxes [*TMA 1970, s 13*]. The inspector cannot demand information under this section if it relates to a tax year more than three years old. Anybody who supplies the necessary information in another satisfactory format would not normally be required by an inspector to repeat that information under the authority of *section 13*. The Revenue have said that they will be discriminating in the issue of notices to solicitors (see Law Society Gazette, 29 May 1991).

Some people receive income on behalf of someone else. If so they can be required to give details to the Revenue. For the Revenue to require a return they must be aware that someone is in this position otherwise they will not know to ask!

This clearly brings nominees into the arena of potential information providers.

PAYE returns

2.19 Employers are required to provide the Inland Revenue with information and this section is effectively the one under which forms P11D and P9D (on which an employer informs the Revenue of expenses paid and benefits provided to directors and other employees) are obtained advising the Inland Revenue of benefits in kind and expenses payments to employees. [*TMA 1970, s 15*]. The PAYE regulations do of course also require an annual return of emoluments paid to an employee and the tax deducted from these.

A cause of problems can be an inspector having difficulty reconciling the PAYE returns to the wages figures in the accounts.

Fees and commissions

2.20 The inspector can require a return of payments made to others. [*TMA 1970, s 16*]. This is an important power for the inspector and is one under which he issues many notices requiring a list of payments made and the names and addresses of recipients. This section has been strengthened by *FA 2000* to gather information relating to non-residents.

Miscellaneous

2.21 There are some other lesser used information-gathering powers relating to income from property and agency fees but those listed above are the ones that the inspector will routinely issue each year to those who he knows are making payments to others.

The details are distributed throughout the tax office network but some are sent to a central location to be collated and then distributed to the individual's particular tax district. An example would be foreign entertainers and sportsmen whose information is collated by the Special Compliance Office in the Midlands. Other particular trades or professions may also be collated centrally in such a manner and information distributed. An example of this that many practitioners will come across is the Inland Revenue subcontractor scheme. The flow of information to the Revenue's Central Information Collecting Office is distributed thereby giving individual inspectors a note of the income that a subcontractor may have received within the subcontractor scheme.

2.22 As well as these formal routine information-gathering exercises, information is also picked up when dealing with other cases. Many investigations commence from information obtained during the course of an investigation into another person. For example, a fairly common situation would be where someone is caught receiving cash that has not been recorded in his accounting records. He accepts this but explains that much of the cash has been used to make payments to those who have introduced business and the inspector compels him to reveal who these people are and the amounts paid. Because the payments are in cash the inspector, perhaps reasonably, assumes that the recipient will not have declared the receipt and so commences an enquiry into the recipient's affairs.

5. Business ratios

2.23 Inspectors are advised to consider a number of business ratios when examining accounts (see Revenue Investigation Handbook, IH 1900). They are told to look out for ratios that are not in keeping with those found in similar businesses or where the pattern of ratios within the same business changes over the years. Inspectors are also on the lookout for ratios that conflict with each other. Such ratios give the inspector clues as to the possible method of evasion that has taken place and therefore help him to direct his focus into particular areas.

Individual self-assessment returns require standard accounts information to be provided in place of a set of accounts. This information is keyed into the Revenue's computers that can then scan for such ratios and identify returns for enquiry. Such a monitoring system also enables the Revenue to be aware of the current ratios a particular business sector is experiencing from time to time, or from region to region, and can therefore easily spot those businesses whose ratios are out of line with similar businesses in the same area. These are the sorts of cases that are selected for enquiry. Unfortunately, it is unlikely that the inspector will say that an unusual ratio is the reason for the enquiry, thereby denying the practitioner the opportunity to establish why and so satisfy the inspector that, even though the ratio may be an unexpected one, it is correct in this particular client's case. The sort of business ratios that the inspector is looking out for include the following; greater detail on how each one is calculated can be found at Appendix C.

Gross profit rate

2.24 Without doubt this is the one that every practitioner who deals with the Revenue will have come across. The inspector says he has taken a case up for investigation because the gross profit margin is less than expected for a particular trade. See also the Revenue's Investigation Handbook at IH 1905.

Over many years the Revenue have gathered information from industry and commerce from which they have built up an experience of gross profit margins that are likely. They have also monitored the gross profit rates of businesses in a particular town or locality. Each year in setting the District compliance plan a decision may be made to make enquiries on every business of a particular category that has a gross profit margin below a certain level. For example, pubs in Birmingham may be declaring gross profit margins that range between say 28 per cent at the lowest and 60 per cent at the highest with the average being 40 per cent. It may therefore be decided that an enquiry will be made on every pub in Birmingham that submits a return showing a gross profit margin of less than say 38 per cent. It does not of course follow that there is something wrong with those accounts but because the results are below average for the particular trade in that particular area, the inspector feels that there is a risk to the revenue worth exploring.

Gross profit is most likely to figure in the selection of smaller cases where relatively modest amounts have a greater distorting effect on the ratio. Gross profit ratios are only valid when dealing with a business that buys and sells products but other businesses have gross ratios that are used by inspectors. For example taxi drivers are frequently selected for investigation because the ratio of their fuel costs to their takings is below that expected. A manufacturing company may have its production wages ratio as an important factor. Some examples of typical ratios are listed in Appendix O.

Profitability

2.25 This head effectively looks at the net profit of the business as a percentage of the turnover. When dealing with companies it is normal to add back directors' remuneration before carrying out the calculation. In other words the inspector is trying to establish what the proprietor gets out of this business. As with all ratios, he will look at the trend for this particular business over a number of years and will try to take into account other external factors that may have affected matters. See also Revenue Investigation Handbook, IH 1915.

The inspector will also begin to compare one ratio with another. If the gross profit margin has stayed steady or even increased but the net profit margin has declined, it may indicate evasion linked to the expenses of the business rather than the sales of the business.

The inspector is looking to make a judgement: does it seem likely that this person would continue to put in the time and effort to achieve the profitability being shown? For example would a baker continue, year on year, to arise early in the morning and spend his day in a hot bakery to have the worries and hassle that go with running a business simply to generate profits below the wages he could obtain by being an employee?

Stock ratios

2.26 The inspector will look at several ratios relating to stock and work in progress. The ratio of stock to purchases is used to establish a number of days' purchases on hand at the end of the year and the inspector will also look at stock turnover during the year to establish the number of times stock is turned over. The inspector knows that certain industries should have a high stock turnover and in others it would be slower. For example a fresh food retailer would obviously be turning over his stock rapidly where a business with far more durable goods would turn over stock at a much lower rate. See also Revenue Investigation Handbook, IH 1917.

The inspector therefore considers the type of business he is looking at but is able to compare these ratios with other businesses of a similar nature both nationally and in the same locality. He is also looking at the fluctuations and variations with this particular taxpayer as the years go by.

Debtors

2.27 A calculation of debtor days will be done as well as looking at the relationship of creditors to purchases and creditors to stock. See also Revenue Investigation Handbook, IH 1919, 1925.

These will be compared to the industry norm and an investigation could be triggered if there are significant variations.

Liquidity

2.28 The two common ratios, i.e. current ratio and quick ratio, will both be calculated and if the business seems to have been illiquid for a number of years the inspector will wonder what, if anything, has been done to correct the situation. If there appears to be a lack of concern or a lack of action, the inspector may wonder if this is because the proprietor has no particular worries due to the fact that he knows that the accounts do not reflect the true position. See also Revenue Investigation Handbook, IH 1930.

Return on capital

2.29 The inspector is warned to take care when using this to ensure that he puts the correct figures into his calculation. It is therefore likely that he will add back directors' remuneration when dealing with a close company. It is however a difficult ratio for the inspector if he is using it to compare the business with others, because unless all assets are correctly valued, an inaccurate result is obtained. What he may therefore use it for is to establish if anybody in their right mind would continue with an investment that is producing very poor returns because it may indicate that something is missing from the accounts and that the real returns being made are healthier than is apparent from the accounts information. See also Revenue Investigation Handbook, IH 1933.

Wages

2.30 Is the ratio of wages to sales or the amount of sales per head of productive staff sensible? If the result of such an exercise is that staff appear to have plenty of relaxation time the question may be asked why are so many employees retained when a reduced number working at peak efficiency could produce the same results. One answer an inspector of taxes may think applies is that not all sales are recorded. See also Revenue Investigation Handbook, IH 1934. Whilst on the subject of wages, inspectors are likely to check an employee's previous employment history and previous addresses because in the past this has revealed family members being employed and the inclusion of domestic staff on payrolls.

2.31 The inspector will produce a table of the ratios he believes to be useful for the case he is examining. This enables him to see changes and patterns much more easily. See the example below.

Example

2.32

Year End	*31/03/97*	*31/03/98*	*31/03/99*	*31/03/00*	*31/03/01*
Sales (£)	115,000	118,000	123,000	131,000	140,000
Cost of Sales (£)	51,750	50,740	60,270	66,810	70,000
Gross Profit (£)	63,250	67,260	62,730	64,190	70,000
Mark up (%)	122%	132%	104%	96%	100%
Gross Profit (%)	55%	57%	51%	49%	50%
Interest (£)	3,750	3,100	2,900	3,800	4,100
Wages(£)	23,000	23,750	23,900	21,750	21,800
Packaging (£)	750	825	1,475	1,650	1,950
Repairs (£)	450	625	6,750	950	625
Net Profit (£)	25,000	29,000	21,000	28,500	32,000
Drawings (£)	15,000	17,500	25,000	30,000	35,000
F & F Additions (£)	1,100	950	7,500	150	450

This schedule quickly identifies the following:

1. Gross profit percentage is falling. Is there an obvious reason for this?
2. Wages have fallen. Has client found a way to pay off-record to avoid NIC?
3. Packaging costs increased in 1999, at the same time gross profit dropped. Did client start to divert sales this year or was there a change in the way trade was conducted?
4. Repair expenditure in 1999 was high. It coincides with drop in gross profit and increase in packaging. Did something happen in the business? Could the additions be private items?
5. Drawings exceed net profit for the last three years. Is this an indication that sales are understated?

6. Expect the Revenue to argue for a restriction on interest allowable on basis that the overdraft has funded private spending.

6. Level of drawings and capital introduced

2.33 If the drawings the proprietor takes from the business, or director's remuneration in the case of a company, appear insufficient to fund a basic lifestyle, or one that would appear to fit the impression the inspector may already have of the client, that is a factor in selecting a case for an enquiry. It is of course open to much debate as to what is a basic requirement and of course this will vary from region to region as well as from town to town and even from area to area within a town.

The inspector knows what his own income is and can make a judgement based on his own experiences. He may also have regard to statistics such as the *Family Expenditure Survey* published by the Department of Employment. This surveys expenditure habits across a variety of circumstances and so gives likely expenditure figures. A comparison to the national insurance retirement pension may be made in more extreme cases. It is widely accepted that it is difficult to live off the old age pension and so a self-employed person apparently living off a similar, or lesser amount, will attract attention.

The inspector does of course know what other people in the same area are taking to live off and he can therefore compare one business with another. He can also discover from the Revenue's computer records what the average drawings are for a particular profession or business in his area or throughout the country. It may therefore be decided to take up for investigation any accounts for, say, a doctor in a particular area whose drawings are below the average for all doctors in that area.

Before embarking on an enquiry, the inspector will try to establish if other income was available; for example a spouse may be in employment.

The Revenue seem to regard proprietors who draw less than the wages paid to their employees with some suspicion and these cases are therefore likely targets for enquiry. An inspector of taxes may wonder why someone would have the risks attached to self-employment if employment could be found that pays more and without the risks of being in business.

2.34 A frequent cause of an investigation is the appearance of capital introduced into a business. The accounts, or an analysis of the director's loan account reveal this. The inspector will routinely ask for the source of this to be revealed and will press for supporting evidence. Within the last couple of years the author was involved in a case in which £10,000 introduced into an ailing business resulted in an investigation that led to a settlement of £500,000 and another in which £100,000 introduced into a start-up situation led to an investigation settlement of £1,250,000!

7. The intelligence officer

2.35 Once known as the Schedule D compliance officer, the Revenue employee in each district who is given the task of finding information relating to taxpayers in his area is now called the intelligence officer. This probably more accurately describes what this individual does. His task is to try and find those who are not known to the Revenue yet are working, and to find evidence that those who are known to the Revenue may not be fully declaring their income. See also Revenue Enquiry Handbook, EH 219.

The sort of activities that these officers undertake is really only limited by their own imagination but typically may include the following.

(*a*) Scrutiny of local newspapers to find interesting articles relating to businesses. A good example of this sort of activity was the reasonably well-known local entrepreneur who claimed he was not resident in the United Kingdom any more and each year proved this by submitting to his tax office details of the days he had spent in the UK. Unfortunately for him he had attended a high profile wedding that was featured in the local newspaper and he had been photographed. When his statement of days in and out of the UK were submitted, the inspector immediately compared this with the known information and that client now very much regrets having stated he was out of the UK on the day of that wedding.

(*b*) Small advertisements are a useful source of information. Very often these will merely contain telephone numbers but the intelligence officer will establish to whom that number belongs. I suspect this is becoming a less fruitful area for the intelligence officer since the introduction of pay and go mobile telephones. It may not however simply be advertisements by local tradesmen. The author once spent a considerable amount of time attending a meeting at a local tax office with a client who he thought was a farmer. However, as a sideline this farmer had been purchasing damaged, but repairable motor cars, repairing them and then selling them through adverts placed in his local newspaper. The Revenue had spotted numerous advertisements and from this had details of a considerable number of cars he had bought and sold.

(*c*) Much information can also be gleaned simply by observing what is going on in the local area. A drive around the country lanes reveals farmers selling produce at the farm gates. A builder's van in a householder's driveway with building work clearly being undertaken tells the intelligence officer to expect to see some income from a job at that house if that year's tax return is selected for enquiry. A quick look at the records will reveal that there may be an omission. Extensive building work being undertaken, such as a house extension, may be traced to a local trader's home and this may be noted for comparison with the known drawings when the next return is submitted (see Revenue Investigation Handbook, IH 1250).

(*d*) Advertisements in shop windows may also be noted and information fed through to an individual's file for consideration when a return is received.

2.36 Intelligence officers are encouraged to establish informal relationships with those who may be prepared to provide information. This may be with the local authority to provide copies of any licence applications for e.g. street traders, or taxi drivers.

Much of their work may be regarded as snooping and there is the possibility that some of it may cause the Revenue problems under the Human Rights legislation or even under the *Data Protection Act 1984*.

8. The tax compliance record

2.37 There is a definite link between dishonest taxpayers and poor compliance with routine tax obligations.

When one pauses to think about this it really does seem obvious. A good conscientious taxpayer who endeavours to complete tax returns and submit them on time, ensures that his business operates PAYE correctly, submits all the necessary annual returns on time and hands over the monthly, or quarterly, deductions without having to be prompted by the collector of taxes, is more likely to have ensured that the business accounting systems are accurate and reliable and so will have submitted a correct and accurate tax return.

On the other hand those with a cavalier attitude to the completion and submission of tax return forms and those who use the PAYE deductions to supplement their bank borrowings also tend to be the ones who are casual about ensuring that the necessary detailed information is available to produce accurate accounts and tax returns.

It follows therefore that those taxpayers who have a consistently poor compliance record in respect of the timely submission of tax returns and the payment of taxes when due are targeted for enquiries.

When the last Conservative Chancellor announced the 'spend to save' initiative, the Revenue said that a good proportion of the extra money being made available to it was to be applied to PAYE compliance. Finding those with PAYE compliance problems not only nets the Revenue more money from the PAYE scheme but also identifies good targets for full investigations. Accountants are in a good position to stop their clients falling foul of the PAYE rules and so can educate their clients thereby removing yet another potential investigation trigger.

9. Technical matters

2.38 Technical matters are more likely to give rise to an 'aspect' enquiry but these can so easily turn into full investigations.

An unexpected or unusually large debit in the profit and loss account is always likely to attract the inspector's attention and one may therefore expect him to make an enquiry. If lucky he may confine this to an aspect enquiry relating to that particular item but that cannot be guaranteed.

A common example would be a large repairs debit. With one of these the inspector senses that some or all of the expenditure may be of a capital nature.

Enquiries about stock and stock valuations may arise and the inclusion of provisions or reserves are always likely to create some correspondence.

On the subject of provisions it does seem that some practitioners are not aware of FRS 12, which requires some significant disclosures in accounts relating to reserves (an FRS is a Financial Reporting Standard).

FRS 12 would not of course apply to an unincorporated business but reserves and provisions are just as likely to be made in their accounts as in a limited company's.

Directors' loan accounts

2.39 Overdrawn directors' loan accounts attract liability under *ICTA 1988, s 419* and the failure to declare such liability on the corporation tax self-assessment return is likely to give rise to an enquiry.

Overdrawn directors' loan accounts have been problematic for accountants over the years because they can create a double tax charge; as well as a *section 419* liability an individual liability may also arise on the director under *ICTA 1988, s 160* (tax on beneficial loans).

In the past it was frequently found that loan accounts were hidden in trade debtors. This is of course incorrect in terms of accounting standards and those accountants who persist may find their clients the subject of Revenue enquiries.

Failure to notify

2.40 *TMA 1970* places an onus on everyone liable to pay tax to notify the inspector of taxes. Those who do not notify commit an offence and are subject to penalties (see 3.6 below). When discovered and returns brought up to date, such offenders are likely to find their returns the subject of an enquiry.

Private adjustments

2.41 Some items posted to the profit and loss account are not wholly business items but have some private use also. Good examples are motoring expenses, telephone costs and in some circumstances, heat and light bills.

2.42 Recent experience in the author's office has been of a marked increase in cases in which virtually the only issue was the extent of the private adjustment. It seems that Inspector's are responding to the demand for more enquiries by going for easy adjustments. Rarely is it found that the accountant has reviewed these and has been using the same fraction for many, many years, the origin of fractions used is usually lost in the mists of time. Some reasonably sized settlements have been seen, one in the region of £12,000.

Our clients are supposed to keep sufficient records to enable an accurate tax return to be prepared. This means the private adjustments also so apart from the taxman's attentions we may have a disgruntled client if he hasn't been advised. This is an area that accountants can address quite easily and so help avoid problems for clients, and themselves.

10. The accountant

2.43 Some accountants have developed a poor reputation for the standard of their work. Accounts and tax returns submitted by such an agent may be selected for enquiry—the fact that this agent is involved being a factor in the inspector's decision.

The revenue adjudicator makes frequent reference to the work of incompetent accountants in her annual report and calls for tax advisers to be regulated to protect the public, and the Revenue, from them.

Giving reasons

2.44 A few years ago the inspector had to say why he had selected a case for investigation and he frequently found himself in arguments over the basis for his reason. This at least had the advantage of being able to focus one's mind on what was causing the inspector some concern and so enabled resources to be directed effectively to properly defend a client under suspicion.

The modern legislation no longer demands the inspector has a reason for making an enquiry and the Inland Revenue have said that their inspectors will not give reasons (see Revenue Enquiry handbook, EH 302; note that this applies to self-assessment enquiries but not if the Revenue open a case under the 'discovery' provisions (see 3.17 below)). This may be useful for the Inland Revenue in that 'fishing expeditions' can be undertaken without the agent being aware of that fact. Given the huge variety of possible reasons why a case may have been selected for an enquiry, it is impossible for the agent to effectively direct resources. Carrying out the sort of reviews that are outlined above may provide some clues but it does make for a more confrontational system.

That is the complete opposite of the stated aim of the Revenue who believe that not giving reasons makes enquiries less confrontational. A survey of practitioners (Lathams Tax Investigations/AccountingWeb survey 2000) revealed that an enquiry without a stated reason is a source of dissatisfaction with the self-assessment system, but until the Board of Inland Revenue instruct their inspectors to give reasons or the Revenue are forced to by a change in legislation the fact is that in the vast majority of cases the practitioner will not know why the inspector has chosen a particular client.

Main points for investigation prevention

1. Advise clients on keeping accurate records
2. Ensure private use adjustments are reasonably accurate and reviewed from time to time
3. Review accounts results for variations
4. Be aware of causes of investigations
5. Provide additional information with tax returns to explain variations
6. Apply intelligence to tax return entries
7. Advise clients on the importance of good compliance with PAYE
8. Keep your own knowledge fresh and up to date
9. Ensure accounts comply with commercial standards

Chapter 3

Opening an Investigation

Summary of chapter

3.1 This chapter looks at the following:

- the legislative background to investigations;
- the modern self-assessment procedures (with a brief comment on the regime prior to self-assessment);
- the process from the requirement to notify the Revenue of a tax liability and the making of tax returns;
- 'repairing' or correcting returns;
- the time limits within which the Revenue can start an 'enquiry' and the Revenue's ability to 'discover' that closed years are wrong and need reopening; and
- the prospects, and procedures, for stopping an enquiry.

Pre-self-assessment (pre-1996/97 for income tax; pre-1 July 1999 for corporation tax)

3.2 Self-assessment has changed the administration of the tax system quite significantly. Before its introduction the Inland Revenue spent most of their time using information provided on tax returns to calculate assessments and then put more resources into making an assessment and collecting the tax demanded. Although the system has now changed it is still possible that some investigations will commence into those earlier years not covered by the new legislation. This would be particularly relevant to companies who only came into the new legislation for accounting periods ending on or after 1 July 1999.

3.3 The scheme of things prior to self-assessment was reasonably straightforward. If a tax return had not been received for completion, and a person had a liability to pay tax, there was a statutory obligation to advise an inspector of taxes within a certain time limit, these being:

- *Income tax.* 12 months following the end of the year of assessment in which the liability arose (e.g. if there was income taxable in the tax year

1992/93 the inspector of taxes had to be notified by 5 April 1994). [*TMA 1970, s 7* as originally enacted].

- *Corporation tax.* 12 months from the end of any accounting period in which liability arose (e.g. if a company had profits in an accounting period that ended on 31 December 1994 it was obliged to advise the inspector by 31 December 1995). [*TMA 1970, s 8*].
- *Capital gains tax.* 12 months following the end of the year of assessment in which the liability arose (e.g. if there were capital gains taxable for the tax year 1992/93 the inspector of taxes had to be notified by 5 April 1994). [*TMA 1970, s 11A*].

Once the inspector of taxes was aware there was liability he would send a tax return for completion. This would be completed and returned to the inspector for examination.

3.4 The inspector had to make an assessment of tax due using the figures on the return of income unless he was not satisfied with the return. If not satisfied, he could make an assessment to the best of his judgement. [*TMA 1970, s 29* as original enacted]. The Inland Revenue's power to investigate was taken from this simple statutory requirement to be satisfied with the figure being assessed.

In most cases the inspector was dealing with a business that had submitted a set of accounts to support the figure of profit entered on the return form. He would, therefore, write saying he was not happy with the return and wanted more information to be able to satisfy himself that the return was correct. He said why he was not satisfied, i.e. gave the reason for his investigation. This would often be because something in the accounts caught his eye e.g. low gross profit rate, low drawings, perhaps some capital introduced.

This system worked well for many years but the self-assessment system has changed it all.

The self-assessment regime (1996/97 onwards for income tax, 1 July 1999 onwards for corporation tax)

3.5 Self-assessment takes away much of the processing work from the Revenue. The scheme is for a taxpayer to calculate his own tax bill and pay it without waiting for an assessment from the inspector of taxes. The need for the inspector to be satisfied with a figure before he could assess is redundant, and so *TMA 1970, s 29* was amended. There must, of course, be some way for the Inland Revenue to check tax returns otherwise the tax system would rely completely on every taxpayer's honesty and correct interpretation of complex legislation. It is this system of checking tax returns that is examined in this chapter.

The self-assessment system basically requires that a taxpayer makes an assessment of his tax liability and notifies this to the inspector of taxes by a certain date, known as the 'filing date'. This is done by completing the tax return that has been provided by the Inland Revenue. The system now applies to all persons be they individuals, companies, trustees or partners.

Notification of liability

3.6 Of course, the taxpayer will only get a return to complete if the Revenue know of him so there are still statutory requirements to notify the inspector if there is a liability to pay tax but a return has not been received. These provisions are similar to those existing pre-self-assessment but with some changes to fit the new timetables for filing returns and paying tax. They are:

- *Corporation tax.* 12 months from the end of the accounting period for which there is liability (e.g. if there is liability for an accounting period ending on 31 December 2000 and no return has been demanded for that period the Revenue must be advised by 31 December 2001). [*FA 1998, Sch 18, para 2*]. This six month limit has however been usurped by a new three month limit introduced from 31 January 2001. This applies for NIC purposes. Anyone commencing self employment must now advise the Revenue within three months of end of the month in which it commenced. EG self employment begins 10 January 2001: Revenue must be informed by 30 April 2001. If not then a £100 penalty is incurred. Although this is for Class 2 NIC purposes the notification will be treated as advising of commencement for income tax purposes.

  Apparently this is part of a package to help those starting up in business according to the Paymaster General! (The Social Security (Amendment) Regulation 2001/45)

- *Income tax and capital gains tax.* Six months from the end of the year for which there is liability (e.g. if there is a liability for the tax year 2000/01 and no return has been received for that year the Revenue must be informed by 5 October 2001). [*TMA 1970, s 7(1); FA 1994, s 196, Sch 19, Pt 1 para 1*].

Corrections and amendments to returns

3.7 The legislation provides a nine-month period of time (measured from the date of delivery of the return) for the Inland Revenue to correct obvious errors that have been made in the completion of the return. [*TMA 1970, s 9(4)(a)* for income tax; *FA 1998, Sch 18, para 6* for companies].

The Revenue will mainly make such corrections from the information they already hold but may on occasions contact the adviser, or taxpayer, for clarification of a particular point. Such a call is not the commencement of an enquiry but an attempt to get the amendment correct. It should be noted that there is therefore no obligation to respond to such a call but there is a risk that the Revenue may then regard the return as incomplete and late filing penalties may be incurred. There appears to be no good reason to be awkward in these situations and it is recommended that there is a spirit of co-operation unless there is a good reason to behave otherwise.

FA 2001 introduced a right to reject Revenue corrections.

3.8 The taxpayer may also make amendments to a return that has already been submitted. [*TMA 1970, s 9(4)(b)* for income tax; *FA 1998, Sch 18, para 15* for corporation tax]. A taxpayer's ability to amend his return lasts for 12 months from the 'filing date' but does however come to an end once an inspector has given notice that he intends to make an enquiry into a return that has been submitted. [*TMA 1970, s 9(5); FA 1998, Sch 18, para 15(4)*]. Any action the Revenue have to take to implement a taxpayer amendment is not an enquiry into the return in the Revenue's opinion (Revenue Tax Bulletin Special Edition, August 1997, p 5).

The Revenue can enquire into the amendment but there is some concern over their possible reaction. Although the legislation permits the taxpayer to correct or amend a return that he has submitted within the 12-month limit the Revenue may argue for penalties relating to the original submission of an incorrect return (see Revenue Enquiry Handbook, EH 665). To do this the Revenue must be of the opinion that the original submission was fraudulent or negligent.

Negligence was defined in the case (not a tax case) of *Blyth v Birmingham Waterworks Co 1856, 11 Ex 781* as 'the omission to do something which a prudent and reasonable man would do'. Negligence is not an easy allegation to defend. If there is a need to amend a return the question of why it was incorrect in the first place arises. The Revenue are notoriously reluctant to accept innocent error explanations and are therefore more than likely to argue for a penalty (see Revenue Investigation Handbook, IH 5065 and Enquiry Handbook, EH 627). The Revenue's attitude seems to make the right to amend a return ineffective.

There is a distinction between someone who fraudulently submits a return, then thinks better of it sometime later and someone who discovers he has made a mistake. Does the legislation give such a person the right to correct his return without fear of punishment (other than interest and surcharges for not paying the correct amount on time)? There must be an argument that it does and in worthwhile cases it may be worth appealing on this point.

What is the position of the taxpayer who delivers his return early, well before the filing date, and then discovers he has made a mistake and corrects it by delivering an amendment before the filing date? He has delivered full and correct information by the date demanded by the statute but has in fact made an incorrect return. The Revenue would seem prepared to charge a penalty for negligence. This does not seem to be fair and reasonable and could lead one to conclude that it is best to delay delivery of clients' returns until shortly before the filing date. This then gives a chance to correct any errors that come to mind without having risked a negligence penalty. The Revenue are keen for returns not to be delayed until the last minute because they want to spread their workload as much as possible but they have only given assurances on early submission not increasing the risk of enquiry, there are no assurances from the Revenue on this penalty situation.

The practical experience of the author is that Inspectors accept taxpayers amendments without question and do not argue for any penalty.

Enquiry powers

3.9 The investigative powers now possessed by an inspector of taxes following the introduction of self-assessment come from the inspector's power to enquire into a return. [*TMA 1970, ss 9A, 12AC* for income tax; *FA 1998, Sch 18, para 24* for corporation tax]. It is useful to note an effective change in the wording of the investigative powers. The old *section 29* provided that an inspector of taxes had to be satisfied with a return and if not satisfied could make a best judgement assessment. The new enquiry powers give the right to 'an officer of the Board' or the Inland Revenue. This effectively means that many enquiries can legally be made by lower-ranking Revenue officials without the need for an inspector of taxes to sign out the letters and give the appearance of conducting an enquiry.

The enquiry powers are similar no matter what the status of the taxpayer, i.e. individual, partner, company or trustee. There are some differences between individuals and companies but these do not really change the underlying rights of the Revenue. An enquiry may be commenced into a return, any amendment to that return or any claim or election related to the return, but written notice of the intention to make such enquiries must be given.

In practice, this notice is given by a letter sent to the taxpayer telling him that an enquiry into the tax return is being made, enclosing the relevant Code of Practice 11 (COP 11) for individuals, or Code of Practice 14 (COP 14) for companies, relating to self-assessment enquiries and advising that a letter has been sent to the agent, if any, requesting the information required.

These Codes of Practice are quite good and set out the Revenue's procedures and the taxpayer's rights in reasonable detail. They are worth reading. The inspectors' compliance with these codes is mandatory, the Inland Revenue Enquiry Handbook at EH 83 saying, in bold, 'All local office enquiries into SA returns must be carried out in accordance with our published Code of Practice'.

An inspector can depart from the terms of the code only on the authority of his head office (EH 83).You can therefore insist that he sticks to the guidelines and provides reasons and explanations for his actions whenever the code says that this will happen. If you are faced with a maverick inspector, and there are some around, refer him to the code and complain to his manager if he persists or if his breach is serious. If the local office manager cannot give satisfaction consider an approach to the adjudicator or even the ombudsman.

The enquiry window

3.10 The Revenue have a strict time limit within which to make an enquiry. For most normal circumstances this time limit expires 12 months from the filing date.

For all taxpayers, except companies, the filing date is 31 January following the end of the tax year concerned. Thus for the tax year 2000/01 the normal filing date is 31 January 2002. A later filing date than 31 January only applies if the Revenue have sent the return for completion after 31 October following the end of the tax year (e.g. after 31 October 2000 in respect of a return required for the year 1999/00), in which case the filing date is three months from the day on which the notice to make a return is given (e.g. if the Revenue send a return relating to the tax year 2000/01 for completion on 1 December 2001, the filing date would be 29 February 2002). [*TMA 1970, ss 8(1A), 8A(1A)*].

If the Revenue have issued a return late then it is possible that your client has fallen foul of the failure to notify liability time limits (see 3.6 above).

Companies have a different rule but it remains within the general theme of having a year to get the figures together in normal circumstances. The filing date is the last day of whichever of the following periods is the last to end [*FA 1998, Sch 18, para 14(1)*]:

(*a*) 12 months from the end of the period for which the return is required;

(*b*) if the period of account is less than 18 months, 12 months from the end of this;

(*c*) if the period of account exceeds 18 months, 30 months from the start of this; or

(*d*) three months from the date the return was served.

The Revenue may commence an enquiry into a return within certain defined periods as indicated below.

For individuals, partners and trustees

3.11

Return made	*Enquiry window*
If the return was delivered (or amended) on or before the filing date.	12 months beginning with the filing date.
If the return was delivered (or amended) after the filing date	The quarter day next following the first anniversary of the day the return was delivered. The quarter days are 31 January, 30 April, 31 July, and 31 October.

[*TMA 1970, ss 9A(2), 12AC(2)*].

Examples

3.12

(1) A return for 2000/01 has a normal filing date of 31 January 2002. If it is delivered to the Revenue on or before 31 January 2002 the enquiry window will expire on 31 January 2003, i.e. 12 months beginning with the filing date.

(2) A return for the year 2000/01 was only sent out for completion by the Revenue on 1 December 2001 and so has a filing date of 29 February 2002 (return issued after 1 October so filing date is three months from issue of the return). The enquiry window will expire on 28 February 2003, i.e. 12 months beginning with the filing date.

(3) A return for the year 2000/01, sent out for completion by the Revenue before 1 October 2001, is delivered to the Revenue on 1 March 2002. Its normal filing date was 31 January 2002. The enquiry window expires on 30 April 2003, i.e. the quarter date following the first anniversary (1 March 2003) of the delivery of the return.

For companies

3.13

Return made	*Enquiry window*
If the return was delivered on or before the filing date.	12 months from the filing date.
If the return was delivered after the filing date or return amended	The 31 January, 30 April, 31 July, 31 October next following the first anniversary of the day the return was delivered or amended.

[*FA 1998, Sch 18, para 24*].

Examples

3.14

(4) Company delivers its return for the period of account ending on 30 October 2000 on 29 September 2001. The filing date is 30 October 2001 (i.e. 12 months from end of period of account) so the enquiry window expires on 30 October 2002, i.e. 12 months from the filing date.

(5) Company delivers its return for the period to 30 October 2000 on 1 December 2001 when the filing date was 30 October 2001. It has therefore delivered its return after the filing date so the enquiry window will expire on 31 January 2003, i.e. 31 January next following the first anniversary (1 December 2002) of delivery of the return.

(6) Company delivers its return for the period to 30 October 2000 on 29 September 2001 but delivers an amendment to that return on 30 October 2001. The enquiry window expires on 31 October 2002, i.e. 31 October following the first anniversary (30 October 2002) of delivery of the amendment. It is to be noted that the enquiry window is extended beyond the norm even though the amendment was made by the normal filing date. This differs from the non-company rules.

3.15 If the Revenue is outside these time limits then an enquiry into the return cannot be made, in normal circumstances. This was very much brought into issue in February 1999. Accountants arriving in their offices on 1 February, a Monday, opened their post to find notices of enquiry into many of their clients. Many of these were dated 29 January, i.e. the previous Friday, and issued by second-class post. It was obvious that clients could not possibly have received them within the statutory deadline, i.e. 30 January 1999 (this being a Saturday). After an outcry, and much column space in the taxation journals debating the issue, the Revenue announced that those notices would be withdrawn, accepting that the legislation was to be interpreted as the taxpayer receiving the enquiry notice by the 30 January and not the Revenue merely having issued it before then.

This interpretation was further emphasised by the Special Commissioners in the case of *Wing Hung Lai v Bale [1999] STC (SCD) 238*. In this case a *section 9A* notice had been issued on 27 January 1999. The Special Commissioner accepted that the accountant had received his copy on Monday 1 February 1999 and that the taxpayer had received his notice on Tuesday 2 February 1999. The decision was that the notice was invalid. This was because the service of a *section 9A* notice is governed by *Interpretation Act 1978, s 7* which says that 'service is deemed . . . to have been effected at the time which the letter would be delivered in the ordinary course of post'. It had therefore to be decided what the ordinary course of post was in this case. The Special Commissioner looked at two helpful notices. The first was a practice direction from the Queen's Bench Division on 8 March 1985 in which it was said 'to avoid uncertainty as to the date of service it will be taken (subject to proof to the contrary) that delivery in the ordinary post was effected (*a*) in the case of first class mail, on the second working day after posting, or (*b*) in the case of second class mail, on the fourth working day after posting'. Working days are Monday to Friday, excluding any bank holiday. The second was a Code of Practice by the Post Office. That promised delivery of second-class post within three working days of posting and also defined working days as Monday to Friday. Therefore the notice could not have been delivered within the ordinary course of post by 30 January because three working days took it to Monday 1 February 1999 and four working days to Tuesday 2 February 1999.

3.16 Some accountants and their clients do, however, appear to have taken the view that it would be easier to answer the Revenue's queries than spend time and money arguing, and were also perhaps fearful that to argue would jeopardise future dealings with that tax office, or lead to them being singled out for attention in some way. Many have the view that it would only mean an enquiry the following year instead so objecting was pointless. This is an understandable reaction, but, in the author's view, in the long term it does damage. Parliament has decided that the Revenue must operate within certain statutory limits. By refusing to insist on the correct and accurate implementation of the rights that Parliament has given to individual taxpayers, those rights are watered down and so may eventually disappear. The Revenue are rarely slow in seeking retribution for breach of time limits e.g. penalties for late filing of returns or failing to notify liability on time. It is therefore a duty of the agent to ensure the Revenue are operating within the rules and to defend the point if so required.

Discovery

3.17 All is not entirely lost to the Revenue if they fail to give notice of an intention to enquire into a return that has been made. *TMA 1970, s 29* provides for occasions when the Revenue makes 'a discovery'. If the Revenue discovers that profits have not been assessed, or have been insufficiently assessed, or relief has been given when it shouldn't have, the inspector may make an assessment to correct the position.

However, even though the Revenue may discover that tax is due for a year that is not the subject of an open enquiry, and cannot be because the enquiry window is now closed, an assessment may only be made if:

- tax is due because of fraudulent or negligent conduct on the part of a taxpayer, or a person acting on his behalf e.g. his accountant [*TMA 1970, s 29(4)*]; or
- the inspector could not have reasonably been expected to be aware of the situation on the basis of the information before him. [*TMA 1970, s 29(5)*].

Once the enquiry window has closed for a period a client can now consider his affairs in order unless he has committed an offence or the Revenue could not have been aware that tax was due. The legislation is helpful in making the decision whether the inspector had sufficient information to have made a correct decision at the proper time. *TMA 1970, s 29(6)* details the circumstances under which information is made available and it is worth listing these:

- the information is contained in the tax return or in any document that has accompanied the return;
- it is contained in any claim that has been made or any document accompanying such a claim;
- it is contained in any documents that are produced to the Revenue for the purposes of any enquiry into the return; or
- it is information that could reasonably be inferred by the inspector from information that has been provided.

References to returns not merely include the returns for the year concerned but also for the two immediately preceding periods.

These provisions provide very important defences to put a stop to an investigation.

3.18 For periods before 1996/97 (or 1 July 1999 for companies) the case of *Olin Energy Systems Ltd v Scorer 1985, 58 TC 592* provides a defence against discovery. The case concerned a company that had losses from a trade that had ceased. In the computations submitted to the Revenue they had carried these losses forward and set them against profits of a different trade. The inspector issued an amended assessment reflecting this computation and so determined an appeal by agreement. A different inspector later decided that this was incorrect and issued assessments to correct the position by withdrawing the losses. The company appealed and eventually the House of Lords agreed that they were protected by *TMA 1970, s 54(1)* (determination of appeals by agreement), saying that the computations were sufficient to alert a competent inspector to the fact that the loss claim was incorrect. The question to be asked was would a reasonable man have concluded that the inspector had decided to admit the claim having regard to the material in his possession. In this case they concluded that he would. The new *section 29* effectively puts into statute the House of Lords' decision in that case. Note however that the Revenue do not regard themselves as bound by arithmetical errors contained in computations they have accepted (Statement of Practice SP 8/91).

3.19 It is therefore important to ensure that when submitting a return sufficient information is given to permit the inspector to decide if he is to make an enquiry or accept the return. If sufficient information has been given he will be barred from making a discovery assessment, if sometime later he discovers that further tax ought to have been paid.

Obviously it is not desirable either for the taxpayer, his agent or even the Revenue for reams of paper and explanations to be supplied with returns and the Revenue have in fact warned against this. In a Press Release of 31 May 1996 they say:

> 'Taxpayers and agents should be aware that the submission of accounts and computations or other documents may not provide protection against a discovery assessment . . . there may be so much material that the Revenue officer "could not have been reasonably expected, on the basis of the information made available to him . . . be aware" [*TMA 1970, new s 29(5)*] of the particular point of liability, unless the taxpayer or agent had explained its relevance. Where voluminous information beyond the accounts and computations is sent in with the return, therefore, it is recommended that there should be a brief indication of the relevance of the material.'

If therefore some deduction has been made, or some relief claimed, where it is known from experience that it is an area which the Revenue would usually look at and debate (e.g. a capital v revenue argument in relation to some repairs expenditure or a question of departure from commercial accountancy principles), it is perhaps good advice to add some note on the face of the return relating to the point in question. If the inspector chooses not to open an enquiry it can then later be argued that he accepted the return in full knowledge of the situation or that it could reasonably be inferred from the information given what the position was. In those circumstances your client should be able to regard that period as closed once the enquiry window has passed.

3.20 It can however be difficult to decide on a disclosure. You may be genuinely certain that the stance you have adopted is correct. You know that if a note is made on the return it is likely that there will be an enquiry and you and your client may be put to a lot of inconvenience and expense. On the other hand you know that if the inspector later discovers the facts he will probably want to look into it and debate the issue, although you are of course confident that he will eventually agree with you. If insufficient information was provided your client is faced with an unwelcome demand for tax arrears if the inspector's views prevail.

An added disincentive to provide information is that doing so may signal to the inspector that although you have taken a particular view you are aware that he may disagree with you. It would be almost certain that he will disagree if you tell him that you think he will. Even though you put forward a robust argument the inspector may decide that it is unlikely you would proceed with any appeal because of your obvious doubts.

This is therefore a difficult decision and one that can only be decided on a case-by-case basis having regard to the particular facts of each one.

3.21 The Institute of Chartered Accountants gives plenty of advice to its members in the Members Handbook (paragraphs 3.1–4.9).They emphasise the importance of full disclosure under the self-assessment system if a client is to achieve certainty but also accept that there is a need to avoid incurring unnecessary costs. A warning is given about those situations in which the agent believes his, or his client's, treatment is correct but from his experience knows the Revenue will ask for information or they will challenge the treatment adopted.

Revenue determinations

3.22 The legislation deals with those non-compliant taxpayers who decide they will not make a tax return even though a notice has been served upon them. In these circumstances the Revenue may determine the tax they believe may be due should a return have been made. [*TMA 1970, s 28C*]. The taxpayer is left with no choice but to either pay up or submit his return to correct the position. This can of course give rise to an enquiry window.

Stopping an enquiry

3.23 There is no real process of formal objection to an enquiry being started. The only remedy available is to make application to the Appeal Commissioners for an enquiry to be closed. [*TMA 1970, s 28A(6); FA 1998, Sch 18, para 33(1)*]. The mechanism is for the taxpayer to apply to the Appeal Commissioners for a direction that the Revenue give notice of the conclusion of their enquiry. The Appeal Commissioners are obliged to order the Revenue to close an enquiry unless the Revenue satisfy them that they have reasonable grounds for continuing. [*TMA 1970, s 28A(7); FA 1998, Sch 18, para 33(3)*]. Note that application can be made direct to the Commissioners; it does not have to be directed via the tax office. The Revenue do however anticipate that many will ask them to arrange for an application to be placed before the Commissioners and have instructed their local offices to have procedures in place to ensure such requests are complied with quickly (Revenue Enquiry Handbook, EH 436).

If, therefore, it is thought that the inspector has no grounds whatsoever for making an enquiry, or continuing an enquiry, then this is the procedure that must be taken to put an end to it if the inspector himself cannot be persuaded. This would be especially useful if there is an inspector who has persistently continued an enquiry despite an adequate response to all of his queries. In these circumstances, it is often found that he is acting on some information and applying to the Commissioners for a closure notice may oblige the inspector to reveal some information in order to convince the Appeal Commissioners that he is reasonable in continuing the enquiry. At least the practitioner would then be aware of the real question to be addressed – this is one major flaw in the current procedures in that frequently he will not be aware of what is causing the inspector concern and therefore what to focus on when trying to convince him that all is well.

3.24 The Revenue think this closure procedure may be used by some to try and prevent an enquiry happening (Revenue Enquiry Handbook, EH 437(a)). There is no real point in wasting time and money trying this. The Revenue have the right to make an enquiry without reason and the Commissioners are not given any powers to interfere with the Revenue's decision. They also believe that agents may try to use it as a method of trying to deny the Revenue access to information they have requested (EH 437(b)). The Revenue advise their inspectors that there are rights of appeal against notices to produce information and so a completion application is not appropriate. They are told to suggest that the appeal against the order route is followed, not the completion application.

3.25 There will however be times when it would be appropriate to ask the Commissioners for a completion notice at the same time as an appeal is heard against a production order. An inspector may be asking for information relating to something that has already been dealt with adequately. It would be appropriate to object to his order and ask for a completion notice at the same hearing. Further discussion on completion notices can be found at 8.5 below.

Information

3.26 To make an enquiry, the inspector will obviously want some information and he will initially set out what this is and informally request that it is provided. Inspectors do, however, appear to be trying to think of every conceivable piece of information and questions they may want to ask and cover these in their initial request for information. The result is a very long list of explanations and information required. It can frequently take an advisor a very long time to put a response together and so dealing with this initial request for information can be costly for the client. It is therefore important to examine carefully what has been requested and only provide what the inspector would be entitled to under the terms of the legislation and what is relevant to the entries on the return.

3.27 The Revenue have now selected the client for an enquiry, served written notice of this on the client and informally requested the information they want. The investigation is open.

Main points

1. Three month time limit for notifying self employment.
2. Self amending a return does not protect against penalties.
3. Codes of Practice are mandatory as far as the Inspector is concerned.
4. Time limits for opening enquiries are strictly applied.
5. If a year is closed the Revenue can only re-open it if they make a discovery.
6. Providing Revenue with information protects against a discovery.
7. An enquiry can be stopped by applying for a closure notice.

Chapter 4

The Faster Working Method

4.1 A frequent complaint is the time taken to conclude an investigation. Such complaints are heard on both sides: accountants about delays by the Revenue and inspectors about accountants' delays in producing documents and responding to correspondence. There is some merit in the complaints of both sides. Accountants are usually busy and do not employ staff on the off-chance that there may be an investigation; as a result resources have to be diverted from other work and that is not always easy to do. Life does not stand still for investigations. Equally, inspectors push for information to be submitted then, when they have it, may appear to do nothing with it for weeks and then respond expecting the accountant to drop everything else and deal with his demands.

In an attempt to speed up the time taken to work and settle an enquiry, the Revenue introduced a system for agreeing a timetable that should ensure cases are opened and closed within a six-month period. Six months is quite a speed for most cases, as typical investigations can easily drag on for 12 to 18 months or more. The Revenue set out a model for the timetabling of a typical investigation in Tax Bulletin, Special Edition 2a 1997.

4.2 The general scheme is for the accountant and the inspector to agree a timetable for:

(1) *Fact finding*. In this phase it will be discussed and decided what records and other information is to be supplied to the inspector. It will be agreed who will produce them and the timetable for this.

(2) *Discussions with agent*. The agent will answer any factual queries relating to the production of the accounts e.g. any estimates or balancing figures used? He will deal with any accountancy points such as stock reserves.

(3) *Examination of records*. The time over which the inspector examines the documents provided to him will be agreed and a date for the next stage will be set.

(4) *Discussions on findings*. Your client will be interviewed and there will be a discussion on the facts and the interpretation of these with the agent. Proposals for settlement will be debated and agreed.

(5) *Settlement*. The formalities of settlement will be timetabled. This includes certificates of disclosure, letters of offer and negotiations relating to time to pay arrangements.

4.3 The scheme is to be much welcomed but in the author's experience there is an unwillingness by some inspectors to use it. It seems to be rarely offered; yet the Revenue said it would be offered in every case. In the Lathams Tax Investigations/AccountingWeb survey in March 2000, 30 per cent of respondents had been offered faster working and a slightly higher proportion had only occasionally been offered it. Only 5 per cent had always been offered this opportunity by inspectors at the outset of full enquiries and the vast majority had little or no experience of the fast track being used.

When asked for, there has been a reluctance by inspectors to agree a timetable. They are happy to set the agent a timetable for the things he needs to do but are disinclined to have one set for themselves. In cases where faster working has been agreed, the Revenue have often withdrawn from it as soon as they saw that they themselves could not keep to the timetable. The Board of Inland Revenue seem to believe that the reason they do not get through enough cases is because of non co-operation by agents. That is certainly a factor, although it should be less so now that the Revenue have *TMA 1970, s 19A* (see 7.21 below) to obtain information, but it is possible that a major contribution to the solution lies within their own organisation.

Inspectors appear to be worried that undue haste will mean a lack of quality in the standard of their investigation and so may prejudice their pay or career. That is apart from a professional desire to do the job thoroughly and properly.

4.4 Faster working is worth asking for. It puts pressure on the inspector to get things done and provided you have kept to your side of the bargain, it helps your case during penalty and interest negotiations.

It is, however, a waste of time if the Revenue can opt out of the plan at any time: so should you ask for it? In the author's view you should, but only if you know you can adhere to the agreed timetable yourself. If an inspector refuses to agree to it without good reason, it may pay to have a word with the office manager. If he cannot satisfy you or if a particular office simply refuses to operate the scheme an approach to Revenue head office may do the trick. Argue that taxpayers in your area are being denied benefits that those in other areas enjoy.

Chapter 5

Meetings

Summary of chapter

5.1 This chapter equips you to minimise the risk of surprise and so enables you to agree to meetings with a greater confidence. It looks at:

- how meetings fit into the process of an investigation;
- whether a meeting should be agreed to at all;
- the best place to hold a meeting and the practical reasons for this;
- the topics to be covered at the main meeting and the 'trick' questions the inspector will ask.

Introduction

5.2 At some point the inspector of taxes is, more than likely, going to ask for a meeting with your client. There could be a variety of meetings:

- *A fact finder.* This is an important and vital meeting and will usually take place very early in the investigation process. The precise point will depend on the individual case and the particular inspector involved. It is this meeting that is considered in this chapter.
- *Progress meetings.* These will be to discuss specific points that arise during the working of the case. The inspector or the accountant may request them. These may not occur in many cases.
- *Technical meetings.* These will be to discuss technical issues such as accountancy treatment or the application of tax law to a particular situation.
- *Settlement meeting.* The case will be reviewed together with culpability and penalties. These meetings are examined in Chapter 8.

The main one, and a vital one, is the fact finder. The inspector wants the meeting to establish facts; he is trained in how to conduct them and so is confident. Meetings do not allow the taxpayer time to consider answers in the same way that correspondence does and, importantly, the inspector can judge the responses by reference to the respondent's body language and demeanour. They are quicker than correspondence and permit other avenues to be opened up and explored as they arise. The inspector is also searching for information he can use in a business economics exercise, for example:

- the number of trays purchased by a hot food take-away may indicate the number of meals sold;
- a carpet fitter's expense claim may give a record of jobs performed for a carpet shop; or
- an appointment diary may indicate sales that have been omitted.

He is also identifying third parties for potential enquiries e.g. a supplier's records may show that purchases have been suppressed to ensure the gross profit rate looks reasonable. This has been a popular method with some fish and chip shops that only recorded every other potato purchase and so, although their gross profit margin appeared reasonable, a substantial amount of profit was omitted.

Your client is no expert in this field so the inspector starts with the advantage. Meetings can however be useful for clients; they ensure the correct facts are in the inspector's possession, they ensure that argument in favour of a client has been correctly understood and given due weight by the inspector and can be used to apply logic in bringing a case to a close.

You will need to talk to your client and ensure he is aware of the serious nature of an investigation and ask if he thinks there will be any problems, i.e. does he have a mind to make a disclosure. If he does, have regard to the advice at 5.28 et seq below.

When the inspector asks for a meeting, what should you do? Refuse, resist, go?

Agreeing to the meeting

5.3 Outright refusal to attend a meeting, or resistance to one, can sometimes appear to be good for client relationships.

Sticking up for the client and refusing to be bullied may make a client feel confident that he has a strong ally on his side. All very well, but is it best advice? The reluctance to apparently co-operate and attend a meeting also arises out of the fact that the Revenue will no longer say what is causing them concern and so you cannot focus on the problem. This means your research has to be broader and so more costly and less effective and your client does not know what he is going to be asked. This must make him nervous and there is the potential for the inspector to spring a surprise.

5.4 In some circumstances non-attendance may be the best tactic. The Tax Faculty of the Institute of Chartered Accountants in England and Wales suggest several preconditions for a meeting (Tax Faculty booklet *Questions and Answers on Revenue Enquiries under Self Assessment*, p 15):

(*a*) both sides have the same objective;

(*b*) both sides are equally prepared;

(*c*) you have a good idea of what the meeting will cover;

(*d*) you know what information the Revenue already have;

(*e*) both you and your client can think on your feet;

(*f*) you, but more especially your client, do not feel uncomfortable before the Revenue; and

(*g*) both you and your client are as used to meetings as the inspector.

In the author's view, if this was followed, meetings with the Revenue would be very rare, and he does not fully agree with the Tax Faculty on this. They support their views however by pointing out that the inspector is trained in the psychology of meetings and that the Revenue's advice to inspectors is consistent with the Revenue already believing that the return is wrong and wanting an opportunity to closely question the client in detail. The Tax Faculty also express concern that they believe some of the paragraphs on meetings in the Revenue's Investigation Handbook are omitted in the version released to the public. All this leads the Tax Faculty to conclude that the Revenue do not view meetings as an opportunity to gather facts but as a tactic in winning fights.

5.5 The Tax Faculty advise that the Revenue have acknowledged that there is nothing to compel a taxpayer to attend a meeting and that one cannot be penalised for lack of co-operation if attendance is refused because this is simply insisting on one's legal rights. The Revenue have agreed that this will not be viewed as non-co-operation if the questions are put in writing and there is no unreasonable delay in answering them (*Questions and Answers on Revenue Enquiries under Self Assessment*, p 14).

5.6 Frequently, however, the client eventually starts to doubt the wisdom of the advice he is getting. This is especially as the Revenue adopt a more formal approach to make progress and he begins to realise that he must produce certain documents and give relevant explanations, even though he has been paying his agent, on advice, to resist the Revenue.

Justifying a refusal

5.7 So under what circumstances could a refusal to attend a meeting be justified?

Legal right

Firstly remember that the Revenue have no statutory right to demand a meeting; the client must be made aware of this. It should however also be realised that the lack of a meeting will not stop the Revenue putting questions in writing and demanding replies using their information-gathering powers (see Chapter 7). Additionally it may eventually result in the client being asked questions in a more formal manner during an appeal hearing.

Illness

5.8 It could be that the client is ill and so unable to attend. If so the inspector will be sympathetic, especially if medical evidence is produced. To progress the case correspondence may be the only real alternative. There are some mental illnesses that may not stop the client walking about and even seemingly going about his normal everyday business but would make it unwise to have him answer questions. The author was involved in a case in which the client was suffering from depression and his doctor advised that the condition would result in his patient not being able to give a proper account of himself, so making any meeting worthless. It is important to seek medical advice and support in such circumstances.

No Code of Practice

5.9 Leaving aside the medical reasons for refusal, the author would be wary of attending any meeting if no Code of Practice had been issued by the Revenue. It is important to know how the Revenue is viewing the case. If Code of Practice 9 has been issued then the Revenue suspect serious fraud and specialist advice should be obtained; the same applies to Code of Practice 8 although at the stage of issuing this the Revenue do not suspect serious fraud. No Code of Practice may indicate that the Revenue are considering a criminal investigation, although if so they should advise that the meeting will be under caution and give the opportunity for legal help to be obtained, or that the inspector is not acting within the Revenue's guidelines. In all of these circumstances the Special Compliance Office would be involved (see Chapter 12) so one can be more relaxed with a local office, but do not proceed until they issue a code and insist on this before agreeing to attend a meeting or even entering into correspondence.

Costs

5.10 On a practical level, it is of course important to consider the costs of attending a meeting against the potential costs of refusal. Meetings can usually save on lengthy correspondence.

Co-operation

5.11 In the author's experience a spirit of co-operation is usually the best way to resolve enquiries and investigations. The Tax Faculty itself ends up, despite all that it said earlier about attendance, saying that it is not against meetings and 'that all we are trying to say is that you should not rush into meetings and ought to minimise as far as possible the risk of being caught by surprise'. The author can fully agree with that and this chapter is aimed at minimising that risk.

5.12 Although a spirit of co-operation is often the best way forward, agents must be careful of being over co-operative. An agent has a duty of confidentiality towards his client. This means that he must not give the Revenue information without the consent of his client unless there is an overriding need to do so. Care is therefore needed when attending a meeting without the client. See Chapter 9 for further discussion on this.

Before the meeting

5.13 Having decided to agree to a meeting, should one simply go along and see what the inspector wants? Many practitioners do and neither they, nor their clients, are prepared for the meeting. The scene is therefore set for the Revenue to gain the initiative and obtain a considerable advantage over the client. At this point a client may begin to lose confidence in his adviser and so the client relationship is at risk.

It is impossible to prepare for the meeting in the same way as the inspector. He has access to more information than the agent does, and is not inhibited in the same way by costs. Unfortunately, the professional costs in thoroughly preparing for a meeting can be significant and may be unnecessary. It is a question of professional judgement, after discussion with your client, as to how much preparation work is done. A lack of detailed preparation should not harm your client provided he does not prejudice himself by giving ill thought-out and inaccurate answers to the inspector's questions. There is though much that can be done.

5.14 Ask the inspector if he intends to discuss any technical areas and clear these and any accountancy points with him before the meeting. You may want to consider meeting the inspector on your own, initially, to discuss these. In that way you can establish a link with him and make your own assessment of his character before seeing him with your client.

5.15 The client will be worried and nervous: statistically he is almost certain to end up paying some money to the Revenue, and he may be concerned about other matters. A partner may have been cheating his partners. A husband may have been using money to keep a mistress. There may be a feeling of shame that his family and friends will lose their respect for him. There may be an embarrassment to admit to someone who has been his advisor for many years, that he has lied to him and misled him in the past.

These factors may motivate him to try and cover up the truth, with potentially serious consequences.

It may therefore be appropriate to remind the client of the duty of confidentiality under which both you and the inspector must operate.

Admittedly you may have a conflict if any admission involves other persons you act for but without full and correct facts you cannot properly advise on the best way forward. Inspectors are usually very sympathetic towards the need for discretion and it may best safeguard your client to have any potentially embarrassing matters aired at an early stage.

5.16 Fear tends to arise out of the unknown. Your client has never dealt with the Revenue; he is unlikely to have been the subject of an investigation of any description; he may be angry at the implied suggestion that he may be dishonest; he will be concerned about the possible consequences. If you reduce the elements of the unknown he will be less fearful. Advise your client on what the format of the meeting will be. If you are unsure of what this will be yourself discuss it with the inspector and agree an agenda.

The agenda

5.17 Inspectors often object to agendas but this is usually because they confuse them with a list of specific questions. In general, investigators will not permit themselves to be restricted to specific questions. They need to explore, clarify and understand what is being told to them and this can only be achieved by supplementary questions. An agenda should not be an obstacle to this. In any event, insist; after all it is the inspector who wants the meeting, not you, and it is reasonable to assume that your client would prefer not to have it at all.

The inspector does not want a case that is full of delay as it prejudices his personal targets. If he is reluctant, refer him to Tax Bulletin Special Edition 2a (the one that deals with the faster working method) under the paragraph headed 'Week 17'. This deals with the timetable for meetings and refers to 'areas of discussion agreed in advance (i.e. an agenda, but not a questionnaire)'.

The Revenue advise their inspectors not to agree to meetings that are conditional on a detailed list of questions being provided (Revenue Investigation Handbook, IH 2321). They will agree to advising on the broad areas to be covered and the initial questions but nothing more. This is fine but you should have a detailed list of points to be covered and not generalities such as the list at 5.18 below.

5.18 The broad areas to be covered are more than likely going to be as follows:

1. The business
2. Record keeping
3. Personal and private matters
4. Specific matters

Every case is individual and different it is true, but virtually every investigation will follow a similar structure. Being aware of the structure may help in alleviating some of the client's worries. He knows he can talk about these with confidence and knowledge.

Location

5.19 Inspectors once disliked leaving their offices and insisted that the meeting should be at the tax office. That has changed and they are now more likely to suggest a meeting at your client's premises. Each case has its own characteristics and it is for you to decide on the place that is most advantageous to your client. The author would normally refuse to meet at his client's premises; it is rarely the best place. There is likely to be disruption with calls, your client has difficulty in concentrating on the matter at hand as he sees a customer come in or hears the telephone ring. Importantly, if something arises in the meeting and the inspector asks to see evidence immediately, it is more difficult to resist while you have an opportunity to look at what is being given to the inspector and consider its implications.

A similar objection to having the meeting in your office arises. All your files are there and it is difficult to resist the inspector's request for detail. It is always best to look these things up without pressure and consider how they are best presented.

This leaves us with the tax office as the author's favoured venue.

Of course this may not always be the case. Your client may feel uncomfortable going onto the inspector's home ground where he has been able to arrange his room to create a psychological advantage. If so, your office is probably the next choice. Having said all that, there can be times when your client's premises are favoured. It could be that you believe that the inspector will get a better understanding of the business and that would be an advantage.

Each case is unique and you need to decide each one individually in the best interests of your client.

Pre-meeting advice

5.20 The advice the author recommends giving to the client before any interview is:

(1) Keep answers concise and to the point. Simply answering yes or no will not create the right atmosphere of co-operation, and in any event the inspector will be asking open questions that demand an explanatory response. However, nervous people do tend to talk too much and there is a danger of giving the inspector numerous avenues to explore that will only serve to increase the time taken up with the investigation, and the cost of dealing with it.

(2) If a question is not understood, say so, do not guess at what you think the question is. Correct answers can only be given to questions that are understood. Do not be fearful of seeming ignorant.

(3) Do not guess at the answer to a question. If the full and correct answer is not known, say so, and explain that the answer will be researched and the Inspector informed as quickly as possible.

(4) Above everything else, do not lie. It is better to stay silent than to lie. If it is difficult to answer a question, tell your advisor and seek his advice.

At the meeting

5.21 It is at this first interview that the course of the investigation is set. If the client lies, he puts himself in a very difficult position.

Very often the client's word is all the evidence that is available. If he proves to be unreliable then his evidence will be ignored. In more serious cases lying could result in the Revenue deciding to pursue a criminal prosecution; at the very least it will be prejudicial to penalty mitigation. Inspectors are told to try and prevent taxpayers committing themselves to obvious lies (Revenue Investigation Handbook, IH 2345).

If the client guesses at answers, these guesses may cause problems later on. The inspector will write down details of what is said and will factor these into his thinking and computations. If some ill-considered response has been made it may be difficult to persuade the inspector that information given to him was incorrect. He may think that there is an attempt to change the facts to fit the case.

5.22 Do not hesitate to stop the meeting at any stage if you think the inspector is being aggressive, simply fishing, straying from the agreed agenda or if your client appears to be distressed. Remember you are there voluntarily and the Revenue have confirmed that non-attendance does not affect penalty loadings provided questions are answered in some manner.

The business

5.23 The inspector will be trying to establish the following information.

What is the business?

He will have it fitted into some general classification but it is important that he is aware of what he is looking at.

He has a wealth of notes on different types of business, some abridged details of them are published by the Revenue. The inspector may think he knows about this business but each is unique so it is vital that the inspector appreciates what he is looking at.

How is the business organised?

He will need to know how many branches there might be and who are the key people in the organisation. What are the banking arrangements?

Who has control of petty cash?

Who does what?

What are each director's/partner's and key employee's duties? He may be especially interested in what work a wife does in a business if wages are paid to her.

Who are the customers?

What type of person buys from this business? Is it dependent upon a small number of customers who may squeeze margins? Could the inspector identify a large customer from whom he could obtain details of purchases as a cross-check? Could there be some contra account arrangements?

Who are the suppliers?

Does the business buy from recognised sources or is there opportunity for off-record purchases? If the inspector can identify a supplier he may be able to compare their records.

What is the service chain?

What happens from the purchase of goods for resale through to supply to the customer? Will there be delivery notes?

What security is there?

Does the business have security cameras or tagged goods? If so, there may be evidence of stock losses or a suggestion that these are under control. Are goods easily accessed by thieves? Is an alarm system fitted?

What problems are there, or have there been?

The inspector wants to know of anything that may have affected the business performance. He needs to be aware of price pressure from competition or losses due to theft.

Where does wastage occur and at what levels?

This is an important area, the inspector wants to prevent it being used later to try and explain away any shortfalls that may be suggested by his business model.

5.24 The inspector is trying to obtain a complete understanding of the business he is investigating. This is essential if he is to produce an accurate and credible argument at a later date.

5.25 He is also on the look out for opportunities to pocket cash e.g. from sales of scrap. At the same time he is quietly noting security measures. Tell him that the client has no problem with shoplifting, or staff defalcations, and it is difficult to introduce these as explanations for losses later on in the investigation.

Wastage is an obvious question but it is unlikely that you or your client will have fully considered it, and measured it, before this interview. Unless you have, it should not be discussed because no accurate, and therefore useful, information can be given to the inspector before it is considered and measured.

Records

5.26 It is possible that before the meeting the inspector will have asked the accountant for a simple report on the records. Typically you may have been asked:

- Did you have to estimate any figures?
- Was it necessary to introduce any balancing figures, and if so, what?
- What was the standard of the books and records from which you prepared the accounts?

You will need to take great care when responding. If you report that there are none and the inspector later discovers there are some you could find yourself in a very uncomfortable position.

Estimates and balancing figures will be used to try and discredit the records. The author has seen inspectors jump to the conclusion that any estimate or balancing figure discredits the records. A recent example was a £75 balancing figure (the only estimate or balancing figure in the accounts incidentally) in a set of accounts for a company with a turnover of £5 million. The inspector used this as his launch pad for an investigation and, to cut a long story short, succeeded in obtaining access to the books and records. To complete the story the inspector successfully uncovered substantial personal expenditure paid for by the company and it resulted in a settlement of £20,000. It came to light that the inspector was acting on an informant's information but wanted, indeed needed, to cite another reason for investigating. He would not of course have the same problem under the current self-assessment regime.

5.27 If the inspector has already examined the books and records, he is likely to ask questions on specific entries.

If he has not done so, he will do so soon after the meeting. He needs to understand the systems to follow them properly. He will therefore want to know what records are maintained and still available. He will establish where they are located; he may need to serve a notice under *TMA 1970, s 20* at some later stage.

5.28 He will want to know who is responsible for writing up the records and when they are actually written up. Tell him that they are written up daily and then give him a set of records that are in pristine condition and in the same ink and he will immediately question what has been said. If it is clear that the records given to the inspector were not written up daily they are immediately discredited and your client has problems. Clients will frequently try and explain that these are neat versions written up from original, but tatty, ones. If the meeting is at your client's premises, and I would urge you to avoid this as a venue, expect the inspector to ask for sight of the previous day's record. All that has been said earlier about telling lies applies here.

5.29 The records presented for accounts production are often a summary. The inspector will explore what prime records exist, i.e. what are the records presented written up from? It may be that daily sales come from a till roll; if so, expect the inspector to insist on seeing these.

5.30 The inspector is likely to establish exactly what takes place from a customer handing over money to recording sales in the records. He will explore how purchases are controlled; e.g. are delivery notes checked?

5.31 Expect the inspector to spend some time discussing the control of petty cash expenditure. He will ask who has access to this and on whose authority it is paid out and against what receipts. The Revenue will often find weaknesses in this area with unvouched, or round sum, expenses.

5.32 The type of, and number of non-financial records are of interest because they can support the financial records or in fact prove they are incorrect; so expect the inspector to probe for what may exist in this field. Appointment diaries are a firm favourite and many an inspector will have a tale to tell of how he succeeded in a case by using an appointment diary. The author's experience is that a client has a long and difficult time after an inspector has seen these. Typically, the inspector will see that, say, Peter Howarth was due to be seen on a Monday afternoon some 18 months ago. He cannot however find any invoice to Peter Howarth, has the sale to this person been omitted? The client has then to try and recall what happened with Peter Howarth. Did he actually keep the appointment? If so did it lead to an invoice being issued and if not why not? Was it billed to some other client for some reason? Or could it have been a non-business appointment? There will potentially be several such queries and your client will struggle to recall what happened in each case, resulting in the inspector deciding that they represent omitted sales.

5.33 Delivery notes have proved to be the downfall of some clients. For example, a builders merchant's delivery note states that materials have been delivered to House A but there is no sales invoice addressed to House A. In fact there is no sales invoice around that time that appears to relate to the materials delivered. The inspector has established omitted sales; he has found a cash job.

5.34 The inspector is, of course, probing for areas of weakness that he can concentrate on during his book examination. Discrediting the records is the key to any successful investigation as far as the inspector is concerned. Once the records are discredited, the inspector is on strong ground. Accounts prepared from unreliable records produce an unreliable profit result. It gives the inspector the reason to say he is not satisfied with the profits declared – once an essential feature in the days of the old *TMA 1970, s 29*, but still vital for any inspector facing a hearing before the Appeal Commissioners or an application to have his enquiry closed down. Once the inspector has valid grounds for disregarding the returned profits, he can substitute his own estimate. Such an estimate must be just and reasonable.

Personal and private matters

5.35 This is always a controversial and delicate area, seen by clients as an invasion of their privacy. Inspectors are told to be tactful (Revenue Investigation Handbook, IH 2130).

In the past, some inspectors have gone to ridiculous lengths under this heading, asking how much is spent on milk, children's spending money and other trivia. These days, most inspectors are not as inquisitive, usually because business economics are used in preference to capital statements. Nevertheless, some questions must be anticipated. The number and detail will depend on whether the inspector thinks a capital statement, or a simpler means test, is needed. Capital statements are often not a very good investigation tool in most cases but they still have a place in some. The essential ingredient of an effective capital statement, or means test, is in getting as much detail of cash expenditure as possible.

5.36 A client will rarely remember what he has spent. Just think of yourself for a minute; how often have you puzzled over where the cash in your wallet, or purse, has gone over the last day or so? It is far more difficult to recall facts over a year or more ago. The Revenue do recognise this difficulty and ask their own inspectors to consider their own spending for the previous month as an example. They also warn inspectors not to rely on a profit recalculation using personal and private expenditure without some supporting back up unless there is no choice (Revenue Investigation Handbook, IH 2130).

If it becomes clear that a full review of the private side is needed it would be wrong to have your client give incorrect replies or guesses. It would be better to politely decline to guess and explain to the inspector your reasons and offer to research private expenditure with your client and provide accurate details in a few weeks' time. You are unlikely to find this offer being resisted; indeed the Revenue encourages their inspectors to have the accountant prepare capital statements (Revenue Investigation Handbook, IH 2093).

Closing escape routes

5.37 What will be covered at the meeting are what are often called the 'bolt holes, i.e. those easily given explanations which cover the unexpected and which can be difficult to verify. Typically these are:

- *Cash hoards.* The inspector will ask how much cash is currently on hand, both business and private. A difficult question is the highest amount of cash that has ever been held at any one time. Here the inspector is anticipating that he may, during a cash flow test, prove that cash must have been available.
- *Gifts and legacies.* Most legacies are documented in some manner although there can be occasions when they are not. Cash gifts from relatives, especially if abroad, are often mentioned. The inspector will ask if there have been any. If so, expect him to be detailed in his questioning relating to these. If non-resident relatives are involved he may refer to the exchange of information clauses in a Double Taxation Agreement as a hint that if a false story is persisted with it may cause problems for the relative from their tax authorities.
- *Gambling wins.* The frequent mistake made by clients is to think that the inspector is trying to find out how much is spent on gambling so he can include it in his capital statement or means test. Whilst this is true, he is really interested to know if there have been any wins that may explain the appearance of cash at some stage. If your client intends to put forward a betting win story he is best advised to do it at this meeting and to give details e.g. horse, race meeting, the odds, and the name of the bookmaker.

These are important areas. In a few weeks' time the inspector may produce a cash flow and ask how some particular item has been funded. Your client, suddenly realising that his undeclared cash receipts are in danger of being discovered, explains it by saying he had cash saved up at home and may explain its accumulation by a gambling win or a gift. Inspectors are told to treat such claims with suspicion and it will be a difficult task getting the inspector to accept the tale at the best of times (Revenue Investigation Handbook, IH 2201).

Betting wins

5.38 The Revenue experience is that many such claims are false and subsequently withdrawn. Others are not persisted with when firmly challenged but those that do persist tend to find their story rejected by the Appeal Commissioners and the courts. Extracts from some judgments indicate the difficulties you will face:

> 'He alleged that these were betting wins . . . it was for him to prove that . . . The Commissioners merely had his statement. Other statements made by him . . . showed that statements of his were . . . unreliable . . . the Commissioners . . . said: You have not discharged this burden and therefore

> the assessments must stand. They were under no duty to take any other course.' (Harman J in the case of *Kilburn v Bedford 1955 36 TC 262.*)
>
> 'In my view the answer to this appeal is . . . simple. The Commissioners, having considered all the evidence before them found quite categorically that they were not satisfied that the whole sum . . . had been derived from betting wins...The onus was clearly on the appellant . . .' (Wynn-Parry J in the case of *Roberts v McGregor 1959 38 TC 610.*)

If, at this opening interview, the client has denied such a cash hoard, or such a source of cash, he is in severe difficulty. It is difficult enough to convince the Revenue; if there have been lies then one must be extremely pessimistic about the outcome. The words of Harman J reproduced above from *Kilburn v Bedford 1955 36 TC 262* make this absolutely clear.

It would have been better to tell the truth (it always best to do so or say nothing), i.e. that he had a source of cash. Why? Because just think about the advantage that has now been handed to the inspector:

- The client has lied. His protestations that the inspector's estimates of unrecorded cash takings are excessive are ignored by the inspector who points out that the client cannot be relied upon. If pushed to formal appeal before the General Commissioners they are going to find it difficult to accept your client's assurances, if this is all the evidence there is. He has proved to be an unreliable witness.
- If the truth had been told at the outset, the inspector is going to find it difficult to add to the disclosed figures. Other, unsubstantiated, explanations have more chance of being accepted. As it is, the inspector jumps to his own conclusions and it will be a difficult task to have him change his mind.

Handling disclosures

5.39 It is better if your client tells you of a disclosure to be made before he makes it. You need to decide how best to make the disclosure and what the Revenue's likely reaction might be. Having it sprung upon you in the meeting is not the best time. If it happens, stop the interview so that you can explore what has happened and the amounts involved with your client.

5.40 If your client is to make a disclosure be a little careful. Whilst the Revenue encourage disclosure, and do tend to treat such people more leniently than those who deny, the current climate for voluntary disclosures is a little uncertain.

Consider the words of Dawn Primarolo, The Paymaster General, when announcing the Revenue 'hot-line' for those wanting 'confidential advice' from the Revenue in relation to their past tax offences and when commenting on the criminal offence clause for fraudulent tax evasion introduced at a very late stage into the Finance Bill 2000.

> 'The new statutory offence will be just one in a package of measures aimed at cracking down on the informal economy. Our message is simple—get the confidential advice and help offered by the Inland Revenue to help join the legitimate world of work, or face the consequences in six months time.' (Inland Revenue Press Release, 27 June 2000.)

Since then, however, there has been the Revenue Press Release of 18th January 2001. This announced the successful prosecution of Frank Moran but the release contained the following announcement by the Revenue:

> '4. The Inland Revenue is also committed to ensuring that people pay the right amount of tax at the right time. Anyone who has used offshore bank accounts, in a similar way to Moran, or understated their profits or income by any other means, should make an early voluntary disclosure to the Inland Revenue.
>
> 5. Taxpayers who make a voluntary disclosure by coming forward before the Inland Revenue starts an investigation can normally expect to settle with the Inland Revenue for tax, interest and penalties.
>
> 6. The amount that has to be paid by someone who comes forward voluntarily is usually considerably less than would be payable under a confiscation order, which is normally sought in prosecution cases. Additionally, the matter is dealt confidence and there would be no criminal record against the individual concerned.'

This makes it quite clear that voluntary disclosures will not be prosecuted so in the vast majority of cases there will be nothing to fear but it would just be as well to be sure your client has adequate protections in place under the Code of Practice the Inspector is working under. If not, or there is doubt, it would be best to seek some specialist expert advice before proceeding with an interview at which your client will make a disclosure of tax irregularities.

Specific matters

5.41 The inspector may have something specific that he wants to explore. It may relate to some information he holds and wants to check out. It may arise from his examination of the books and records, if he has had an opportunity to examine these before the meeting. It is difficult, if not impossible, to properly prepare for anything that may arise under this head.

Some help may be obtained by asking the inspector if there are any specific points he wishes to bring up at the meeting. If he says there aren't but he proceeds with some, you will feel on stronger ground to object and refuse to deal with them at the meeting. Of course this will depend upon the nature of the questions and the potentially serious consequences of them.

This part of the meeting does however give your client an opportunity to say things that are relevant and have not already been covered e.g. to point out that he is not of UK domicile if an offshore account is involved.

It is also a good idea to indicate any possible means problems that exist at this stage. There may be an advantage in reducing the inspector's enthusiasm for the case.

Preparation

5.42 Good preparation starts even before the client is investigated. It starts with your own files.

Ensure your working papers are neat and easy to follow. Ensure journals are properly explained with cross-references to supporting evidence. This will make supplying information quicker and cheaper. It will however be difficult to remember why a particular adjustment was made in a few years' time. If the adjustment appears to be suspect you may find yourself in some difficulty with the Revenue.

If, when preparing accounts, your client tells you of something relevant to the figures, note it down. It could be an uninsured loss, a theft by an employee, a bad purchase that had to be thrown away, an event causing disruption to the business e.g. road works, a flood.

5.43 The first thing to do when the inspector gives notice of a full enquiry is to review your file for such notes and ensure the inspector is told of anything relevant.

A useful exercise is to schedule out the last six years' tax returns and accounts. This enables trends, fluctuations and ratios to be quickly spotted and assists in focusing on danger areas in discussions with the client, and in forecasting the areas the inspector is likely to be focusing on. See the examples below.

Example: Tax return summary schedule

5.44

	1996/97	*1997/98*	*1998/99*	*1999/00*	*2000/01*
Salary	25,000	25,000	25,000	30,000	30,000
Bonus	5,000	15,000	50,000	25,000	20,000
Expenses	12,000	12,000	12,000	12,000	12,000
Rents	3,000	3,000	0	0	2,000
Interest	750	800	500	5,000	5,500
Pension Premiums	2,500	2,500	2,500	5,000	5,000
Expenses	12,000	12,000	12,000	12,000	12,000
Spouse	*1996/97*	*1997/98*	*1998/99*	*1999/00*	*2000/01*
Wages	20,000	20,000	20,000	25,000	25,000
Bonus	10,000	20,000	50,000	15,000	15,000
Interest	350	500	4,000	4,250	5,000

This schedule may cause you to review the following points with your client before seeing the inspector.

1. What does the wife do in the business? Are her wages the result of tax planning or does she genuinely earn what she is paid? (It is of course possible to have the roles reversed.)

2. The significant increase in interest for the spouse in 1998/99 and client in 1999/00 will need enquiries into source of capital for such an increase.

3. Expenses have the look of a round sum amount of £1,000 per month and with no fluctuation over the years do appear to be a withdrawal of petty cash as a 'perk'.

4. Rents are not declared for 1998/99 and 1999/00. It is possible that this is an error in the accountant's office, or possibly the client owns the property from which his company trades. Often the client thinks his accountant knows about this and so does not tell him about it at tax return time.

5. Other points may arise but the example illustrates how scheduling out helps quickly to see trends, possible omissions and even technical topics.

Example: Accounts schedule

5.45

Year End	*31/03/97*	*31/03/98*	*31/03/99*	*31/03/00*	*31/03/01*
Sales	115,000	118,000	123,000	131,000	140,000
Cost of Sales	51,750	50,740	60,270	66,810	70,000
Gross Profit	63,250	67,260	62,730	64,190	70,000
MU%	122%	132%	104%	96%	100%
GP%	55%	57%	51%	49%	50%
Interest	3,750	3,100	2,900	3,800	4,100
Wages	23,000	23,750	23,900	21,750	21,800
Packaging	750	825	1,475	1,650	1,950
Repairs	450	625	6,750	950	625
Net Profit	25,000	29,000	21,000	28,500	32,000
Drawings	15,000	17,500	25,000	30,000	35,000
F & F Additions	1,100	950	7,500	150	450

This schedule quickly identifies the following:

1. Gross profit percentage is falling. Is there an obvious reason for this?

2. Wages have fallen. Has client found a way to pay off-record to avoid NIC?

3. Packaging costs increased in 1999, at the same time gross profit dropped. Did client start to divert sales this year or was there a change in the way trade was conducted?

4. Repair expenditure in 1999 was high. It coincides with drop in gross profit and increase in packaging. Did something happen in the business? Could the additions be private items?

5. Drawings exceed net profit for the last three years. Is this an indication that sales are understated?

Expect Revenue to argue for a restriction on interest allowable on the basis that the overdraft has funded private spending.

Main points

1. Consider whether you will agree to attend a meeting at all. Think about the preconditions recommended by the Tax Faculty, and balance these against the wishes of your client and the desire to bring the enquiry to a close as quickly as possible. Remember non-attendance does not prejudice penalty loadings.
2. Assess the fitness of your client to attend a meeting.
3. Take care not to give the Revenue information that your client has not authorised.
4. Ensure the inspector has issued a Code of Practice.
5. Have an early discussion with your client to establish any possible problem areas.
6. Consider asking the Revenue for a list of points to be covered at the meeting.
7. If you decide to proceed with a meeting remember the basics:
   - Keep answers concise and to the point.
   - Do not guess at what you think the question is. Have it clarified.
   - Do not guess at answers. Decline and research the correct answer.
   - Do not tell lies.
8. Prepare for the meeting by knowing the answers to the following typical topics.
   - i. What the business precisely is.
   - ii. How it is organised?
   - iii. Who does what in the business?
   - iv. Who are the main customers and suppliers?
   - v. What is the service chain?
   - vi. What security arrangements are there?
   - vii. What problems have there been in the business?
   - viii. What is the level of any wastage?

ix. What estimates or balancing figures were introduced into the accounts?

x. What non-financial records are there?

xi. Who writes up the records and when?

xii. How is cash controlled?

xiii. What is the broad level of personal and private expenditure?

9. Consider the most amount of cash ever held at one time.
10. Has your client received any gifts or legacies; is there any evidence of these?
11. Have there been any gambling wins? If so gather the evidence together.
12. Be careful if your client intends to make a disclosure, consider obtaining expert assistance with this.
13. Prepare well by reviewing the last six years' accounts and returns.
14. Decide the venue you want for the meeting.
15. Stop the meeting if your client becomes distressed or the inspector is aggressive.

Chapter 6

The Argument

Summary of chapter

6.1 This chapter gets to the heart of the investigation, the argument over what figure should be assessed. It covers:

- the dangers of accepting seemingly modest proposals too quickly;
- the process of critically reviewing an inspector's proposals;
- a structured approach to substituting your own figures, including a discussion on the standard of evidence you will need;
- a review of the Revenue's investigation techniques and how to challenge them;
- the most effective ways to break an impasse;
- how to tactfully deal with a stubborn inspector; and
- the Revenue's policy on reopening early years of assessment.

Introduction

6.2 Following the fact-gathering phase the inspector will either close his enquiry or put forward proposals for extra profits to be taxed. You may expect him to say that he concludes the profit returned is unreliable because the records from which they were prepared are unreliable, proved by some flaws he has found. He therefore proposes an alternative figure of profit. This will have some sort of logical base. It may be the application of a mark-up rate, it may be the result of a capital statement, it may apply some ratio or other.

At this stage the inspector is likely to be concentrating on one year: the year he has reviewed. Once that year is agreed, he would typically seek to impose the same basis to earlier years that have not been reviewed at all, let alone in detail. This is a danger zone.

Example

6.3 The Inspector proposes to add a modest-looking figure to last year's return, say £4,000. Your client thinks it is uneconomic to pursue an argument;

it's less than £1,000 of tax, so he instructs you to agree. The inspector then hits you with the 'earlier years' argument. He will contend that it is unlikely that the irregularities started in the one year he chose to examine and that on the balance of probabilities, an adjustment is needed for earlier years also.

Let us take a look at the damage this could do. You have just agreed an addition of £4,000 for the year to 31 March 1998. The inspector proposes taking this figure and applying the Retail Price Index (RPI) to it to arrive at the additions for earlier years, but he will restrict himself to the last six years, as follows:

Year end	*Add back*	*RPI*
31/03/00	4,000	168.4
31/03/99	3,865	164.1
31/03/98	3,768	160.8
31/03/97	3,669	155.4
31/03/96	3,545	151.5
31/03/95	3,465	147.5
31/03/94	3,400	142.5

If this is a simple case of a small sole trader liable at basic rate, this translates into income tax assessments as follows:

Year	*Additional assessment*	*@*	*Extra tax*
1999/00	4,000	23%	920
1998/99	3,865	23%	888
1997/98	3,768	23%	866
1996/97	3,607	24%	865
1995/96	3,465	25%	866
1994/95	3,400	25%	850
Total tax payable			£5,255

The Inspector has not yet finished. He wants interest.

Year	*Tax*	*Due date*	*Interest to 01/04/01*
1994/95	850	01/04/95	410
1995/96	866	01/04/96	358
1996/97	865	01/01/98	241
1997/98	866	01/01/99	159
1998/99	888	01/01/00	93
1999/00	920	01/01/01	20
Total interest			£1,281

It is becoming clear that agreeing to the modest £4,000 was not quite as cost-effective as you and your client first thought, and there is worse to come. There is a penalty. More about this later but for the purpose of this example, let's just accept that it will be 35 per cent of the additional tax.

Penalty 5,255 × 35% = £1,839

So, all in all, the figure is:

Tax	5,255
Interest	1,281
Penalty	1,839
	£8,375

This is a long way from the just under £1,000 that came into your client's mind when the additional £4,000 was agreed, and there is worse to come.

The example has so far ignored any possible Class 4 NIC liability. If this is due, there is an additional:

Year	*Additional Earnings*	@	*Class 4 NIC*
1999/00	4,000	6%	240
1998/99	3,865	6%	231
1997/98	3,768	6%	226
1996/97	3,607	6%	216
1995/96	3,465	7.3%	252
1994/95	3,400	7.3%	248
Total Class 4 NIC			£1,413

Interest on late paid Class 4 contributions was introduced with effect from 1992/93. [*Social Security Contributions and Benefits Act 1992, Sch 1, para 6(2)(3)*]. You should take care that it is not applied to earlier years in error.

Year	*NIC*	*Interest*
1994/95	248	119
1995/96	252	104
1996/97	216	60
1997/98	226	41
1998/99	231	24
1999/00	240	5
Interest		£353

So, we now have an extra £1,766 just on Class 4 NIC. This exceeds the original expectation in itself. Then comes the NIC penalty £494 (£1,413 × 35 per cent).

So the total is now:

Tax	5,255
Class 4 NIC	1,413
Interest on tax	1,281
Interest on Class 4 NIC	353
Penalty	2,333
	£10,635

The inspector says he would be willing to recommend a settlement of £10,900.

You are very much wishing you had looked at that £4,000 suggestion more seriously. You start trying to argue your way out of it – will you succeed? You may, but you also may find yourself stuck with the figures. Your client is totally unhappy. He will not pay your fee and you are worried he may leave you also.

Just when you are beginning to forget this sorry episode, the file is in archive, time is healing the wounds, and the client is talking to you again, there comes yet another blow. The local VAT fraud team call to say the Inspector of Taxes has told them about the investigation. They are disappointed that you have not called them to sort out the VAT on these additions. They want to interview your client; it will be tape-recorded.

You have completely overlooked the VAT aspect of these figures but you quickly calculate that VAT on the total additions agreed is £3,292 plus interest (quick calculation of £800) plus penalty (at least 20 per cent so £658). Your client will need to find another £4,700!

In fact your quick calculation is wrong because VAT is due on more than the tax assessments. You have forgotten that because of the introduction of self-assessment, one year dropped out; it didn't for VAT.

6.4 Regardless of the subtleties of the computation, the example serves to illustrate that failing to appreciate the consequences of what is being agreed is very costly. In the example we started with an expectation that our client would pay less than £1,000 but he ended up parting with over £15,000!

One tip for reducing the figures is to deal with the VAT issues at the same time as the direct tax settlement. The Revenue settlement would have been reduced by some £1,600 in the example above (see Chapter 11 for a full review of VAT adjustments).

Reviewing the proposal

The inspector will have spent some time attempting to discredit the accounts. This will be easy if the records are clearly inadequate as demonstrated by the need to introduce estimates or significant balancing figures but the inspector may have to work hard in other cases.

Cash flows

6.5 Cash flows are a good way for the inspector to discover those cash jobs that your client may have thought beyond detection. The inspector will work on the basis that if all receipts are banked, as he has often been told, then cash must be drawn from the bank for personal spending.

He will have established the pattern of this at the interview. 'How do you organise your housekeeping?' he may have asked. 'I give my wife £100 a week each and every week' your client may have said. 'Every week? Has there ever been a time when you may have missed?' the inspector asks. 'No, never. I am a proud man and always ensure there is food on the table for my family' your client retorts.

The inspector then scans the bank statements looking for a period when no cash was withdrawn and homes in to prepare a cash flow for this period. He has computer software to help him with this.

6.6 Such computations are quite damning but it is necessary to carefully review them. Very frequently you will find a problem with the opening cash figure. This is an odd situation. To demonstrate the inspector's cash flow is wrong you have to show that your client's record of cash on hand is incorrect, so his records must be wrong!

Nevertheless it is important to ensure the figures being used are about right.

The private side

6.7 The inspector may choose to attack the case from the private side. He will gather information on your client's lifestyle and spending and produce a capital statement. These are rarely used these days because they are so time-consuming and very inaccurate.

This is basically a set of accounts for the client's private affairs. It measures growth in wealth and spending against known income.

It is a tried and tested investigation tool and is accepted by the courts (*Johnson v Scott 1978 52 TC 383*) but it is time-consuming and expensive to produce and the Revenue prefer accountants to do this for them (see Revenue Investigation Handbook, IH 2093). The accounts are only as accurate as the information used and the critical area will be personal and private spending and so a very careful and detailed review of a client's spending is needed. Clients resent this but it is the only way if accurate figures are to be produced.

6.8 One of the problems is that you will be dealing with history and no records of private spending are likely to exist. The bank statements and credit card statements will help but cash spending will be the problem.

The only way is to establish current spending and, after ensuring there has been no change in lifestyle, apply the Retail Price Index to this to convert it into the likely figure for the year being reviewed.

An aide memoir of areas of expenditure is useful to ensure no aspects are missed. The Revenue produce one for their inspectors to use (see Revenue Investigation Handbook at IH 2145).

Business economics

6.9 Having demonstrated that the accounts are unreliable and cannot be accepted as a basis for assessing liability the problem becomes one of estimating what the likely figure should have been. The inspector will probably use business economics to do this i.e. he will look at how the business operates and reconstruct what was likely to have happened.

6.10 Having received the inspector's suggested addition to the profits for the year under review, you need to know how the inspector has arrived at his figure and why. It is unacceptable for the inspector simply to produce a mathematical calculation of the sales a business could, in theory, make.

There needs to be some underlying reason for setting aside the returned profit and replacing it with another estimated one. Revenue guidance to inspectors says:

> 'Do remember that a business model does not prove conclusively what the profits of a business were . . . If there is no other reason to believe the records are unreliable, the profits shown by the business model are merely an alternative to those shown by the accounts and the Commissioners might consider the latter to be more reliable' (Revenue Investigation Handbook, IH 1975).

These reasons could vary in degree.

(i) There is clear evidence that accounts are incorrect e.g. omitted bank account containing undeclared takings.

(ii) There is overwhelming evidence that figures declared are incorrect e.g. drawings not capable of funding obvious lifestyle.

(iii) Persuasive evidence that margins in the accounts are wrong e.g. gross profit margin on a pub is only 10 per cent when all others have 35 per cent minimum and no obvious explanation is available.

(iv) Balance of probabilities evidence that the accounts are likely to be incorrect e.g. the records are clearly poorly maintained and unreliable and some key ratio (e.g. gross margin) is considerably different from that theoretically expected.

If the books and records from which the accounts were produced are good and reliable and the accounts have been prepared on a technically sound basis then any suggestion that the profit returned be increased, if there is no persuasive evidence that something is wrong, should be resisted firmly (see Revenue Investigation Handbook, IH 1975).

6.11 It is important to be critical about what constitutes good records. Your idea of good records may be that they are neat, easy to follow and a set of accounts can be produced quite easily from them. An inspector of taxes will be more critical. For example, is there a stock figure, was cash on hand counted, when are the records written up and from what?

It should be borne in mind that there is no concept of materiality when it comes to a tax return. To put it crudely, when an accountant is putting together a balance sheet he is only concerned that it is 'about right' and is not bothered about getting it 'absolutely right'. In testing whether he is 'about right' he applies a materiality test that is based upon various criteria. So, for example, if the balance sheet shows net assets of say £20 million but some figure may be £10,000 out, he is not concerned because £10,000 either way on £20 million will not influence anyone's view of the state of the company. If however the net assets were say £20,000 and that figure is out by £10,000, it would be material and he would need to qualify the accounts if he could not resolve the matter. In either case, the Inland Revenue want their tax on that £10,000. So a set of accounts may be perfectly acceptable from many viewpoints but may not be so from a taxation point of view.

6.12 If you have now concluded that, for one reason or another, there has to be a figure for extra taxation it is then a question of trying to arrive at the most likely figure. It is important to remember that the standard is 'on the balance of probabilities'. Many tax inspectors would seem to require absolute proof and that is even beyond the criminal standard of 'beyond reasonable doubt'. This is well demonstrated by an example that many experienced practitioners will be familiar with. A client has been selling widgets and the local inspector asks if any expenditure was unvouched. The answer is that there were no receipts for the purchase of widgets. The inspector says without a receipt he cannot allow the expenditure. This is nonsense. If a man is selling widgets he must have got them somehow. On the balance of probabilities he had to buy them and so there must have been expenditure.

This argument does, perhaps, occur more frequently with the absence of fuel receipts. It is obvious, however, that once it is accepted that there is a vehicle and that it is used, then fuel must have been purchased for it. The problem is estimating what the expenditure was likely to have been, on the balance of probabilities.

Of course every single case is different but each one needs to be approached with a questioning, open and critical mind.

6.13 It is also vital to consider whether what the inspector is saying is factually correct.

The author was once asked to look at a case in which the inspector was wanting to settle at £350,000. The case involved a pub and the inspector had taken the current year's price list (1993) and applied it to the purchase invoices for an earlier year (1989). His explanation? He did not know the prices charged in 1989 and so could only go on information available and there was no evidence that the taxpayer had increased his prices since 1989. As well as this there was a serious arithmetical error in the inspector's computations. That case eventually settled for £35,000 and all it needed was a questioning review of the figures being put forward by the Revenue.

So carefully check the facts the inspector is using:

- are they correct?
- is the inspector making links that are not just factually unproved but just plain impossible?
- is the arithmetic correct?

6.14 Assuming that you are now satisfied that the inspector is comparing like with like, hasn't flown in the face of the known facts and is arithmetically correct, what is the next step? You should consider:

- what it is you are trying to prove (i.e. demonstrate);
- what information you need to achieve this (i.e. evidence);
- where this information (evidence) can be obtained; and
- if it is not readily available whether it can be created.

Always keep in your mind that you are dealing in probabilities; conclusive direct evidence is not always required.

Example 1

6.15 In the case of a pub, typically the inspector will have reviewed the gross profit margin and produced his own model of what he would have expected. This is when accuracy of replies at the first interview becomes vital.

The first point is that, very rarely will he have been able to check this accurately for the year under review. All necessary data is unlikely to be available. He is likely to have based it on recent purchases and sales because data is available e.g. the price list displayed in the bar.

An immediate observation is therefore that any result achieved is not directly related to the period being investigated.

- Have prices been increased beyond those imposed by the brewery?
- Has the sales mix changed?

It is likely that the inspector has taken a sample period, not a full year.

- Is this sample period representative of a full year? If the Christmas period has been included, it may not be.
- If the period around Budget time is taken and an increase in duty has been announced, it may be that the client increased prices immediately but would not, of course, be faced with the increase until his next delivery and so enjoyed a short period on an increased margin.
- It would be wrong to take these periods and apply the results to the entire year. The longer the sample period taken, the more accurate the result but the more time and work that needs to go into it.

Example 2

6.16 In one case – a greengrocer, the inspector had produced some figures for a greengrocer following a gross profit exercise. These figures were exceptionally high. The client had however built an extension on his house many, many years before. He had done all work himself using reclaimed materials and took three years to build it.

The inspector consulted some tables for the year planning consent was given that gave construction costs per square metre and concluded that my client could not have afforded this out of declared drawings and savings for that year. Unfortunately after applying the Retail Price Index to this figure it came within 5 per cent of his proposed assessment for a more recent year. He had 'proved' his figures using two methods, and was confident.

Firstly he had produced a gross profit calculation using the prices from one outlet, a town centre shop close to his office. He had overlooked the fact that there were other outlets, mainly market stalls with cheaper prices and, importantly, a wholesale trade with even lower prices.

Secondly the building costs used by the inspector assumed a full range of professionals were employed as well as first rate builders using good materials from mainstream merchants.

This client had not used an architect, as was proved from the planning application. He had done the labouring himself, as was proved by witness statements from neighbours as well as photographs of him working on the building. Witness statements were also used as evidence that the work had been spread over several years, as were the photographs to a limited extent because they showed work progressing through different seasons. This proved that the expenditure was spread. Many materials used had been reclaimed or purchased at auction and evidence of this was gathered.

The inspector agreed to close his investigation after presentation of these facts.

6.17 Assuming you are not happy with the inspector's figures, what should you do? Quite simply you should produce your own figures. Do not use the inspector's figures as a base, but research your own using the following process.

- Decide on the sample period to use. If possible agree this with the inspector. If he has agreed the sample period, a potential area for conflict is removed. Do not however let the inspector dictate this. Remember you are building up your client's case; take the period you believe produces a supportable result that you would be prepared to present as evidence to an Appeal Tribunal if necessary. Note that this must be a supportable result and not necessarily the most beneficial result. There is little point in selecting a period that produces the lowest gross margin if it is easily discredited; you have wasted your time and all but destroyed your client's case.

- Having decided the period, research your own price list. You may find differing prices depending on the particular bar or lounge. If so, you may have to do more than one computation. Apply these prices to all relevant purchases, taking note to apply the correct VAT treatment (see Chapter 11 for a full review of VAT adjustments).
- Take account of other factors e.g. wastage. The only way to get the right wastage figure is to measure it. It is different at every establishment so there is only one way; understand the processes and measure each one. Don't forget to calculate the effect of other factors such as free staff drinks, happy hours, promotions, tokens from game machines. You must do this, with the help and assistance of your client. He must be involved in the process because only he has the necessary knowledge of the business. It also makes him feel more in control of what is happening to him.

6.18 If having undertaken the above exercises you produce a figure that is similar to the inspector's it should be possible to agree a settlement quickly. If different, your figures will have been better researched and be more accurate than his and so should provide the basis of agreement.

What should you do if your figures greatly exceed the inspector's? Quite frankly something is likely to be wrong with your calculations if this happens. If your client knows he is making more than the inspector suggests, he is unlikely to pay you to do an extensive business economics exercise just to prove the point, although fees may not be an issue if you are not charging or an insurance company is indemnifying (see Chapter 9 for a discussion on fees and insurance schemes).

Remember you are trying to either demonstrate that the profit returned is about right or agree an estimate of what it was likely to have been. It is for the inspector to propose the profit he believes to be assessable, if he is not accepting the self-assessment return, and ultimately assess this. So unless you know that the inspector's figure is grossly understated you should move towards agreeing the inspector's proposal. If however you know that your client's accounts are incorrect and by how much, you have a more difficult task to perform (see Chapter 10 for a review of disclosure requirements).

6.19 It is not possible to go through every trade and come up with a standard approach. Each trade is different and has its own variations and problems; these need to be searched out. Butterworths Tax Investigations contains data on many different businesses and may be a useful reference. To the extent that there is a standard approach it is as follows.

- Is the inspector's proposal acceptable?
- If not, what evidence is needed to reduce the inspector's figures or prove your own alternatives?
- Having identified what evidence is needed, set about gathering it, remembering you are trying to establish something on the balance of probabilities.

The impasse

6.20 Most cases settle by mutual agreement for one reason or another but on occasions there is an impasse: the inspector has reached a point at which he will move no further; likewise you or your client refuse to agree with the inspector. What next?

The case is now heading for the Appeal Commissioners, so it is useful to take a fresh look at the case through the eyes of an Appeal Commissioner. It is as well to remind ourselves of a sad fact – we have to prove the inspector is wrong, he does not have a burden of proof. [*TMA 1970, s 50(6)*]. It is a sort of 'guilty until proven innocent' situation.

6.21 The first thing to do is read over the file. Ask yourself if you fully understand the inspector's argument and how and why he has calculated the proposed figures for assessment. If you do not fully follow his workings or arguments, go back to him for clarification.

Having satisfied yourself that you fully understand what the inspector is saying, ask yourself if you are happy with any technical points the inspector is arguing. If not ask him for a note of the authority for his view. This may be a reference to statute or case law, and you can then have a look at this and decide if you agree. It can be the case that we all have some mistaken view of a particular point and when challenged to prove it find we cannot.

Let's take a common example as an illustration. The inspector may be saying that he cannot allow any unvouched expenditure (see 6.12 above on this point). Ask the inspector to quote the authority for his view, and he will struggle to find any. There is no statutory provision that says this and the author is not aware of any case law saying this. It is of course for the taxpayer to show that he did spend the money and a receipt does this; without it the more difficult task of demonstrating that it was probable the money was spent is necessary but the assertion that unvouched expenditure is not allowable is not correct. The author has recently come across inspectors who are quoting *TMA 1970, s 12B* as an authority for their view that unvouched expenditure is not allowable. This section is the one that requires records to be kept for the purposes of completing an accurate return. However that is all that the section says; nowhere does it say that unvouched expenses are not allowable. Failure to have retained receipts may result in a penalty for breach of *section 12B* but that is different from saying 'no receipt, no allowance'.

The inspector may have done what came naturally to him without too much thought about the strength of his ground. Once he realises that the ground beneath him is shaky, he may be more receptive to argument. In technical arguments it is important to remember that profit remains that calculated on commercial accountancy principles (see *Johnson v Brittannia Airways Ltd 1994 67 TC 99*). If the accounts prepared comply with these then that is the profit to be taxed unless the *Taxes Acts* step in and change something e.g. the

Taxes Acts do not allow depreciation so we add this back in the tax computation and apply capital allowances instead.

6.22 The next step is to consider the case you have made out for your client. Have you gathered evidence to support your argument? Sadly, in many cases, very little substantive argument is made. After peeling away the layers of generalised denial, has your case been presented in a better manner? If not, it is time to think about what you are trying to demonstrate and gather the information (i.e. evidence) to support it. Remember you are trying to establish the balance of probabilities, not prove beyond all doubt.

6.23 If you have gathered your evidence and put the case, consider if there is another way of presenting the same facts and evidence:

- Has the inspector understood your argument?
- Is he aware of your argument?
- Have the important pieces of information been lost in a mass of lesser material and so not had the impact you intended?

Consider other ways of proving the same point. If two methods arrive at similar answers, it provides very persuasive argument: e.g. if a review of your client's means produces a similar result to a gross profit exercise, it is likely that the figure computed is about right.

6.24 If, after taking all of these steps, you cannot think of any way to break the impasse, it is time for one of two things. Either look to be agreeing figures with the inspector or start thinking towards an appearance before the Appeal Commissioners.

At this stage, you may consider asking a colleague to have a look at the case and give a view. Someone who is not involved with the case, does not know the client, and has no feelings towards the inspector, can provide a good indicator of how independent Commissioners may view the case. You could consider asking an investigation specialist for a view or for advice.

If the conclusion is that you have a good case but the inspector is being stubborn or not giving sufficient weight to your evidence, try telling him so.

6.25 If it is downright stubbornness or stupidity that is the problem, think about an approach to his manager. Before doing this, try telling the inspector that an approach (i.e. complaint) is being considered but that you will delay this for seven days to allow him to consider the evidence and argument you have presented. In this way, you give him an opportunity to come to his senses and back off without the consequences of a black mark against him. It is important to realise that you may come across this inspector again in another case and it does no harm to try and maintain goodwill between your practice and the Revenue.

Thankfully the vast majority of inspectors behave in a reasonable and responsible manner but they are as human as the rest of us and can have their moments of 'red mist'.

There are, however, examples of unacceptable behaviour on a worrying scale, illustrated in several recent cases. The case of *Scott & Scott t/a Farthings Steak House) v McDonald (Inspector of Taxes) [1996] STC (SCD) 381* involved an investigation in which several inspectors had become involved, including the district inspector. It is a frightening tale of bullying by inspectors and even threats being made towards the acting agents who turned to a specialist firm for help. Even they found themselves faced with aggression on a scale they had never experienced. The case was taken before the Special Commissioners who strongly criticised the Revenue and awarded costs to the taxpayer. The second example is that of the disgraced inspector, Allcock, who was found to have accepted money and favours and was sentenced to a term in prison. In *R v CIR ex p Kingston Smith [1996] STC 1210* a judge could have sent the deputy chairman of the Board of Inland Revenue to jail for ignoring his injunction. The Revenue had raided the offices of Kingston Smith (a reputable firm of accountants) with a search warrant to obtain documents relating to a specific client. The Revenue wanted to remove the computer hard disk but this contained information on all clients, not just the one subject of the warrant. A court injunction was obtained stopping the Revenue from proceeding until the matter was clarified. The Revenue ignored the injunction and continued with their search. The judge was angry and said 'no citizen should be placed . . . [in the position Kingston Smith found themselves] . . . when he is dealing with a public body'.

6.26 If this has all failed, then the case can only be settled by the Appeal Commissioners, assuming, of course, that the inspector has issued an assessment, or an amendment to your client's self-assessment, against which an appeal can be made. An assessment, or self-assessment amendment, is the only way he can break an impasse himself. If one hasn't been made, the only remedy would be an application to close the enquiry under *TMA 1970, s 28A* but if the dispute is over figures, this is not the right forum. Now, do not lose sight of the fact that it is your client who is taking the inspector before the Appeal Commissioners, not the inspector taking your client. Take the initiative and contact the Clerk to the Commissioners yourself requesting an appeal to be listed for hearing. Do not leave it for the Revenue to organise the hearing; signal to the inspector that you are confident, pro-active and ready for the hearing.

Reopening earlier years

6.27 Once the inspector has established the omission for one year he must decide whether to reopen earlier years.

To reopen a year he has to make a discovery. There is however case law that supports the view that it is reasonable to conclude that if one omission is established it means that earlier accounts could be unreliable (*Rossette Franks*

(*King Street) Ltd v Dicks 1955 36 TC 100*). There is also a presumption of continuity i.e. that if someone's lifestyle and business remain unchanged it is reasonable to infer that his habits have remained unchanged (*Jonas v Bamford 1973 51 TC 1* in which the judge said 'once the inspector comes to the conclusion that, on the facts which he has discovered Mr Jonas has additional income beyond that which he has so far declared to the inspector, then the usual presumption of continuity will apply. The situation will be presumed to go on until there is some change in the situation, the onus of proof of which is clearly on the taxpayer.').

6.28 Under normal circumstances the Revenue can make an assessment up to five years from the 31 January following the end of a tax year e.g. an assessment for the year 1999/00 can be made at any time up to 31 January 2007. [*TMA 1970, s 34*]. If there has been default the time limit is extended to twenty years! [*TMA 1970, s 36*].

The law in this area has changed several times over the years; it was once necessary to obtain an Appeal Commissioner's consent to raise out of normal time assessments. Years before 1983/84 remain under the old rules but it is unlikely that many cases will go back as far as that.

No assessment on a deceased person can be made more than three years from 31 January next following the tax year of death [*TMA 1970, s 40*] e.g. A client dies on 1 March 2000 i.e. in tax year 1999/2000. No assessment can be made after 31 January 2004.

6.29 The Revenue have internal guidance on how far their inspectors should go back but refuse to make these known to the public.

For small amounts they will settle for the year being reviewed and not seek to reopen earlier years. This could be for additions below say £1,000. Larger amounts will have them seeking a settlement covering the previous six years but only in more extreme cases are they likely to go beyond this to the full twenty years.

Main points

1. Agreement to reasonably modest sums for the year under review can result in large sums being paid to the Revenue.
2. It is important to critically review any proposals made by the inspector, they have been known to make incorrect assumptions.
3. Consider preparing your own computations in co-operation with your client.
4. Remember that the standard of evidence required is on the balance of probabilities.
5. It is not correct to say that unvouched expenses cannot be allowed.

6. An impasse can be broken by having an independent person review your case.
7. If faced with a stubborn inspector consider ways of making a complaint.
8. Be prepared to proceed with an appeal hearing if the case warrants it.
9. Consider if it is necessary to review private spending.
10. Be aware of the various cash flow tests that will be applied by the inspector.
11. The normal time limit available to the Revenue is five years but in investigation cases of a serious nature they can go back 20 years.
12. Assessments cannot be made on a deceased person after three years.

Chapter 7

Powers of the Revenue

7.1 The inspector does not often have to resort to the use of formal powers to progress an investigation and to obtain the information he wants. Most cases are worked within the spirit of co-operation that is encouraged, but the presence of these powers encourages co-operation. These powers are many and varied. It is necessary to know how far the Revenue can go in obtaining information and what to do if faced with a formal order.

This requires a detailed look at the statutory provisions. If you just need to have a general overview of the sort of powers the inspector has, simply read the overview below. If you then need to know more about the powers go to the detailed analysis.

Overview of chapter

7.2 The inspector's first power is the one that can require a person to complete a tax return. Persons other than companies have, in normal circumstances, until 31 January following the end of the tax year concerned to complete a return and deliver it to the Revenue (e.g. a return for the tax year 2000/01 must be with the inspector by 31 January 2002). Companies usually have twelve months from their year end. There are variations for those who are not asked to complete a return until near the deadline and for companies who have varying accounting periods. There is a system of penalties for failing to deliver a return on time.

7.3 Once the inspector has the return he has the right to check its accuracy by giving written notice that he is to enquire into it. There is no right of appeal against the inspector's decision to do this, and he does not have to say why he has decided to check the return. A taxpayer does have the right to ask an Appeal Tribunal to order the inspector to stop his enquiry.

7.4 The inspector will ask for information so that he can check the return. He will, initially, ask for this to be produced voluntarily but if refused or unreasonably delayed he can order its production within a set time limit. There are penalties for defaulting on such an order. The law allows the inspector to demand the production of any documents, or particulars, that are relevant to the return and are reasonably required. He could therefore require information to be collated for him or for a question to be answered. He cannot demand anything that is not relevant to the return he is checking (e.g. information relating to an earlier tax year) nor can he demand something that is unreasonable. A taxpayer does have the right to appeal against such an order or for further time to comply with it. This power is sufficient for most investigations but if not there are some wider ranging ones that the inspector could use. [*TMA 1970, s 19A*].

7.5 If the inspector needs documents or particulars for a year not covered by the powers linked to tax return enquiries he can use *TMA 1970, s 20(1)*. To use this he has to obtain the consent of an Appeal Commissioner having first given the taxpayer an opportunity to voluntarily produce the information. He must give at least 30 days for production of the information. In some serious cases the Revenue can insist on immediate production and do not have to give a warning of what information they want. Penalties can be incurred if there is a failure to comply with an order.

7.6 Sometimes the inspector believes that a third party has documents that will help his investigation. This may be a bank, a customer or supplier for example. He can order that person to produce such documents after first having informally requested them and then having obtained the consent to an order from an Appeal Commissioner. Certain protections are given to the legal profession and to accountants and tax advisors but these are not extensive. Penalties can be imposed for failing to comply with the terms of an order.

7.7 It is a criminal offence to destroy, conceal or falsify a document once the Revenue have said they would like to see it. The courts can impose a prison sentence of up to two years for this.

7.8 In serious cases the Revenue can obtain search warrants and have a power to order an advisor to hand over documents if a judge agrees.

Detailed analysis

To require notification of tax liability [*TMA 1970, s 7* (income tax and capital gains); *FA 1998, Sch 18, para 2* (companies)]

7.9 This is not something to be done when the inspector so orders but is something that must be done without prompting.

The first step in the tax system is to ensure that the Inland Revenue are aware of who is supposed to be paying tax. It is not left for the Revenue to go out and find these people, although they do of course do this. The legislation directs that any person liable to tax must notify the Revenue within strict time limits. These time limits are:

- for income tax and capital gains tax, six months from the end of the tax year (e.g. for 2001/02 the deadline is 5 October 2002) [*TMA 1970, s 7(1)*];
- for corporation tax, 12 months from the end of the accounting period. [*FA 1998, Sch 18, para 2(2)*].

7.10 There are penalties for failure to give such notice.

- For income tax and capital gains tax: the maximum penalty is 100 per cent of the tax due and unpaid by the following 31 January (i.e. for the year 2001/02 if notification of liability has not been given by 5 October 2002 and the tax due for 2001/02 has not been paid by 31 January 2003). [*TMA 1970, s 7(8)*].
- For companies: the maximum penalty is 100 per cent of the tax due and unpaid 12 months after the end of the accounting period. [*FA 1998, Sch 18, para 2(3)*].

Prior to 1988/89, the penalty was a maximum of £100 for each offence.

This means that a penalty for late notification of an income tax or capital gains tax liability can be avoided by ensuring that if the notification deadline is missed, the tax due is paid by the following 31 January.

7.10A There is however a new notification requirement effective from 31 January 2001. This relates to Class 2 National Insurance contributions (i.e. the NIC liability of the self employed). It requires a person commencing self employment to notify the Inland Revenue within three months from the end of the month in which they commence. [*The Social Society Contributions (Amendment) Regulations 2001/45*]. There is a £100 penalty, for failure. This notification will also be accepted for tax and Class 4 NIC purposes.

7.11 Prior to this new requirement arguments arise over what is a notification.

Cases have been seen in which a business with employees had not notified the Revenue separately from their PAYE section of the fact that they were in business. PAYE was being operated on employees' wages, with the full knowledge of the Revenue, yet no returns were being issued on which to make a return of income because the Revenue claimed they were not aware of the client's liability.

It can be dangerous to assume the Revenue know that returns need issuing; it does not follow that because there are employees, there will be profits chargeable to tax (see IH 5063 for Revenue policy if PAYE is being applied).

7.12 The legislation merely says that notice must be given, it does not specify the manner in which this must be given, but *ICTA 1988, s 832* says that the word 'notice' must be interpreted as meaning notice in writing. The Revenue, however, take the view (see IH 4626) that it is not necessary to advise in writing to comply with the legislation. It is difficult to reconcile this with *section 832*.

It is therefore the author's view that there is a requirement for the notification to be in writing and it would be wise to follow this up if there is no acknowledgement within a reasonable period. The author would suggest 28 days, this being the Revenue's published service standard for responding to correspondence.

The requirement applies to each and every year so if the Revenue suddenly seem to forget about your client it is no defence to say that they were aware of him in previous years. If a return is expected, and needed, but none is issued by the Revenue it would be wise to contact the local tax office before the failure to notify offence deadlines are triggered. The fact that a return had previously been made in fact prejudiced the taxpayer's argument in the case of *Barney v Pybus 1957 37 TC 106* because it showed he was aware of the requirement to submit returns.

7.13 Any penalty can be mitigated, or even waived, under the usual mitigation powers given to the Revenue. [*TMA 1970, s 102*]. The guidance given to inspectors in 'failure to notify' cases is only briefly set out in IH 5525 but is approached in the same manner as all other tax-geared penalties (see Chapter 15).

Co-operation can reduce the penalty by 40 per cent, and is usually easier to obtain in failure cases than others. The Revenue believe that most cases will attract the full 20 per cent reduction for disclosure, or even 30 per cent if it was a voluntary disclosure by your client. They see size and gravity as being more difficult and will be influenced by the length of time involved. In the author's view the penalty will also be affected if there was a reasonable excuse for the failure. You can, however, expect any 'reasonable excuse' argument to be considered critically and what may be reasonable in one case may not be in another. For example, a young man leaves school at 16 with a poor academic record. He commences a small business washing cars. He has never heard of the Inland Revenue or VAT and his income is small. His failure might be regarded as reasonable. Someone in their 30s, with experience of life, may not be able to convince the Revenue that he had never heard of taxation (see also IH 5063).

To require completion of a tax return (*TMA 1970, s 8* (personal returns), *s 8A* (trustee's returns), *s 12AA* (partnership returns); *Finance Act 1998, Sch 18, para 3* (companies))

7.14 There are some differences in the wording of the main statutory provisions but, in essence, a person can be required by the Inland Revenue to make a return of income and gains for any year. Once required to complete a return there are deadlines for the delivery of the completed return to the Revenue. These time limits are:

- for individuals and trustees, 31 January following the end of the tax year (e.g. for the year 2000/01 the return must be delivered by 31 January 2002), with the proviso that there will always be at least a period of three months for returns issued for completion after 31 October.
- for companies, the latest of:

(a) 12 months from the end of the accounting period;

(b) if the period of account is less than 18 months, 12 months from the end of this;

(c) if the period of account exceeds 18 months, 30 months from the start of it;

(d) three months from when the return was issued.

In all cases there is a requirement to deliver the return to the officer or inspector requiring its completion. The Revenue only regard a return as being delivered if it is handed over to the office that issued it or placed in the office letter box. Merely putting it in the post is not delivery until it is received in the Revenue office (see Revenue Company Taxation Manual, CT 10315). If a deadline is approaching and the relevant Revenue office is many miles away, it would be wise to speak to the inspector to see if he will agree that it can be handed in at a local office.

7.15 The legislation also requires that accounts, statements, documents and reports be delivered with the return if so required. [*TMA 1970, ss 8, 9; FA 1998, Sch 18, para 3(2)*]. Individuals and trustees have a protection in that only those reasonably required are covered. Companies have no such protection.

What is meant by 'reports'? *Hansard* records that these are mainly, but not exclusively, those required by the *Companies Act*, especially the directors and auditors report (Standing Committee Debates 21 June 1990, cols 378, 384).

7.16 Inevitably there are penalties for failing to deliver on time.

Individuals and trustees

7.16A For individuals and trustees, it is £100 rising by a further £100 after six months. If the return is over a year late then, in addition to the £200, a further maximum penalty of 100 per cent of the tax liability that should have been on the return. [*TMA 1970, s 93*]. The penalty can never exceed the tax due on the return however.

The Revenue can opt out of the extra £100 after six months by applying to the Appeal Commissioners for a direction that the taxpayer be put on a daily penalty, maximum £60 per day, from notification of the direction. [*TMA 1970, s 93(3)*]. This penalty cannot be imposed once the failure has been remedied.

The fixed monetary penalty (£100/£200) can never exceed the actual tax liability for the year outstanding at the filing date. [*TMA 1970, s 93(7)*].

Note, however, that the tax linked maximum penalty does not apply to the partnership tax return, only to those of individuals and trustees. This is logical. There will never be any tax assessed on a partnership return so having a tax related penalty would mean there could never be a penalty for a failure to deliver the partnership return.

Companies

7.16B For companies, if the return is late, a £100 penalty is incurred unless it is over three months late in which case it is £200. Persistent late filers have a stiffer penalty. If late filing penalties have been incurred for the previous two accounting periods, the penalties for the third year are £500 and £1,000. [*FA 1998, Sch 18, para 17*].

There is no provision for the Revenue to seek daily penalties from a company but there are tax-geared penalties. If the return is not delivered within 18 months of the end of the accounting period (in most cases this will mean up to six months late), a penalty of 10 per cent of the tax unpaid at that point, providing it is delivered within 24 months of the end of the period. Otherwise the penalty is 20 per cent of the tax unpaid at the 18-month point. [*FA 1998, Sch 18, para 18*].

Reasonable excuse

7.17 A penalty may be waived if there was a reasonable excuse for the late return. [*TMA 1970, s 118(2)*]. Given the length of time there is to complete returns, it will be difficult to persuade the inspector that it was not possible to complete it on time. If there are genuine difficulties, tell the inspector in good time and agree on how to proceed.

A common reason for late submission is that figures are unknown because of an ongoing Revenue investigation. This is a peculiar excuse but it is no excuse at all as the case of *Dunk v Havant Commissioners 1976 51 TC 519* reveals. In that case, the taxpayer complained about penalties for failure to submit returns, arguing he did not have the necessary information to do so. The court was unsympathetic because every taxpayer had a responsibility to make a return and it was open to him to include estimated figures and explain that his return was unreliable. The Revenue published their practice as regards estimated returns in Tax Bulletin October 1998. This is that provisional figures are accepted on condition that reasonable efforts were made to get the correct figure and that the actual figure is supplied as quickly as possible thereafter.

Another favourite excuse often put to the inspector is that the income was returned elsewhere, perhaps on someone else's return. Walton J was not impressed with this argument when he considered the case of *Nicholson v Morris 1977 51 TC 95*. He ruled 'it is idle for any taxpayer to say to the Revenue, "Hidden somewhere in your vaults are the right answers: go and dig them out of the vaults." That is not a duty on the Revenue. . . .'

To enquire into returns [*TMA 1970, s 9A* (income tax and capital gains tax), *s 12AC* (partnerships); *FA 1998, Sch 18, para 24* (companies)]

7.18 Once a tax return is received, the Revenue have a period of time within which they can make enquiries into that return as described in Chapter 3.

7.19 The Revenue only get one chance to enquire into a return. Once they have closed the enquiry, that return cannot be enquired into again. That does not, however, prevent the Revenue from taking action if they discover that fraud or negligence has resulted in a loss of tax (see Chapter 3).

The general scheme is that a taxpayer who is honest and takes reasonable care to ensure his tax returns, and other information supplied to the Revenue, are correct should be confident that his tax affairs are in order. Those who are dishonest or careless can never rest easily as the Revenue can approach them for many years to come, so they can never regard their affairs as in order. It is difficult to find fault with this scheme of things.

7.20 Under the old system, before self-assessment, the inspector had to say why he was making enquiries. Under the new legislation he does not have to and in fact is instructed by the Board of Inland Revenue not to give any reasons (see Revenue Enquiry Handbook, EH 302). Note however that the legislation itself does not prohibit the Inspector giving his reason, it merely says he does not have to. It is Revenue policy not to.

As there is no mechanism for appealing an enquiry notice it may be appropriate in cases where your client's records are good and both he and you are happy that all is well to put forward an argument for closure of the enquiry and insist the Inspector justifies his reasons for continuing by saying what is causing him concern.

To call for documents (Part 1) [*TMA 1970, s 19A* (income tax, capital gains tax and partnerships); *FA 1998, Sch 18, para 27* (companies)]

7.21 The power to enquire into a return would be rather lame if the inspector was unable to access the documents that enable him to check the accuracy of a return. It comes as no surprise therefore to find legislation to enable him to do this. This basically provides that an inspector can order the production of documents and particulars. It is important to understand this power, because a client who has done nothing to cause any suspicion of wrongdoing, may become the subject of one of these. It is a potentially draconian power.

Experience says that the more documents the inspector looks at the longer the investigation will take; more questions arise that need to be researched and answered, and so the costs increase. It is therefore important that the Revenue only obtain those documents that they are entitled to, unless other material positively helps the client settle the matter.

The Institute of Chartered Accountants in England and Wales Faculty of Taxation supports this view. They say, '. . . it cannot be in the interests of your client to volunteer information that could lead to a long and unjustified enquiry into his affairs. It is important to use common sense' (ICAEW Tax Faculty booklet, Questions and Answers on Revenue Enquiries under Self Assessment, p 12).

7.22 First of all, the Board of Inland Revenue require their inspectors to informally request any information and give a reasonable period for its production. In practice, inspectors are allowing a period of 30 days. They are advised not to issue reminders but, on expiry of the period given, to issue a *section 19A* notice direct to the taxpayer.

Experience to date shows that inspectors are following this procedure with enthusiasm. There is therefore a risk of difficulties with a client if he suddenly receives a formal notice with an accompanying letter saying that it is because you have not responded to a request for information.

7.23 The inspector can only ask for anything that is relevant to the figures on the return and is reasonably required. What is relevant? Well it must obviously relate to the entries on the return. Some documents are obviously relevant – a statement of interest or the financial records of a business. Others are less obviously relevant. Private bank statements of a businessman, for example, may have no direct relevance to the figures reported. Inspectors are told to be prepared to justify requests that are not obvious (EH 319).

Private bank statements are a difficult area; if they contain business receipts then they will be relevant, if they were examined when preparing accounts or the tax return they will probably be relevant, but otherwise it is the author's view that they are not and their production should be resisted.

It seems the Revenue itself is unsure because it tells its officers that the legislation does not specifically give access to private bank accounts, so there are no hard and fast rules that the information can always be obtained (EH 398).

The author's views on this are agreed by the Faculty of Taxation who in section 15 of their guidance leaflet (Questions and Answers on Revenue Enquiries under Self Assessment) say,

> 'This is a grey area. If business receipts or payments have gone through the private bank account the Revenue is . . . entitled to see the . . . statements. If no such items have passed through . . . and the . . . statements are not the only independent source for checking other entries on the return it will normally be sensible to resist the request . . .'.

Some documents however must be irrelevant. A request for non-financial records must be suspect e.g. diaries, correspondence.

On the subject of diaries see the comments of the Faculty of Taxation at section 17(f) of their leaflet: 'the Revenue say that if an officer wants to check travelling and subsistence costs ... the officer has a right to examine "work diaries" as well as hotel bills etc. We think that this is questionable unless the diary is used as a prime record to record expenses.'

7.24 There is an emphasis in the wording of the statute on the purpose of the production of records. The legislation says they are to be produced 'for the purpose of determining whether and, if so, the extent to which the return is incorrect or incomplete', but note this wording is absent from the company equivalent. [*TMA 1970, s 19A(2)(a); FA 1998, Sch 18, para 29*].

The emphasis is on finding out if the return is wrong, not satisfying the inspector that the entries are correct. That was the general scheme before self-assessment.

It must therefore be open for an inspector to argue that he wants work diaries, for example, because they would help him to determine the extent to which the return is incomplete.

We now have the benefit of some reported decisions on section 19A notices but it has to be realised that each is decided on its own merits and cannot set a precedent. Some 'grapevine' reports of cases taken before the General Commissioners indicate mixed results. They do however serve as an encouragement to appeal those cases in which you genuinely believe the information demanded is unreasonable or irrelevant.

Some reported Special Commissioners cases have indicated a requirement for the Inspector to demonstrate that the information is relevant to establishing if the return is incorrect.

The message must be to consider what the Inspector has demanded carefully, if you cannot see the relevance then ask the Inspector to justify his demand, if still unconvinced then appeal the point to the Appeal Commissioners.

7.25 The Revenue do not believe that accountancy working papers (referred to by them as the 'link papers') can be obtained under *section 19A* because they are not in the power or possession of the taxpayer. They do, however, advise that a request for 'particulars' may be made to explain the link between a figure in the records and a figure on a return (EH 389). The subject of ownership of accountants' papers is a difficult area, but it would be safer to assume that by some method or other the Revenue could obtain access to them.

7.26 The time given to comply with a notice must be at least 30 days. An inspector may agree further time if appropriate. The writer's experience to date is that further time will not be agreed, no matter what the circumstances. Fortunately there is an appeal process. The client can appeal within 30 days of the formal notice on the grounds that:

- all or some of the information required is not reasonably required;
- documents required are not within the client's power or possession; or
- insufficient time has been allowed for compliance with the notice.

If the Commissioners confirm any part of the notice it must be complied with within 30 days of the date of this decision. So if you know that it will take more than 30 days to get the information together, you cannot afford to wait for the appeal decision before commencing work. It is worth pointing out that if an appeal is lodged on the basis that a record does not exist or it has been destroyed, your client risks a penalty for failing to keep proper records. [*TMA 1970, s 12B(5); FA 1998, Sch 18, para 23*].

7.27 It is worth noting that inspectors are not allowed under *section 19A* to:

- insist that taxpayers attend meetings;
- require that documents are delivered to the Revenue's office – they need only be produced;
- gain access to premises;
- obtain documents brought into existence for an appeal hearing;
- obtain documents relating to a year not under enquiry;
- obtain information about someone else's return;
- get information from third parties; or
- ask for general information.

(EH 403.)

There are, however, other powers that enable the inspector to do many of these.

7.28 Failure to comply with a notice brings a penalty. [*TMA 1970, s 97AA; FA 1998, Sch 18, para 29*]. Inspectors must write giving 14 days to comply or penalty proceedings will be commenced according to their guidance manual (EH 684). The initial penalty is £50 and will be imposed by the Revenue. After that a daily penalty can be imposed. A limit of £30 a day is put on Revenue imposed penalties. If the Revenue think the case is deserving of a higher figure they must go to the Appeal Commissioners who can impose a penalty of as much as £150 per day, while the failure to comply continues. Penalty notices are appealable. Those by the Revenue can be appealed to the Appeal Commissioners. Those imposed by the Appeal Commissioners can be appealed to the High Court.

To call for documents (Part 2) [*TMA 1970, s 20(1)*]

7.29 This provision is in many ways similar to *section 19A* and *FA 1998, Sch 18, para 27* and it is expected to be used only in rare cases when this legislation does not apply. This would be when the Revenue are investigating under the discovery procedures (see Chapter 3 above) and not under the return enquiry powers, or if an enquiry under *section 19A* or *FA 1998* does not permit an order for the information required but *section 20* may.

Section 20(1) requires a person to deliver documents in his possession or power relevant to his tax liability. It may also require the production of particulars e.g. answers to factual questions or the production of a statement of assets.

An inspector must first informally request the information he wants and then obtain the consent of an Appeal Commissioner before he can issue a formal notice. The Appeal Commissioner must be satisfied that the inspector is justified in proceeding, before he can give such consent. The enquiry production powers have no such policing by the independent Appeal Commissioners and so are easier for the Revenue to use.

The taxpayer has no right of attendance at the hearing before a Commissioner for such a consent. The inspector must, however, provide a written summary of his reasons for seeking a consent, but not to the extent that it would identify an informant, or if the Commissioner has directed that reasons need not be given because doing so would prejudice the Revenue. [*TMA 1970, s 20(8E)(8H)*].

A period of at least 30 days must be given to comply with the notice. [*TMA 1970, s 20(8D)*].

7.30 On a practical note, there is little point, in a normal case, of having a *section 20(1)* order issued against a client. If the inspector's informal request is relevant and reasonable there can be no justification in prejudicing any penalty mitigation by being unco-operative. There will, however, be the exceptional case in which the inspector's request is seen as unreasonable or he is asking for particulars that are not relevant to the assessment of tax. It may cost an excessive and unreasonable amount in fees to comply with a request having regard to the case and the relevance of the details asked for.

In these circumstance it is important to set out any objections, with reasons, in writing and ask that the inspector lays the letter before the Commissioners when seeking consent. He is obliged to present the Commissioner with full facts and the letter is relevant and so must be placed before the Commissioners (see *R v MacDonald and CIR ex p Hutchinson and Co Ltd 1998 71 TC 1*). It is the only chance to influence the decision, because the hearing is ex parte i.e. neither client nor agent are allowed in.

Before writing the letter, make sure you talk over the pros and cons of non-co-operation with your client. He may be unimpressed further down the line when the inspector tells him that the penalty mitigation is not as high as it might have been because of the Revenue's need to obtain formal orders to obtain information if that was the first he knew of it.

To call for documents (Part 3) [*TMA 1970, s 20(2)*]

7.31 This power requires great care. The inexperienced frequently mistake it for a search warrant but it is nothing of the sort. It is a very similar power to *section 20(1)*. In fact the only difference in wording is that 'the Board' may require the production of documents or particulars instead of 'an Inspector'. 'The Board' is of course the Board of Inland Revenue and this power is usually only used by the Special Compliance Office and even then very infrequently.

The subtle differences from *section 20(1)* are that 'the Board' does not have to give informal notice that it intends to make such an order, and is not required to obtain the consent of an Appeal Commissioner to the making of an order. [*TMA 1970, ss 20(7), 20B(1)*].

In fact, the only restriction is that 'the Board' can only issue a notice under *section 20(2)* if the case is serious. [*TMA 1970, s 20(7A)*]. Also there is no requirement for any period of time to comply.

The only remedy if you are aggrieved by a *section 20(2)* notice is to apply for a judicial review of the Board's decision, something that is easier said than done when faced with such a notice.

7.32 What often happens is that the Revenue arrive at a client's premises, usually in some numbers, without having advised you that they are doing so. The inspector in charge will hand over the *section 20(2)* notice. This will demand the production of documents or particulars and will provide that they are produced on that day i.e. immediately. He will then ask that he and his team be allowed entry to collect these documents.

The client, probably stunned and confused, possibly with staff and customers around, is unlikely to carefully read the notice or to notice the subtleties of being asked for consent to enter. He thinks he is the subject of a search warrant and that he has no choice but to let the Revenue team in. Once in they will ask if they can open cupboards, look in handbags etc. and are typically allowed to by the client.

If the client does have the presence of mind he will tell the inspector either to wait outside while he collates the information required or advises the inspector that he will deliver the information to his office within the next day or so. Hopefully he will also call his agent so that he can do all of this for him.

7.33 *Section 20(2)* does not give the right of access to premises. It does not even give a right to inspect premises, let alone search them. All it does is require the production of information. The author understands that the Board of Inland Revenue do not condone the practice illustrated above. This is however a practical book that aims to present tax investigations as they happen in the field and not the mere theory behind them. The author has experience of clients being visited with *section 20(2)* notices as described.

7.34 As indicated earlier, judicial review is the only legal remedy to a *section 20(2)* notice. It is, however, hard to imagine a client calmly reading the notice, referring to the legislation, and then challenging the inspector on his 'reasonable opinion' or on whether the details demanded are 'information relevant' or on the meaning of 'serious prejudice' [*TMA 1970, s 20(2)(a)(7A)*], following which he advises the inspector to wait outside while he instructs his solicitor to apply for judicial review. Such things are for you to consider and advise on when you get the call from the client, but if the Revenue have been and gone by this time, and this is likely, there is probably little point because they will already have achieved their aim.

7.35 The investigation expert is not, unfortunately, the one who usually gets the call and so the opportunity for a knowledgeable specialist to consider the merits of such a notice are few and far between. In practice, the client will usually call after the Revenue has left with their sack of papers.

To call for documents from a third party [*TMA 1970, s 20(3)*]

7.36 The workings of this power are very similar to *section 20(1)* i.e. consent of a Commissioner is needed, an informal request is to be made first, time to comply must be given.

One difference is that *section 20(3)* only permits the Revenue to obtain documents in the third party's possession or power, one cannot be required to furnish particulars. So an inspector can demand to see, for example, invoices relating to transactions with someone but cannot ask for a list of transactions to be provided, unless such a list already exists.

Inspectors are told to be sensitive about using *section 20(3)* because of the burden that may be placed upon the third party or because of the sensitivity of telling someone else about an investigation (IH 8080). If third party information is needed, the inspector should ask the taxpayer to obtain it for him. There may however be times when the inspector may think this is not a good idea. He may know that it will not be obtained or may think there is a risk of collusion with the third party. In those cases the inspector may simply proceed under *section 20(3)*.

Unless the case is very serious, the inspector has to tell the taxpayer that he has served a notice under *section 20(3)* and give him reasons for doing so. [*TMA 1970, s 20(8E)*]. He can however be exempted from doing this if fraud is suspected and a Commissioner agrees there are reasonable grounds for such a suspicion. [*TMA 1970, s 20B(1B)*]. It is unlikely that such a case would be working in a local district; if fraud were suspected it is more likely that the case will be working with the Special Compliance Office, but the changing nature of investigation practice within the Revenue makes it unsafe to make such an assumption. Certainly if you do learn of a *section 20(3)* notice for which your client has had no reason provided to him you should be concerned and either seek advice from a specialist investigation practitioner immediately or try and find out the reason from the inspector.

7.37 The inspector can be exempted from giving reasons for less sinister reasons. These are simply:

(*a*) to protect the identify of an informer; or

(*b*) the Commissioner giving consent to the *section 20(3)* order has directed that certain information need not be disclosed because giving it may prejudice the assessment or collection of tax. [*TMA 1970, s 20(8G)*].

Note that this does not exempt the inspector from telling the client he has made an order only that he not give his reasons. Although *section 20(8E)* does not in itself say that a copy of the order must be given to the taxpayer, *section 20B(1A)* says that one must be provided.

7.38 The taxpayer involved must be named in the *section 20(3)* notice. [*TMA 1970, s 20(8)*]. It may sometimes happen that an inspector is not aware of the identity of the taxpayer on whom he requires information. If so, he may use *section 20(8A)* to obtain the consent of a Special Commissioner to the issue of a *section 20(3)* notice without naming the taxpayer. He can only ask for this if:

(*a*) he does not know the taxpayer's identity;

(*b*) there are grounds for believing that the taxpayer may have failed to comply with the *Taxes Acts*;

(*c*) that failure is serious; and

(*d*) the information is not readily available elsewhere.

Anyone served with such a notice may object within 30 days on the grounds that compliance would be onerous. If that matter cannot be agreed with the inspector, it is referred to the Special Commissioners for a decision. [*TMA 1970, s 20(8B)*].

7.39 An inspector cannot give a notice to a barrister, advocate or solicitor but the Board of Inland Revenue can [*TMA 1970, s 20B(3)*] and these cannot be required to produce anything subject to 'professional privilege'. Legal professional privilege is a complicated area.

7.40 A notice does not oblige anyone to produce a document that wholly originates more than six years before the notice unless there is a reasonable ground for believing that fraud may be involved. In that case there is no time limit, but only if a Commissioner approves of this.

If the taxpayer has died, *section 20(3)* cannot be used after six years have elapsed since the death.

A protection is available against the production of audit working papers. [*TMA 1970, s 20B(9)*]. This protection is however a little weak. It only applies to papers that are the property of the auditor and were created by him in connection with the performance of his functions as auditor under any enactment. In other words, the auditor must have been appointed because of a statutory need. Partnerships, sole traders and very small companies have no protection therefore, but the Revenue voluntarily extends the protection if an audit to statutory standards has been performed (Revenue Statement of Practice SP 5/90). The protection is not general, it only applies to papers created for audit purposes. If accounts are being prepared at the same time as the audit, the papers in respect of accounts preparation are not protected.

A working rule adopted in the author's practice to distinguish between the two types of papers is that if the paper is one that the client could have created himself from his prime records then it is probably not protected. If the client could not have created the paper himself then it is the auditor's property, created for the statutory audit, and so is protected.

A similar protection is available for communications between a tax advisor and his client that relate to advice about his tax affairs. [*TMA 1970, s 20B(10)*].

Note however that this protection is for notices served on an auditor or tax advisor. The tax advisor's client does not have a protection for the same correspondence, so the mirror image of the correspondence could be obtained from the client.

This has led one specialist tax journal (The Schmidt Report) to suggest that all advice should be taken offshore and conducted orally and even recommends that if there is correspondence to destroy it. This is a bit extreme and would seem to assume that the client has illegal evasion in mind. The reason most people want a protection is not to prevent the Revenue uncovering evasion but to avoid the Revenue discovering any argument in their favour. For example: you are advising your client on a transaction and giving your view on the tax consequences of this. You may rehearse your argument and any counter-argument you think the Revenue may have. It is for the Revenue to decide on any counter-argument themselves without assistance from you. You do of course have an obligation to ensure the Revenue have sufficient facts to decide on the position they may wish to take.

All of these protections are however swept away if the person receiving the notice has assisted in the preparation of 'any information, return, accounts or other document' delivered to the Revenue and the document demanded explains such information etc. that has been delivered. [*TMA 1970, s 20B(11)*].

A more detailed review of the relationship between accountants, advisors and the Revenue is at Chapter 9.

7.41 Recipients of *section 20(3)* notices have, on occasions, turned to the courts for judicial review. In the main, the courts have supported the Revenue in its use of *section 20*. In fact Lord Lowry in the House of Lords decision of *R v CIR ex p T C Coombs & Co [1991] STC 97* thought that successful judicial review was practically impossible. This was mainly because the inspector would have to have acted irrationally before the court could intervene, but his reasons for making an order are reviewed by the consenting Commissioner who must therefore have concluded that the inspector was acting reasonably.

7.42 If faced with a *section 20(3)* precursor it is vital to make written representations to the inspector arguing why he should not proceed and ask that he put those representations before the Commissioners. He is bound to do so following the *Coombs* case and the more recent case of *R v MacDonald and CIR ex p Hutchinson & Co Ltd 1988 71 TC 1*. The time to influence the decision to issue the *section 20(3)* notice is before it happens. There is little chance of changing it after the event.

There have been some successes, such as in R *v O'Kane and Clarke ex p Northern Bank Ltd [1996] STC 1249*. In that case, a *section 20(3)* notice on the bank demanded too much information relating to a named individual. The notice did not specify documents but asked for every piece of information held by the bank. The court held that this was 'unfair and oppressive'.

However have regard to *R v CIR ex p Ulster Bank Ltd 1997 69 TC 211*. In this case, the court approved of the Revenue's precursor request for information required under *section 20(8A)* covering a period from 12 October 1979 to 12 April 1991 relating to unknown taxpayers and unspecified accounts. The bank estimated it would take five years for one man working full time, to comply with the request at a cost of £346,000! The Court of Appeal was unimpressed. As this was a Court of Appeal decision it has greater authority than the *Northern Bank* case.

If the author were to offer any hope that *Ulster* does not make *Northern* redundant it would be that *Ulster* concerned *section 20(8A)* which is really a fishing expedition section whereas *Northern* concerned *section 20(3)* relating to a named individual regarding whom the Revenue went fishing.

Ulster Bank appears to be suffering from *section 20(8A)* for it was back in Court again for judicial review arguing that the Board of Inland Revenue could not delegate authorisation for such an order to an Inspector. Once again Ulster was unsuccessful (*R* v *Commissioner of Tax ex p CIR; R v CIR ex p Ulster Bank Ltd ([2000] STC 537)*.

Section 20(3) was again before the Court for Judicial review in *R v CIR ex parte Lorimer ([2000] STC 751)*. This concerned an order for banks to produce accounts relating to a solicitor's clients, it was argued these were privileged documents but the Court disagreed. Legal privilege did not apply when the solicitor himself was being investigated.

An important case for the Revenue is *R v CIR ex p Banque International a Luxembourg SA [2000] STC 708*. They again succeeded in surviving an attack on a *section 20(3)* notice, this time on a Human Rights issue concerning the right to confidentiality and privacy. The judge observed that the *Human Rights Act* allowed interference by the Government for the protection of the taxation system and revenue. The Judge also quoted Mr Justice Lightman in *R v CIR ex p Archon Shipping Corp ([1998] STC 1151)*: 'the Courts should be astute to avoid giving by the avenue of judicial review, what is, in reality, a second look at the commissioner's decision.'

7.43 A note of caution for anyone with an informal request for information on a third party. Do you have a statutory, professional or contractual obligation to ensure client or customer confidentiality? If so, you cannot provide any information voluntarily without the consent of the third party. You will have to advise the Revenue of this reason for non-compliance and await the formal notice.

To call for the papers of a tax accountant [*TMA 1970, s 20A*]

7.44 This power is only relevant to agents; it does not affect your clients directly. It basically permits the Inland Revenue access to all of your clients' files if you yourself have committed a tax offence. If you are subject to one of these orders, you are most likely to already be under the guidance of experts. If you have not done so already get expert help.

Essentially, if you have been convicted of a tax offence, or have a penalty imposed upon you under *TMA 1970, s 99* for assisting in the preparation of incorrect accounts, information or returns then you can be the subject of this section.

Destruction of documents [*TMA 1970, s 20BB*]

7.45 This section makes it a criminal offence to falsify, conceal, destroy, or otherwise dispose of a document that has been required by a notice under *TMA 1970, s 20* or *s 20A*. It also makes it an offence if an opportunity to deliver the documents voluntarily prior to a formal order has been given. It is also an offence to permit the falsification, concealment, destruction or disposal of any such document.

The only real difference is that under an informal order the request is treated as having expired after a six-month period. For the formal order it is treated as having expired when two years have elapsed.

The penalty is a criminal one and carries a rather stiff maximum penalty of a two-year jail sentence and a fine.

Search warrants [*TMA 1970, s 20C*]

7.46 It is under this section that the Inland Revenue have the power to obtain search warrants and execute them. The legislation only permits the Revenue to apply for a warrant if there are reasonable grounds for suspecting that serious fraud is involved. The officer applying for the warrant has to give evidence on oath that there are reasonable grounds and that evidence is likely to be found on the premises specified. Also the officer has to swear on oath that he is acting with the approval of the Board of Inland Revenue in that particular case.

It can be seen therefore that a warrant would only be applied for in the most serious of cases and after a considerable degree of internal scrutiny by the Inland Revenue at a very high level. This prevents the local inspector simply obtaining the search warrant any time he wishes.

The warrant must be approved in England and Wales by a circuit judge, in Scotland by a sheriff and in Northern Ireland by a county court judge.

It goes without saying that if you or your client is the subject of a search warrant, then you are facing a very serious case indeed that is heading for a prosecution in the courts. In such circumstances, urgent expert legal help is needed.

While you are waiting for such help and assistance to arrive on scene, you should take some elementary steps to ensure that the warrant is valid. It seems obvious, but check that the officers have come to the correct address. If the warrant says that the premises at No 22 can be searched and you are in No 24 then no matter what the officers try and persuade, the warrant is not valid for a search of No 24.

The warrant must be exercised within 14 days of it being granted. It will specify the number of officers that are permitted to search the premises and it will also specify the hours within which a search may be conducted. Check these things and if there are more officers than authorised or the Revenue are outside their permitted hours, then demand that they leave the premises immediately.

7.47 The warrant permits a search of the premises and permits the seizure and removal of documents that are relevant to the investigation, subject to legal privilege. Legal privilege is a complex area that has been the subject of much recent debate following a Special Commissioners' decision. It is a difficult area that is best left to the legal experts to deal with.

Once documents have been removed, the officer in charge of the search must provide a record of what has been taken. Documents taken can only be retained for as long as necessary and must be returned if a photocopy will suffice as evidence.

The Revenue, having taken away many books and records, can cause enormous problems to a business. The legislation permits access to the seized documents, albeit under Revenue supervision, and permits the taking of copies of any document required. [*TMA 1970, s 20CC*]. There is one proviso and that is that the Revenue can refuse copies and refuse access if they believe that this would prejudice an investigation or a trial.

7.48 Search warrants by the Revenue are still a rarity but have been used more frequently in recent years. More importantly, they have been used against major firms of accountants and solicitors by Revenue officers investigating what tax practitioners would customarily have described as tax avoidance schemes.

Unfortunately accountants and tax advisors cannot control the activities of their clients so if the Inland Revenue suspect one of your clients of serious fraud, sufficient to justify obtaining a search warrant, they may also seek a warrant to search the advisor's premises to obtain your file and any other documents relating to that client. This will of course mean that an agent could be faced with having to deal with a search of his premises, even though he or she is blameless. It is therefore advisable for agents to have procedures in place to deal with a search should it occur.

At its most basic, this should ensure that staff at the reception desk know precisely who to call should the Revenue present themselves. There should be a sufficient number of senior people in the organisation familiar with the legislation and the basic checks to be carried out as described above.

The telephone numbers of appropriate solicitors and specialist tax investigation advisors should be readily available both to the senior people who may have to deal with the warrant and to the reception team who may be faced with dealing with it in the absence of any assistance within the office. An urgent call should be made to the solicitor or investigation expert.

The good news for advisors is however that search warrants against them are likely to be very rare in the future following *Finance Act 2000*. This introduces a new power [*TMA 1970, s 20BA*] to require production of documents if a judge agrees.

Orders for delivery of documents (Part 4) [*TMA 1970, s 20BA*]

7.49 The Revenue have recognised that search warrants on third parties such as accountants, solicitors and banks are an unnecessary blunt instrument that causes distress. They have therefore introduced legislation to avoid this.

The search warrant is replaced by an order to produce documents. The procedure is similar to a search warrant in that a senior Revenue official must approve an application to a judge for a production order. Instead of a team of officers turning up at your office with a warrant you will receive an order to produce specified documents within a time limit.

The Revenue must tell you they are applying for an order and you have the right to attend this, they only need to give you three days notice though. It is a criminal offence to tip off the client. Failure to comply with the order is also a criminal offence it being deemed a contempt of court, so you face the possibility of imprisonment.

Information power re transfers of assets abroad [*ICTA 1988, s 745*]

7.50 This section and its associated capital gains tax equivalent at *TCGA 1992, s 98*, is a power specifically to support the anti-avoidance sections at *ICTA 1988, s 739* onwards, commonly known as 'Transfer of Assets Abroad'.

This power permits the Board of Inland Revenue (n.b. not a local inspector of taxes) to require any person to provide particulars that are thought necessary for the purpose of these anti-avoidance sections. A period of at least 28 days must be given to comply with a notice. The particulars that may be required include:

- details of any activity carried on for others;
- anything the Board think proper to investigate whether or not the recipient of the notice believed the activities to be within the anti-avoidance provisions or not; and
- details of any activities taken part in personally.

Solicitors are let off the hook a little. If all they did was give advice, then they are only effectively required to give the name and address of their client and anyone else who is involved in a transfer.

Appeal Commissioner's powers (precepts) [*SI 1994/1811* (Special Commissioners) and *SI 1994/1812* (General Commissioners)]

7.51 There are provisions for the Appeal Commissioners to order the production of documents, or the attendance of witnesses, necessary for an appeal hearing. It is quite some time since the author last saw the Revenue obtain documents or information by asking the Commissioners to use their powers, once the routine way for the Revenue to proceed.

Failure to comply can bring penalties imposed by the Commissioners.

It should be noted that this is not a power of the inspector, in fact you have exactly the same power as him in this circumstance i.e. you can ask the Commissioners to order the Revenue to produce a document that you believe is relevant to settling any appeal.

Force of personality

7.52 As we have seen, the inspector has a number of powers that enable him to obtain information, charge tax, and punish those have not fully complied with the rules. The inspector usually prefers not to have to use these formal powers but rely on co-operation, this being encouraged by the fact that the powers are there. This has advantages for the inspector beyond making life more relaxed and speeding up the progress of cases.

Inspectors often find they just need to ask for something and it is provided. There appears to be a general assumption that they can have what they request.

In Revenue circles this is sometimes referred to as 'the force of personality' and is regarded as an unwritten power.

It is wrong to assume that the Revenue is entitled to everything they ask for: such assumptions can prove costly.

Legal privilege

7.53 Privilege protections have been examined under each head where the legislation specifically provides them. There is however the question of common law legal privilege. This is a complex subject and there is a need to consult the expert lawyers on the subject when the need arises.

Those served with *section 20* notices sometimes run off to the Courts claiming legal privilege protection but they have generally found the Court unsupportive.

7.54 In the past year there have been two important cases on this subject.

Firstly there was *R v CIR ex p Lorimer [2000] STC 751*. In this case a solicitor was served with third party notices relevant to an investigation into his own affairs. It was held that legal professional privilege does not apply if the solicitor himself is the subject of investigation.

The next was *R (re Morgan Grenfell) v Special Commissioner [2001] STC 497* in which the Court of Appeal ruled that privilege was excluded from *section 20*, except where it was expressly preserved.

This may differ when action is taken under the criminal procedures but if faced with a civil production order assume that there is no privilege unless the specific legislation provides it. Examples are the protection of audit papers and correspondence with a tax advisor as discussed above.

Main Points

1. The 'failure to notify' legislation requires the Revenue to be told of liabilities each year. It cannot be assumed that they know just because a PAYE scheme is being operated or because returns were issued in earlier years.
2. Penalties will be incurred if a return is deliberately delayed while an investigation progresses and knowing that the Revenue have the information elsewhere in their system does not excuse a failure to make a return.
3. There are strict time limits for opening self-assessment return enquiries and any notice must be examined to ensure it falls within time and evidence of receipt retained to support your argument.

4. The inspector can call for the production of documents or particulars from your client but under the self-assessment legislation only those relevant to the return under enquiry and which are reasonably required. Demands for information not used in the preparation of the return or of a non-financial nature must be considered critically.

5. For periods not covered by the self-assessment system, or perhaps if that system does not go far enough, the inspector has another power to obtain documents or particulars. This time he needs the consent of an Appeal Commissioner before he can use it.

6. The Board of Inland Revenue do not need such consent and their power to order immediate production of information can be mistaken for a search warrant.

7. Third parties can be ordered to produce documents if an Appeal Commissioner so consents. The Revenue has to tell the client that they have made an order on a third party unless so doing would prejudice their cases or disclose an informant. The courts are supportive of the Revenue's power but have refused general fishing expeditions.

8. An accountant's audit papers are protected from disclosure unless they are vital to understanding an entry in the accounts.

9. Likewise a tax advisor's correspondence with his client is protected but remember that the mirror image of your file in your client's hands has no such protection.

10. It is a criminal offence to destroy any document once the Revenue have said they would like to see it.

11. Search warrants served on agents are likely to become even more rare now that a new power to order production of documents in criminal cases has been introduced.

Chapter 8

The Settlement

Summary of chapter

8.1 In this chapter the process of settling liabilities with the Revenue is explained. The author looks at:

- each of the forms your client will be expected to sign and advises on what should and shouldn't be done;
- the wording of offer letters;
- statements of assets and the certificate of disclosure.

Introduction

8.2 The point will be reached when the inspector's investigation is complete. You and your client have provided him with all the information he has asked for and can have. You have considered his proposals and the debate with the inspector on the amounts to be assessed has been completed. You have agreed with the inspector the number of years that are to be involved and have agreed the additional sums chargeable to tax for those years, commonly referred to as 'the add back'.

The next stage will be computations of the tax that has been lost for all of these years together with a calculation of interest taken to the date upon which it is expected that your client will settle his liabilities.

You will now be sent some documents that the Revenue will require completing. You may also at this stage be sent a draft of the settlement offer; the wording on these varies.

This is a very important stage of the investigation. All forms that your client will be asked to complete and sign are extremely important and it is essential that the advisor fully understands them, agrees that they are relevant, and explains them fully and properly to the client before inviting and advising him to sign them.

Basis of settlement

8.3 The Inland Revenue could now proceed formally. By that it is meant that they could amend the self-assessment return or make assessments for the amount of tax that is due. They can determine the amount of interest that is due on that tax and they could determine the penalty that is due. All such amendments, assessments and determinations could be appealed of course but the Inland Revenue are looking for a less confrontational and more agreed basis of settlement.

In place of such formal proceedings they will invite your client to make them an offer. This is often when your client begins to feel confident because suddenly the terminology is within his experience. Jargon such as 'offers' and 'deals' are frequently within his daily language. The Revenue system is not the same as that prevailing in commercial life.

The Revenue are looking for a lump sum offer that is less than the maximum due in law but which covers the tax, the interest and the penalties. Once such an offer is made and accepted by the Inland Revenue there is a contract between your client and the Revenue to pay that sum. The payment then loses its character of being tax, interest or penalties but is merely a contracted sum. Inspectors often refer to a 'contract settlement' to describe such a settlement.

8.4 Once an offer has been made and accepted, it should be regarded as final. There is, in all practical terms, no going back on it to correct mistakes, misunderstanding, or changes of mind. Over the years the author has often been asked to comment upon a settlement that has been agreed with the inspector of taxes but unless it is possible to set the contract aside for some reason (e.g. duress) it is a futile exercise. If your client wants a second opinion or you have doubts upon how the Revenue are settling the case, then advice should be taken before making the offer.

8.5 If matters cannot be resolved in this way, then the Revenue will follow the formal procedures. Under self-assessment these provide for a taxpayer to be told when the Revenue have concluded their enquiry into his return [*TMA 1970, s 28A(5)* and *FA 1998, Sch 18, para 32*], the system being that the inspector gives written notice of this. Most practitioners will now be familiar with such notices. Once the inspector has issued such a notice he is barred from asking any more questions and he is stuck with the tax assessed for that year unless he can use his discovery powers. [*TMA 1970, s 9A(3)* and *FA 1998, Sch 18, para 24*)]. This provides clients with certainty that their affairs are in order.

8.6 There is a concern over the Revenue's practice of not issuing a completion notice if there is to be a contract settlement (see Revenue Enquiry Handbook at EH 535). The Revenue's reason for this appears to be that following the normal procedures will cause all outstanding liabilities to be included on the statement of account and cause collection action to begin by the issue of demands to your client, perhaps before they have finalised the contract settlement. The Revenue prefer to account for investigation settlements separately from normal liability.

Without a completion notice your client's tax affairs remain open and the inspector can repeat visit the open years. This is not a satisfactory position.

The Revenue told the Chartered Accountant's Tax Faculty that in practice they would regard such a year as closed (see p 23 of Questions and Answers on Revenue Enquiries under Self-Assessment published by the Faculty of Taxation in 1998). They hoped the Revenue would publish an assurance on this. 'Taxation' of 15 October 1998 reported that it was thought the Revenue was intending to do this. The author can find no such published assurance. It does not seem to be a difficult thing to do, simply write to the taxpayer and tell him the enquiry has finished and state the conclusion is all that the legislation demands! To deny this because of some internal administration problem does seem unacceptable.

It is of course open to you to request that the Revenue do issue a closure notice, and to force this by applying to the Appeal Commissioners if the inspector refuses. It is unlikely he would refuse; his instructions are to issue one if so requested but to warn that this may cause collection procedures to commence (EH 544). This of course means that your client will then receive statements in the post demanding payment of large sums of tax when he believes all is under control and within the contract offer. Clients tend to be unnerved by such demands and you may be faced with having to placate them and explain how the Revenue cannot apparently cope with the necessary accounting very easily.

The Revenue's reason for this would however seem to disappear after the contract settlement has been made, accepted and paid. It is therefore the author's suggestion that at this point you request the closure notice. You may need to be prepared to help the Revenue match up payments that have been made because it is possible your client could be pursued twice for the same tax. Good client relations will depend upon your having warned the client this may happen and the fact that you have taken action to protect him.

The statement of assets and liabilities

8.7 At this stage the inspector is likely to request a statement of your client's assets and liabilities at a current date (see Revenue Investigation Handbook, IH 2175). You may have provided statements of assets during the investigation, typically one at the commencement of the period under review and one at the end of the period under review. The one at a current date is the easiest to complete because it asks for the assets as of today so cash can be physically counted and there is little risk of something being forgotten in the mists of time. The purpose of this is two-fold.

Firstly, it provides the Revenue with an absolute statement supported by signatures, and the certificate of disclosure, at a current date. Should your client ever be unfortunate enough to suffer another investigation at some point in the future, the inspector has a starting point with this statement of assets and so this will provide a very useful reference point for the future. Additionally, it does focus your client's attention on something he may have overlooked or rather cleverly concluded was outside the year under investigation and so need not be disclosed. Your client is faced with signing this form at the same time as he signs the certificate of full disclosure (see below) with your warnings ringing in his ears on the possible consequences of having failed to disclose fully.

Secondly, it assists the inspector when considering the means that your client has to meet an expected offer and so alerts him to the possibility of problems he may have in obtaining a signed offer because your client cannot meet the obligation upon him that it would impose. The inspector can consider the assets, their value and the extent to which they will be readily converted into cash. He can consider their value as security for loans and so can put himself in a position to properly debate a problem with you and your client. It is hoped that if there is a means problem you would have notified the inspector well before now.

8.8 The inspector will probably provide a stencil prepared by the Inland Revenue for the purpose of completing statements of assets and liabilities (form MS 142). The form does contain some notes of guidance but despite that, clients get very confused when asked to complete it unaided and the author receives many queries even from accountants who are used to completing it.

Bear in mind what is being asked for. Unless the statement is being prepared to establish current means, values are usually irrelevant. The inspector is interested in what has been paid for an asset and the source of the funds for this. When it comes to insurance policies, what is especially relevant are any single premium policies or any bonds that have been purchased with a lump sum. Once again the inspector is really only interested in surrender values or disposal values if there is a question of means.

Household goods and house contents frequently cause confusion and are usually best dealt with by simply referring to the house contents insurance policy and noting the insured value on the statement. The policy will usually highlight any specific items that are separately insured or have to be individually declared to the insurance company.

The liabilities section should not be overlooked.

If there is difficulty over a certain item or there is uncertainty as to what information to enter, do not hesitate to discuss it with the inspector. If you disagree with him and an unreasonable amount of work has to be done to satisfy him, you could consider going your own way, producing the statement as you and your client think fit but ensuring that the basis upon which it is completed is made clear on the face of the form.

8.9 Standard statements usually call for the inclusion of the assets of minor or dependent children. Prior to 6 April 1990, it was standard to demand information relating to a spouse. However the introduction of the independent taxation of spouses makes it a little more difficult for the inspector to demand this. Spouses are independent persons and if not under investigation personally may refuse co-operation. The inspector can of course always revert to *TMA 1970, s 20(3)* (see Chapter 7 above) but this does cause him some difficulty because his powers only permit him to demand the production of documents from a third party. He cannot require a third party to produce particulars and the production of a statement of assets would be asking for the production of particulars. The inspector may however ask for a statement of gifts to establish if any assets have been transferred between spouses.

8.10 When considering the statement of assets remember that it includes assets held by nominees or otherwise held on behalf of your client and also includes assets outside the UK.

8.11 If at this point your client advises you of an asset that has not previously been disclosed and has an impact upon the investigation, stop and consider what approach you are going to take. The inspector is obviously going to have to be told about it but the manner in which you make this approach would have to be considered carefully. See Chapter 10 on voluntary disclosures.

8.11A Should you agree to the completion of a statement of assets? The answer must depend upon the circumstances of each case.

If the Revenue have demonstrated a good case for suspecting the returns are incorrect it would be difficult to resist demands for statements relating to the year under enquiry, indeed the Inspector may use his powers under *section 19A*, or *section 20(1) TMA 1970* (see Chapter 7).

The inspector will frequently ask for one 'at a recent date'. This would usually fall into a year outside of the one under enquiry and so should be refused unless it serves some useful purpose. This could be that there is a means problem or you judge that, on balance, it is better to produce it and argue for greater penalty mitigation.

The certificate of full disclosure

8.12 Towards the end of the investigation, the inspector is likely to ask your client to sign a certificate of full disclosure (see IH 3020).

This is a vital document. There is no obligation in law for your client to sign it and you should explain this to your client. The logic for the inspector requesting it is quite simple. When your client submitted his tax returns he certified them to be correct and complete. It has now been found that the certificate on the return was incorrect. Your client has corrected that by disclosing to the Revenue the figures that should have been reported on his tax return, or by providing the inspector with information from which the inspector has calculated the figures that should have been declared in the first place. The Revenue therefore think it is reasonable to ask that the final figures agreed as correct for assessment for each year, coupled with the tax return that was submitted, be certified to be correct i.e. that the inspector is now aware of all matters that are relevant to calculating and agreeing a liability.

This is logical and quite reasonable but the potential consequences of signing a certificate that later proves to be incorrect can be severe. The Revenue have a policy of considering all false certificates for prosecution. All materially incorrect ones are referred to the Inland Revenue's Special Compliance Office for them to consider what action is to be taken. Material in this regard should be taken to be an omission of assets amounting to more than £5,000 or an omission of profits or income exceeding £5,000 (see IH 3031).

8.13 The inspector most commonly asks for the certificate round about the time he is inviting the offer in settlement. Some inspectors, however, will request the certificate when they believe that the case is ready for conclusion but before they sit down to calculate the tax that is due. The latter is the more logical time and is the time recommended to inspectors in their Investigation Handbook (IH 3023). But, in practice, it is usually at the settlement time that it is requested.

8.14 It is very important to note that the inspector should not ask for a certificate of disclosure if nothing has been found to be wrong with your client's tax returns, or if the omissions are minor and involve only the latest tax return (IH 3023). This is logical and fits in with the Revenue's view that the certificate should be signed as a replacement for the signature on the tax returns that were proved to be incorrect. You should also note that a certificate should not be requested if the offence is one of a failure to notify liability provided the correct returns were submitted to remedy this failure. Again this is logical because the signature on the tax return certifies them to be correct and there is no evidence that they are incorrect.

8.15 It would be usual to find the inspector asking each partner in a business, and each director of a close company that has been involved in an investigation to sign a certificate. What you must do is consider each request and decide whether it is relevant and reasonable having regard to the nature of the case and the omissions and the involvement of the individual concerned. In particular, if one partner or director has clearly had no involvement in any wrongdoing, it would probably be unreasonable to ask that person to sign a certificate of disclosure.

If a certificate is requested, look at it carefully before agreeing that you will put it to your client for signature. There are a variety of certificates in circulation. They are of varying length and complexity and are designed to suit the individual case; they are reproduced at Appendix D. As always with pre-printed standard forms, all may not suit the particular circumstances of your client. For example, a certificate that asks for confirmation that details of all gifts have been declared when these have never been mentioned by the inspector, never discussed, and no details ever provided relating to any gifts, would not be appropriate. Likewise, confirmation that details of all bank accounts operated have been declared whether still open or closed over a particular period will not be appropriate if the inspector has never asked about these and none have been involved in the investigation. Of course, if your client tells you about some gifts or about some bank accounts that the inspector was not aware of and which would have an impact upon the figures that have been agreed, then the inspector should be advised of these. But that is a separate matter from signing a certificate that includes confirmation of such disclosure if none has been made because the points were not covered in the enquiry.

This is particularly relevant when considering the period that is covered by the certificate. Commonly there is a thorough investigation of a recent year and the results of that investigation applied to previous years under some negotiated formula. There may have been a complete disclosure of everything relevant to the year being investigated but no disclosure of anything relating to the earlier years. It would therefore be inappropriate to certify that a complete disclosure has been made of all bank accounts, gifts or whatever else is included on the form that relates to those earlier years when none of them have been subject to the investigation in detail. You should also carefully note the period that is covered on the certificate of disclosure and ensure that the period covered is relevant to the particular case you are dealing with.

8.16 Frequently certificates are simply signed without their contents being carefully considered and you must bear in mind the potentially serious consequences for your client if something later comes to light. The serious nature of this document leads the Revenue to advise their inspectors personally to hand over the form to the taxpayer directly and explain its significance. The Investigation Handbook recommends that inspectors do not invite immediate signature but ask that the form be taken away and be considered carefully before being signed and returned (IH 3029). In practice, many inspectors will invite its completion in a letter and rely on the Revenue's form 94E, now reproduced on the reverse of pre-printed certificates, to alert the taxpayer to the potential seriousness of the form. The inspector may also ask you to ensure that your client appreciates its significance and the potentially serious consequences that could follow from an incorrect certificate.

Regardless of which method the inspector takes to request the certificate, you do have a responsibility to your client to ensure that the form is relevant, appropriate to the particular case, and that your client does appreciate what he is signing. The author recommends that you make a detailed file note and preferably confirm your advice to him in writing before obtaining a signature and especially before sending a completed form to the inspector.

8.17 You may now be satisfied that the certificate requested is relevant and appropriate but are conscious that there is no statutory obligation upon your client to sign this. Given the potentially serious consequences of an incorrectly signed certificate, should you advise your client to sign it at all or merely advise the inspector that a certificate will not be signed? It could be that you believe it is appropriate for your client to sign it but your client may be reluctant to.

Is a refusal to sign a reasonable stance to take? The inspector cannot force the signature but a refusal to confirm that all facts, income and all things relevant have been disclosed is going to make the inspector concerned that he is not aware of all facts. He will therefore return to his file and carefully review it. He will be looking for clues that there may be something he has missed. There may be something he has not asked about because he concluded it was unlikely to be relevant in this case. If so, he may now look at this and request, or demand further information. He may have simply accepted your client's assurances in some areas but he may now decide that he should not accept such assurances and obtain independent evidence, if available. Your client may therefore expect the investigation to continue; it is unlikely that settlement will now take place within the near future. Should the inspector turn up something during this period that was relevant he may, if it is large enough or serious enough, refer the matter to the Special Compliance Office and the case could become very serious for your client from that point on.

At some stage, however, the inspector is going to be satisfied that he has everything that he is ever going to get and will be prepared to agree settlement of the case.

Signing a certificate will therefore bring a case to a conclusion far more rapidly and will most certainly reduce the costs in handling an investigation. You may also expect it to be reflected in the mitigation of penalties under the headings of co-operation and disclosure.

Whether or not the extra trouble and expense that may follow a refusal to sign is justified because your client will be in a stronger position should the certificate ever turn out to be false, is really going to depend on the individual facts of each case. It is vital to proceed with caution.

The letter of offer

8.18 Figures have been agreed, the interest calculation is correct, the tax computation is accurate and technically correct, you have discussed liability to penalties and the extent of mitigation with the inspector and have arrived at the figure mutually acceptable to you, your client and the Inland Revenue. All that is now needed is to formalise a settlement. What will usually happen is that the inspector of taxes will invite the taxpayer to make an offer to settle his liabilities to tax, interest and penalties. It must be stressed that this has to be a free will offer i.e. one that your client makes freely and not under duress.

It is a rare occasion indeed that the quantum of an offer debated with the investigating inspector comes back rejected by his head office (settlements over certain limits have to go to HQ for acceptance), but it does happen on occasions and sometimes in a surprising manner. There was one occasion during the author's days as an inspector of taxes when head office returned a file with instructions to invite a lower offer. It was thought that he had been too harsh in the mitigation of penalties. This also does serve as a reminder that if you genuinely believe the inspector is being too mean with penalty mitigation then you do not have to go along with the offer that he suggests but submit an offer which you believe to be fair and just for consideration.

Wording of the offer

8.19 The letter of offer must be taken seriously. All too often the inspector of taxes will produce one for signature and this is then signed with little regard to its actual wording and terms. It is true that most of the time there is no major consequence arising out of this, or indeed any consequence at all, but if this offer is to conclude the case, it is important to get it right.

What is now happening is that your client is about to enter into a contract with the Inland Revenue to pay them a sum of money in consideration of the Revenue not taking proceedings to collect any liability to tax, interest or penalties. Your client will make an offer and the Board of Inland Revenue will accept it thereby creating a contract.

This contract replaces the liability to tax, interest and penalties and substitutes a new liability under the law of contract. This practice was given judicial approval in the case of *CIR v Nuttall 1989 63 TC 148.*

8.20 Care is therefore needed and accuracy is important. The Inland Revenue assist their inspectors with the wording of suitable offers and have produced several standard versions that are acceptable in the majority of cases. These are reproduced at Appendix 1 of the Inland Revenue's Investigation Handbook; indeed the Investigation Handbook also reveals the guidance given to inspectors in relation to letters of offer (IH 6100 et seq). The law of contract in Scotland is slightly different to that in England and Wales so variations are produced for use in Scotland. Notwithstanding this, the Inland Revenue recommend their inspectors to adopt the wordings suitable under English law because it would seem that Scottish contract law is slightly more lax than the English versions (some standard models are reproduced at Appendix E).

8.21 The danger in having standard wording is that that wording may not be entirely suitable in all cases. If so, the wording and the terms must be adapted accordingly to fit the particular terms your client is offering to the Inland Revenue. The Revenue produce a checklist to aid their inspectors (IH 6105). This ensures that any letters of offer that have been drafted by the taxpayer or his advisors contain all the essential elements required by the Revenue before they will consider the offer for acceptance. The main points are set out in Appendix P.

8.22 An offer must be clear and unambiguous. Essentially both sides must know exactly what they have offered and accepted and it is clearly desirable to avoid any possibility of misunderstanding.

The author has frequently been involved in trying to settle disputes between clients and the Inland Revenue when the client insists that some liability the Revenue is now trying to collect was covered in an investigation settlement but the Revenue denies this. This usually occurs when a new inspector is on the scene and cannot see from the letter of offer that something was included, nor can he see from his colleague's file notes that there was any agreement on the matter.

A typical example of this may arise when a company settles an investigation into its affairs but some PAYE matter was mentioned in passing to the investigating inspector. The client, having been told that making an offer settles all outstanding matters up to a certain date, now believes that the PAYE matter is also settled, the inspector having decided not to pursue any enquiries in detail and not to pursue any liability. An offer is made but does not have regard to the settlement of PAYE liabilities, the Board of Inland Revenue accept the offer and everyone goes away quite happily having put the past behind them and now getting on with life. The client is however encouraged by the apparent lack of interest shown by the inspector in some relatively minor PAYE failing, fails to correct the bad habits and continues with them. A new and different Revenue officer discovers this failure a few years later and demands payment of the outstanding liabilities for all years involved. This of course now includes years that were included in the settlement. The inspector agrees that he will certainly not try and collect tax that has been the subject of a previous settlement or agreement. He has, however, little knowledge of the previous investigation settlement and undertakes to review the papers. The inspector subsequently advises that he has scrutinised the investigation papers but can find no reference to the PAYE matter and in particular it is not included in the offer letter in any shape or form and so, unfortunately, he must pursue the liability. Your client is unhappy; he blames you, refuses to pay your fee, and moves off to another firm of accountants.

This letter of offer is the only opportunity to ensure that all matters that have been agreed are registered as agreed. Take great care therefore in ensuring that the wording is unambiguous. A warning that it isn't may be when your client starts asking many questions about it, particularly if he is asking you to explain what it all means.

The gross offer

8.23 The offer must contain consideration for something in order for a contract to be established. Your client will be offering to pay the Inland Revenue in return for the Revenue agreeing not to take proceedings. It is important to emphasise to the client that this does not refer to criminal proceedings. It refers to the civil proceedings to assess or amend and take proceedings in the court to enforce payment.

8.24 The offer must contain a list of the duties that are covered by the offer. It must contain the gross offer before deductions or reliefs. This will frequently prompt your client to question the figures because he may have paid the Revenue something on account as the investigation has progressed e.g. it has been agreed that the Revenue should be offered £100,000 to settle an investigation during the course of which the client has made payments totalling £50,000 on account of the eventual settlement. The letter of offer now reads 'I offer to pay you £100,000 in consideration of no proceedings being taken against me in respect of the duties set out in the statement below which I acknowledge to be unpaid'. The fact that £50,000 has already been paid should be recognised in the letter of offer by inclusion of the expression 'of which £50,000 has been paid on account' or alternatively in a schedule of terms of payment. It is however necessary that the gross offer is included.

Another example would usually relate to *ICTA 1988, s 419* liabilities when settling investigations into the affairs of a close company. Frequently the debt has been repaid and so *ICTA 1988, s 419(4)* relief is due. The offer should contain the gross liability to *section 419* tax without deducting the relief, and the fact that relief is due should be reflected elsewhere in the letter of offer.

Payment terms and instalments

8.25 The offer letter should also specify when payment will be made. The standard is to offer to pay within 30 days of the date of the letter from the Inland Revenue accepting the offer. Having a payment date pegged to the date of a letter is really the only unambiguous way of proceeding. If one referred to the date a letter was received, there can be uncertainty as to what this date is.

However, the 30 days is not essential. It is your client who is making an offer to settle and so you must have regard to his ability to pay. If cash deposits are on 90 days' notice, for example, it may not be possible to make payment within 30 days and so an offer to pay within that period should not be made. You should be considering a period of 90 days or perhaps, if pressed, 60 days given that there is a significant period prior to making the offer during which it is known what funds are needed, and there is usually a short period of time between making the offer and this being accepted by the Revenue.

Occasionally a specified date is mentioned e.g. 'on or before 31 January 2000'. When specifying a date, you must again have regard to the ability of your client to have the funds in place by then and also to the time it may take the Revenue to process the letter of offer and decide whether to accept it or not.

8.26 It is not uncommon to find that your client is more than willing to make amends and pay the Revenue a just amount of tax, interest and penalties but simply does not have the funds available, nor can he raise them. This does not necessarily prevent an offer being made and accepted. The local inspector has some discretion and if a relatively short period is involved he may be willing to accept an offer for payment in say three to six months' time without too much difficulty.

Longer periods start to be more difficult. Two years can sometimes be negotiated with the local inspector but will require the recalculation of forward interest. There may also be some negotiations on a general increase in the offer to take account of the Revenue's risk in waiting for its money. Periods over two years are usually outside the local inspector's discretion and will have to be submitted to head office for a decision.

It would be a rare and exceptional case for any period in excess of five years to be accepted. Such lengthy periods are usually undesirable both to the Revenue and to your client. It keeps the matter hanging on for many years with the risk that there may be a failure and so the prospect of the contract being in default and the Revenue being able to reopen the matter is present (IH 6052).

The Revenue will not readily accept instalments provisions and will look towards the raising of money or the liquidation of assets and will usually require evidence that efforts have been made before accepting that instalments are the only answer, provided of course they are content that those instalments will be met.

Exclusions

8.27 The letter of offer should also deal with any exclusions. For example, before the days of self-assessment when the basis period for assessment was more complex, there was always the possibility that an unincorporated business may cease trading, requiring a revision of assessments for earlier years, or if in the early years of a business, the possibility of an election to have the assessments for those earlier years on a special basis. Such matters may require the adjustment of liabilities that have been included in an investigation settlement and so the Revenue will not want to be barred from seeking extra tax, nor would they want to deny anyone from benefiting from relief that the legislation permits by having them debarred by the terms of the offer. Suitable wording is therefore usually inserted to deal with such possibilities.

Acknowledgement of default

8.28 The Revenue will demand an acknowledgement of your client's default in the letter of offer. This is usually catered for by wording such as 'I offer to pay you £x as set out in the statement below which I acknowledge to be unpaid by reason of my default'. It can sometimes be the case, however, that your client is willing to make an offer to the Revenue but disputes that he is in default. The Revenue will accept offers which refer to an alleged default e.g. 'I offer to pay you £x in respect of the duties set out in the statement below which is alleged by the Inland Revenue to be due to my default'.

A letter of offer that denies default or fails to acknowledge that the offer is in respect of an alleged default will not be accepted. If default is disputed, the inspector must seek to establish default. This will of course usually be done by the taking of formal proceedings i.e. establishing the tax that is due, then making the penalty determinations which your client may then appeal against and have the issue of his default settled by the Appeal Commissioners.

Side letters and corrections

8.29 The Revenue do not like covering letters accompanying letters of offer that contain conditions affecting the offer. This is not good practice, it is far better to have all conditions relating to the offer in the offer itself.

8.30 It should be mentioned that the use of correcting fluid should be avoided when dealing with letters of offer. If there is a dispute at a later date, who knows whether you made the change, the inspector or your client, whether it was done before the offer was submitted or after the offer was submitted and it adds to the risk of ambiguity discussed earlier.

Awaiting acceptance

8.31 Once the letter of offer has been sent to the Inland Revenue there is a period of time before which they accept it, thereby establishing the contract. During this period there is a window of opportunity to withdraw the offer or amend its terms. If something comes to light that may have a bearing on the offer then the author would suggest an urgent telephone call to the inspector advising him that something has occurred that will cause the offer to be withdrawn or amended and follow that up immediately with a fax, or, if possible, e-mail ensuring that you retain evidence of the time of despatch of the fax or e-mail. It may be that evidence to support some contention being put forward by your client has suddenly been found, or it could simply be that you suddenly realise that a computational error was made.

8.32 The Revenue will regard the offer as fresh for a period of six months (IH 6125). After this period of time they will not accept it but will invite the taxpayer to confirm that he still wishes to make that offer. Clearly, you should not wait six months for the Revenue's acceptance without taking some action. The Revenue's systems, particularly now we are in the age of computers, are such that oversights are usually picked up sometime further down the line. If an inspector has put the letter of offer and the file in a cupboard and completely forgotten about it or has left the office and not alerted his successor to the case, there will be some log in the Revenue's systems of either unsettled appeals, uncollected tax, or an open enquiry and at some point someone will look into the reason why. It is always more difficult to resurrect matters and deal with things from the past and also do not forget that until that letter of acceptance arrives the case is not settled and your client is at risk of another inspector re-opening matters or taking a differing view on technical aspects or a level of penalties.

Once agreed, the settlement should be completed quickly.

Conditional offers

8.33 The Revenue will not accept offers that have conditions to reopen the case e.g. 'I hereby offer to pay you £x but this may be reduced if evidence of my betting wins comes to light'. Nor will they accept a conditional offer e.g. 'I will pay you in 30 days provided I have sold my house by then'. Likewise, uncertain offers will not be accepted e.g. 'I agree to pay you £x in settlement of my liabilities and will pay you as and when funds become available'.

Voluntary restitution

8.34 It will perhaps be rare, but you may come across occasions when the Revenue are time barred from assessing liability but your client wishes to make voluntary restitution and include this in his offer. The offer must contain the duties included in the offer and so include those that are time barred for assessment and the offer must contain reference to the fact that there is voluntary restitution.

Errors and ethics

8.35 Some interesting discussions can sometimes be had with your client, and indeed heated arguments, when you notice that the inspector has made a glaring error in his figures when sending you a letter of offer to consider and put to your client for signature. He may have made an arithmetical error in the calculation of *section 419(4)* relief, he may have made some transposition error when inserting the payment on account figure. This all potentially results in your client paying less than he should. Your client, anxious to pay the minimum possible, argues he has done nothing wrong, he hasn't submitted any incorrect figures to the inspector. It's not for him to check the inspector's figures, he can merely accept them. The inspector must have got it right, so just accept it and say nothing.

It is clear that you should not go along with this. This is for the simple reason, regardless of any ethical question, that it will potentially be an offence under the *Theft Act 1968*.

The Institute of Chartered Accountants has detailed guidance for its members in the Members Handbook and in general takes the view that their members should persuade their clients to disclose errors and that in some circumstances they must disclose errors without reference to the client unless there are 'special circumstances' or the amounts involved are *de minimis*. There is no guidance on what is *de minimis* from either the Institute or the Revenue but the Revenue have said that the Institute's advice on 'special circumstances' presents them with 'major difficulties'.

The Revenue view, predictably, is that the Institute 'ask that members . . . take all possible steps to ensure that their clients pay the correct amount of tax due in law, even where following an error by the Revenue insufficient tax is demanded'.

The Institute say '... unless the amount of tax ... at stake is *de minimis*, he should consider whether he should continue to act, bearing in mind both the importance for trust to exist between the Revenue and the member, and the exposure of both the member and the client to possible criminal or civil penalties should the Revenue not be informed of the error'.

Signing of offers

Individuals

8.36 So having now considered the wording of the offer, got it right, and confirmed that the conditions are acceptable, it now simply needs signing. The correct signing of the offer can also produce complications. In a simple case of a sole trader it is fairly obvious and little complication arises. More complex considerations arise when dealing with partnerships, husband and wife situations and close companies, deceased persons or the ailing client or relative. Self-assessment also complicates matters because assessing rules have changed.

Partners

8.37 Partners, prior to the introduction of self-assessment, were jointly and severally liable for the partnership tax debt. All partners must therefore sign a partnership settlement to the extent that it relates to the pre-self-assessment years. For the self-assessment years, each partner should have his own settlement but there is nothing to prevent a joint and several offer being made to the Revenue if all partners so wish and fully understand the implications. Even in the pre-self-assessment days, however, if any individual partner's liability arose e.g. capital gains tax, or liability on bank interest in addition to partnership tax liabilities it was necessary to have two letters of offer, one from the partnership and one from the individual partner relating to his individual liabilities.

It is therefore necessary to consider what years are involved and who has the legal liability to pay. It may be necessary to have a number of separate offer letters in respect of what you may regard as one investigation settlement.

Husband and wife

8.38 Similar considerations arise in husband and wife situations, although this is becoming less so as time goes on. Prior to 5 April 1990, the husband was responsible for his wife's tax liabilities and so if a wife had erred then her husband was the one who had to make an offer to pay the Revenue. If the settlement straddles 5 April 1990, it may be necessary to have the husband sign an offer up to 5 April 1990 and his wife one following that date.

In some circumstances it may be possible for the husband and wife to make a joint offer that will be acceptable to the Revenue.

Companies

8.39 Company investigations will frequently conclude with a liability on the company and a liability on individual directors and so separate offers are required in a similar way to those required in partnership cases. You may, however, find that the Revenue will seek to have directors joined in an offer from a close company so that they become jointly and severally liable with the company and the other directors for the settlement by their company (IH 2990). This would especially arise if an instalment arrangement was being accepted or a company's ability to pay was dependant upon a director repaying his overdrawn loan account.

Remember that these are free will offers and the Revenue cannot dictate the offer or the form it takes. They are, of course, at liberty to refuse an offer they find unacceptable and take formal proceedings to collect the duties due.

Each case has to be judged on its merits. It is not correct to say that you should never agree that a director is joined in the company settlement. You must, however, fully advise your client on what he is doing and consider if the inspector's request is justified.

Third Parties

8.40 Other odd situations can arise. If the taxpayer has deceased then an offer must be made by his personal representative. In such circumstances it is important to note that the wording on the offer must change. The personal representative has not committed any default and must therefore not make reference to his default but must make reference to the default of the deceased.

It may sometimes happen that you or another agent is authorised to make an offer on behalf of your client. Apart from ensuring that your instructions are absolutely clear and unambiguous and there can be no dispute that you are authorised to make an offer then by all means proceed. But once again, the wording of the offer must be changed to reflect the fact that you are making an offer as agent and are referring to your client's default, not your own.

Witnesses

8.41 The Revenue sometimes asks that offers be witnessed. This apparently is only a necessity in Scotland but overall there can be little objection to witnessing your client's signature and confirming that this has been done. Please bear in mind however that if you are signing to say you witness your client signing it, that you did in fact witness him sign it.

Acceptance

8.42 Within a reasonably short period of submitting an acceptable letter of offer you will receive an acknowledgement from the Revenue that the offer has been accepted. Once the terms of the offer have been satisfied i.e. payment made, the matter is settled and the files may be put away.

The local inspector has delegated authority from the Board of Inland Revenue to accept certain small cases on their behalf (IH 231). When he tells you that it is for the Board of Inland Revenue to decide whether any offer is acceptable or not he is serious. Apart from those cases where delegated authority has been made, all cases must be submitted to the inspector's head office for them to consider the case and the offer and decide if it is to be accepted. True, they are very much influenced by the inspector's recommendation to accept or reject an offer but the Board of Inland Revenue through their head office unit are free to make their own decision and indeed sometimes do, as described earlier.

The task of the head office unit is to ensure there is a uniform standard of investigation throughout the United Kingdom and that the Board's policy on mitigation of penalties is being applied consistently throughout the country. It would not be right if the amount one paid at the conclusion of an investigation was dependent on the area of the country in which you happened to live. If the inspector of taxes in Cornwall is a gentle, kindly soul and is very forgiving, he may be exceptionally generous in his penalty mitigation, whereas there was one occasion that the author, in the North West, was a little harsh in his application of mitigation to penalties. In such circumstances, the head office unit would probably reject any offer submitted by the South West inspector on the grounds that it was insufficient. At the same time, they may reject the North West inspector because he is being too harsh. By this method, the Board ensure that a good degree of uniformity is applied and by and large the system works well.

The settlement interview

8.43 At the end of an investigation, the inspector is encouraged to hold what has become known as 'the settlement interview'. The general idea is that the inspector ensures that the taxpayer fully understands the nature of what has happened, the Revenue's case, the offence that has been committed and the interest and penalties that the Revenue could pursue (IH 6160). Expect the inspector to insist on one of these therefore.

The inspector will start by reviewing the history of the case, what has happened, what he has found and how it has been concluded. If a problem arose because of some action by you e.g. forgetting to add back some non-allowable items then if your client hasn't already discovered this fact, now is the time when he is likely to do so.

The inspector will summarise the tax that has been agreed to be due and ensure that your client fully understands how this has been calculated and that he agrees with the figure. He will review your client's actions and the factors relating to his culpability and will put forward his view of the degree of culpability i.e. fraud or neglect. It is important to the inspector that he establishes default and has agreement to the level of culpability.

In the majority of cases, it is sufficient to establish neglect for all practical purposes and so it is unlikely that he will provoke disputes and arguments by alleging something more serious such as fraud.

If, having put forward his view of the degree of culpability, the inspector receives no dispute or comment from the taxpayer or the agent, he is entitled to assume that lack of disagreement means agreement and records that as such (IH 6162).

The inspector will worry the client by advising him of what the maximum penalties in law the Revenue can proceed for, but then proceed to advise of the factors he has taken into account in considering mitigation of those penalties and advise what in his view will be the appropriate penalty loading. Prior to this however he would have invited you and your client to present any arguments you may have, relating to the mitigation of penalties, and may revise his own views in the light of these.

It is important to put forward your mitigation arguments before settlement is discussed. It is easier to influence the inspector's views than to persuade him to alter an opinion he has already formed.

8.44 Having ensured that your client understands what has happened, how figures have been arrived at and his degree of culpability, he will invite an offer and explain what this entails. If appropriate, he will consider the means of your client because he could not accept an offer or submit one for consideration where he believed the taxpayer had no prospect of meeting his obligation under the settlement agreement.

Finally, the inspector will warn your client as to his future conduct and assist by providing guidance on matters to be corrected (IH 6190).

Attendance at a settlement interview is not compulsory and you and your client may refuse to attend one. If so, there is very little the inspector can do about it and would have to proceed accordingly. He will want to ensure that your client fully understands what is happening. He may ask you to give him certain assurances or may write direct to your client spelling out the things he will cover at interview. An inspector may dispense with the settlement interview in simple and straightforward cases or he may be more ready to do so if he knows the agent involved and the fact that he is very experienced in investigation matters and can be relied upon to accurately relay the Revenue's case to his client and ensure his client fully understands what he is entering into. Even then, the inspector will ask the agent to confirm that he has done these things before he will be willing to consider any offer that may be put forward (IH 6161).

8.45 As a general rule, the author would usually recommend going along with the Revenue's usual procedures. They have developed and adapted them over the years to avoid problems at this stage both for themselves and also for the taxpayer. The Revenue do not want to be faced with angry representations at some later date from someone claiming he was hoodwinked and did not know what he was doing when he made the offer. Such a scenario would be of no benefit to the Revenue and obviously not to the client involved.

If costs are a problem, advise the inspector that there was no objection to a meeting provided he keeps the length of it to a minimum and suggest that the meeting is held at your office to reduce the length of time that you will be engaged with your client. Explain this suggestion is not made to be awkward but out of regard to costs. The inspector should go along with this.

Main points

1. When all liabilities are agreed the inspector will ask for a settlement interview. At this he will review the history of the investigation and give his views on culpability and the level of penalty mitigation.
2. It is sensible to discuss penalties with the inspector before he decides on the level of these. It is easier to influence his decision than it is to change it.
3. As with all other meetings, there is no obligation to attend one of these.
4. Prior to this the Revenue are likely to have requested a statement of assets and liabilities from your client. It is important to get this right; incorrect statements run a high risk of prosecution with local offices being told to report anything in excess of £5000 to Special Compliance Office.
5. The statement demands the cost of assets rather than their current value; use the house contents insurance policy for household and personal items.
6. Discuss any problem areas with the inspector and record what you have agreed.
7. The inspector will ask your client to confirm in writing that he has now declared all facts having a bearing on his tax liabilities by inviting signature of a certificate of disclosure. This is an important document that must be carefully considered before being signed; many Revenue prosecutions arise out of false certificates.

8. Consider the wording and decide if it is appropriate to your client's case and circumstances. The Revenue use pre-printed forms that do not always suit every situation.
9. There is no obligation to sign a certificate so you must decide if you will recommend your client to proceed to sign one. If you do, ensure he fully understands what he is signing and the implications of this. If the certificate is refused expect the inspector to be nervous and perhaps review his case again.
10. Settlement is usually by making an offer to settle the liability to tax, interest and penalties in place of the Revenue proceeding formally. Once an offer is accepted there is a legal contract between your client and the Revenue to pay the agreed amount. The amount payable loses its character of tax and thus it can be difficult to have the case reopened to correct any errors, so it is important to be sure that all adjustments that are expected are catered for in the letter of offer.
11. The Revenue will supply their suggested letter of offer but it must fit the case you are dealing with so it must be carefully reviewed before your client is invited to sign it and any problems resolved with the inspector. There is nothing to prevent you from drawing up your own offer letter.
12. If the client has a problem in meeting an acceptable offer negotiate an instalment arrangement with the Revenue. Periods of up to six months should not be too difficult to obtain in genuine cases. For more difficult problems the local inspector has discretion for instalments covering two years, beyond that he is obliged to involve head office.
13. In partnership cases the Revenue will want all partners to join in the offer. This was perhaps reasonable prior to self-assessment when there was joint and several liability so an innocent partner would have been liable if the Revenue proceeded formally, but not so now. If one partner is innocent of any wrongdoing then it would not be right for him to admit default and be liable for the tax, interest and penalties of his errant partner.
14. Likewise in company settlements the Revenue may seek to have the directors join in the offer to make them jointly and severally liable. Each case has to be judged on its merits but if the settlement is not dependant upon a director repaying money to the company then you should be considering advising your client against this.
15. Husband and wife problems are becoming rare as independent taxation is now over 10 years old but if there is liability straddling 5 April 1990 two offers will be needed if it involves the wife's income: pre-5 April 1990 from the husband and post-5 April 1990 from the wife.
16. The inspector will ask for a settlement interview but you are not obliged to attend this. At this he will review the case and the offence and explain the settlement procedure to your client.

Chapter 9

Accountants' Problems and Fee Protection

Summary of chapter

9.1 This chapter takes a look at:

- Accountancy errors and how they affect clients
- The avoidance v evasion problem
- Client relationships
- The problems that offshore structures can create
- Money laundering
- Fees and insurance schemes

Is the accountant the problem?

9.2 When we speak of tax investigations and settlements, we usually think of a trader who has put cash in his pocket and not recorded it in his books or at a more serious level the businessman who has extracted cash from his company by some devious and unacceptable manner. We recognise those and they sit comfortably with our view of a wrongdoing that has to be corrected and to some degree punished.

Life is not however always so clear-cut. In most investigations there is some adjustment to the degree of private use that something has been put or some item posted to the profit and loss account and not added back; it is agreed to be non-allowable for tax purposes and the tax adjustment follows. To what degree are such adjustments culpable?

Perhaps even more difficult are those adjustments that arise not from what we would traditionally describe as an investigation but flow from some debate with the inspector as to the correct treatment of something in the accounts. It may be following his request for analysis of repairs, following which he successfully argues that the repairs should have been capitalised. Is such an adjustment culpable? Traditionally such adjustments were regarded as 'technical' adjustments not attracting the traditional settlement of tax, interest and penalties, merely agreement on the correct figure to be assessed for a particular year.

In relatively recent times there are signs of a hardening attitude by the Revenue generally towards the behaviour of accountants and tax advisors. This changing approach has manifested itself in the way that the Revenue is tackling avoidance issues and the more frequent prosecution of accountants and advisors.

9.3 The starting point for all tax liabilities is the accounts drawn up on proper commercial accountancy principles. That was established in the courts quite some time ago and has been upheld time and time again (see *Johnson v Britannia Airways Ltd 1994 67 TC 99*).

This puts the onus on the accountant to ensure that accounts are technically correct having regard to standard accountancy principles. If the requirement to make a proper tax return is dependent first of all upon the accounts being technically correct, there is a strong argument for culpability if the accounts are technically sub-standard. For guidance on how accountancy principles affect taxation computations refer to *Tolley's Accounting Principles for Tax Purposes*.

It is probably reasonable in these circumstances for the Revenue to argue culpability and seek penalties.

9.4 There is then the question of the accuracy of the tax computation. There will always be room for debate with certain items. Should it be posted to repairs, should it be capitalised, is it a personal item or can business use be justified? These are not so much the worry although you will have to consider to what extent you provide the inspector with information when submitting the self-assessment tax return.

The real issue surrounds complete 'howlers' and the question of whether these may have been deliberate or not. The author recalls one firm of accountants during his inspector days who seemed to have great difficulty when it came to arithmetical accuracy in tax computations. So much so that it became difficult to accept there was the occasional error, especially as the frequent errors were always in the client's favour; arithmetical errors never seemed to break in favour of the Revenue.

Such accountants bring their profession into disrepute and quite rightly are not tolerated by either the Institute or the Revenue who advise their officers at IH 5068 as follows:

> '... an agent who made frequent errors, always in favour of the taxpayer, could well be thought to be making deliberate mistakes in the hope that they would not be noticed. You would consider the penalty mitigation very carefully and would consider a brief report to Special Compliance Office where records are kept of accountants whose work is considered to be unsatisfactory.'

Such agents do cause problems and it is their client who gets the brunt of it and has to answer and pay the Revenue. There is certainly an onus upon the taxpayer to ensure that whomever he appoints to look after his affairs is competent to do so. Consider what the Revenue has to say at IH 5067: 'an astute businessman who professes to rely on the advice of an obviously incompetent agent is unlikely to be believed by the Commissioners.'

It is well established that a taxpayer cannot hide behind the errors, or misdeeds, of his agent and will be liable to penalties. This is so even if the client has no knowledge of the agent's actions, as held in the cases of *Clixby v Pountney 1967 44 TC 515* and *Pleasants v Atkinson 1987 60 TC 228.*

The avoidance versus evasion debate

9.5 There have been many column inches on this subject in recent years mainly due to the proposals to introduce a general anti-avoidance provision for both VAT and direct taxes. For the purposes of this book there is no real need to review this debate in detail but you should be aware that war has been declared on the tax avoider and his advisors. If in doubt reflect on the following statement made by Dawn Primarolo, currently Paymaster General and so effectively head of the Inland Revenue but who was Secretary to the Treasury at the time:

> 'There is a limit to what we ... regard as acceptable. And that limit is breached when people take advantage of tax breaks in a way Parliament would not have anticipated or intended, use contrived loopholes ... or hide or obfuscate the facts. Those who do so must be prepared for us to ... clamp down ... They must recognise they are playing with fire.'

H M Customs & Excise have a little more extreme stance on avoidance than the Inland Revenue do. They appear to regard all avoidance as offensive and criminal because it is an offence to thwart the intentions of Parliament. The Inland Revenue have a more balanced view but they too are now investigating avoidance at a criminal level.

9.6 We have witnessed in recent times the conviction and imprisonment of tax barristers, a solicitor and accountants, all relating to so-called tax avoidance schemes. Frequently when these 'avoidance schemes' have the surface scratched off them, some element of deceit is revealed and it is this that introduces the criminal element.

Whether an avoidance device is so objectionable that it amounts to an act of dishonesty is essentially a jury matter, as the Court of Appeal pointed out in the case of the tax barrister, Cunningham (*R v Cunningham, Charlton, Wheeler and Kitchen 1995 67 TC 500*, more commonly referred to as *R v Charlton*).

This case shook tax advisors and provoked many articles in the professional press. It involved three accountants and a barrister who had assisted their client to set up a tax avoidance scheme. The scheme involved an offshore company being set up to buy goods overseas and sell them to a UK company at a profit and for the offshore company to receive commissions from the UK company for services rendered. The offshore company was under the management and control of the UK company directors, although this was not obvious to the casual observer. It is a scheme with which tax investigation specialists will be all too familiar. The Revenue had challenged the directors but the barrister had advised them to answer that their books and records were correct.

All were convicted on the basis that they were guilty of falsely representing the transactions to be bona fide commercial ones, and that Cunningham had been a party to deceiving the Revenue.

The defendants were, apparently, decent people but have ended up with convictions and lives in ruins. They argued that this was a case of avoidance, not evasion, although they accepted that their clients did act dishonestly without their knowledge.

The Court of Appeal upheld both conviction and the sentences. They found it impossible to accept that the accountant was not aware of his clients' dishonesty and with regard to the barrister said it was for the jury to assess his credibility and they 'plainly did not believe him'.

It is this 'jury' matter that makes many tax advisors uncomfortable. One prominent tax barrister writing in Taxation magazine on 5 June 1997 was clearly concerned at the make up of the jury in such cases.

> 'They were convicted ... before a jury of ordinary people whose only qualification was that they were on the electoral role, between 18 and 65 and were not peers, lunatics or practising barristers. Such persons would have found it very difficult to understand ...'

He may be right, and many may agree with him, but unless and until the system is changed you will be faced with 'such persons' deciding your fate and so it is in your own interests to decide upon the distinction between evasion and avoidance.

9.7 Clearly those involved in the avoidance field have cause to feel uncomfortable but perhaps they can be guided by the views of the Inland Revenue.

The Revenue accept that it is acceptable for anyone to organise their affairs so as to pay the minimal amount of tax possible on any given transaction. They find artificial schemes that are not connected with a commercial transaction, but done merely to secure a tax advantage, objectionable and indeed frequently find judicial support as far up as the House of Lords, as the now well-known and famous *Ramsay* principle evidences. But even then, the Revenue do not seem to regard the matter as criminal, provided they are aware of all the facts which are relevant to a scheme so that they have a fair chance of making their own decision and reaching an agreement on what the correct tax treatment is.

One thing is therefore absolutely certain: if asked any questions, it is an absolute must that full, correct answers be given. Any attempt to withhold facts or even deceive the inspector makes the Revenue angry. The author's personal approach to this is that if you know, or even just think, that a scheme will only succeed if the Revenue are not aware of the full facts then it is culpable because quite simply you know it is wrong and does not work.

9.8 Many avoidance schemes rely on certain events taking place at a critical time and in a critical order, and either due to oversight or laziness these things are not done at the right times and in the right order. Subsequently documents are drawn up to make it seem as though things happened at the right time. This of course is a deceit and a common cause of the Revenue taking exception to what many refer to as an avoidance scheme.

Client relationships

9.8A Investigation work can put strains on client relationships. Extra fees need to be charged; who is to blame? your client may expect you to cover up for him, or even lie to help him; you may not believe your client's explanations; there may be issues of client confidentiality and questions about the necessary consent to disclose information.

An agent has a duty of confidentiality towards his client. This means that he must not give the Revenue information without the consent of his client unless there is an overriding need to do so.

It was established in the case of *Tournier v National and Provincial and Union Bank of England [1924] 1 KB 461* that these overriding needs may be:

(a) there is a statutory duty to disclose (e.g. a notice under *TMA 1970, s 20(3)* or under the money laundering legislation);

(b) it is in the public interest to make a disclosure (this is a difficult area and the Institute of Chartered Accountants advise members to seek legal advice before making a disclosure (Members Handbook section 1.306)). This may cover a situation where the agent becomes aware of a serious fraud involving a professional person, a Revenue official, or an appeal Commissioner; or

(c) it is in the agent's own interests to disclose (e.g. to defend himself against a criminal charge, or against a civil case).

One safeguard against the client taking action against the agent would be to have a suitably worded engagement letter containing a general consent to disclose all matters.

Offshore problems

9.9 Many of the most serious cases dealt with by the Special Compliance Office include some sort of offshore involvement.

The author comes across an incredible degree of naivety and ignorance amongst taxpayers and advisors when it comes to offshore issues, as perhaps is evident from the *Charlton* case discussed at 9.6 above. Many do seem to genuinely believe that income earned offshore is not taxable in the United Kingdom, that having an offshore company with nominee directors avoids UK taxation, and that setting up an offshore trust always works for taxation purposes.

The question of offshore trusts is complex and perhaps one could be forgiven for being ignorant and confused in that area. When it comes to 'tax dodging' however, many involve cases in which the settlor of a trust purports it to be one set up by a non-resident. So the web of deceit commences and one really need go no further than realise that if there must be pretence to make the scheme work then it can't possibly work.

9.10 The offshore company situation is covered by anti-avoidance legislation that is dealt with in detail in *Tolley's Anti-Avoidance Provisions.* The problem that arises in this area is that the transactions may be genuine but caught by the anti-avoidance provisions and steps are frequently taken to deceive the Revenue and prevent them realising that the provisions apply.

Far more blatantly however, one has UK residents managing and controlling offshore companies from the United Kingdom, but with the pretence that they are managed, controlled and owned by offshore residents. Right from the outset there is a deceit as to the true ownership and control and perhaps not surprisingly, the Revenue find it difficult to accept that a mature businessman, familiar with the ways of the world and business, would conclude that such a set-up genuinely worked for UK taxation purposes.

Nevertheless people do. But when questioned, they frequently give incorrect or misleading answers and so start to dig a far bigger hole for themselves than they were ever in, in the first place. If it is thought that the structure is genuine, then why not tell the Revenue the full facts when asked? The author would therefore advise anybody with such a structure to obtain a second opinion on it, and if invited to answer any questions by the inspector of taxes to obtain expert advice before answering them. Certainly the advice must be that if you cannot find it within you, at this stage, to tell the full and correct facts then say nothing until proper advice has been obtained.

9.11 Offshore situations usually involve significant amounts of tax and you are usually dealing with the Inland Revenue's Special Compliance Office (see Chapter 13). The risk of prosecution is high and it is therefore vital that the very early stages are handled with expert advice from those most experienced at dealing with the Special Compliance Office.

9.12 The author is frequently asked if the UK Inland Revenue can order the production of information from people living overseas. The answer to this is that they cannot. They can only use domestic legislation where that domestic legislation has force. A *section 20* notice cannot therefore be served upon someone resident in the Channel Islands. The Revenue is however making more and more use of agreements for the exchange of information. Such agreements are usually present in double taxation agreements and most certainly are part and parcel of agreements within the European Union. In the year to April 2000 the Board of Inland Revenue's Annual Report reveals that they received some 350,000 pieces of information from foreign Revenue departments, a very significant increase on the 1998's figure of 175,000. This very much serves to underline the increasing co-operation between countries in line with the introduction of all-crimes money laundering legislation and political pressure.

9.13 Tax and offshore issues are complex and can lead to some very serious consequences. The headline prosecution of advisors in recent years has usually involved offshore structures. It is an area in which to proceed with great caution and certainly to take expert advice if challenged or questioned by the Revenue. The author would at this stage draw your attention to question 6 on the individual self-assessment tax return that asks a simple question involving offshore activities and asks for a simple response of yes or no.

Question 6 of Tax Return

Q6	Did you have any taxable income from overseas pensions or benefits, or from foreign companies or savings institutions, offshore funds or trusts abroad, or from land and property abroad or gains on foreign insurance policies?					
		No			Yes	
	Have you or could you have received, or enjoyed directly or indirectly, or benefited in any way from income of a foreign entity as a result of a transfer of assets made in this or earlier years?					
		No			Yes	

Answering 'no' to this question when offshore activities are taking place will make a defence of ignorance very difficult to maintain, and let's not lose sight of the fact that it is the advisor who will probably tick this box on behalf of his client. This underlines the need to ensure that your client actually reads the tax return before he or she signs it. Quite frequently in tax investigations involving offshore activities the UK accountant was totally unaware of the structure that had been set up and what was going on and so he would tick 'no'.

Money laundering

9.14 Money laundering is something all agents must have regard to and acquire a reasonable working knowledge of the legal requirements. Failure to do so could have dire consequences as prison sentences can be expected.

The legislation really requires that you provide information to the police if you suspect, or know, that you are dealing with the proceeds of a crime.

The law is drawn from several statutes, namely, *Criminal Justice Act 1998, Drug Trafficking Act 1994, Prevention of Terrorism Act 1989* and the *Money Laundering Regulations 1993 (SI 1993/No 1933).*

The rules are confusing. It is not at all clear exactly what must be reported. The authorities seem to have a different view from that of many legal advisers. A useful starting point is an article 'Not Doing The Laundry' by Sylvia Courtnage that appeared in Tolley's Practical Tax Service on 8th March 2000 and then the extensive guidance notes from the Institute of Chartered Accountants.

The detailed rules require careful consideration and are beyond the scope of this book. It is, in any event, wise to consider taking legal advice if you have doubts about the application of the law to any particular circumstance.

What you should be aware of is a legal requirement to appoint one person to be the *Money Laundering Reporting Officer*; to train staff in the requirements of the rules; and keep records of transactions. It is also an offence to 'tip off' a client that a money laundering report has been made.

Fees

9.15 Many accountants complain that they lose money on tax investigation work. They argue that they cannot charge their client for all the hours that have been put in because it would cost too much, especially when compared to the fee for accounts preparation or the audit. Some do the job for nothing because they undertake to deal with any Revenue queries arising from their work. It is, of course, open to anyone to make whatever arrangements they like with their clients, but if an investigation is handled thoroughly it means a big investment of your time and this will cost you money because you will not be doing chargeable work for other clients.

Dealing with small aspect enquiries within an overall fee is probably reasonable, but to extend this to a full enquiry has to be avoided if possible. The legislation has created the problem for the client, not you, and in my view it is unreasonable to expect the accountant to pay.

The solution is effective engagement letters that make it clear that full enquiries will be billed separately.

9.16 Another potential solution is to consider using one of the insurance schemes that have been around for quite a few years. These basically work by you paying a premium to buy insurance that covers your fees in the event of an investigation into any of your clients. Typically a premium will be worked out specifically for you based on your client profile.

There are a number of these schemes around with new players coming into the market from time to time; all have variations but in essence a plan is put together by someone who then finds an underwriter to insure it and he administers the policy for the underwriter.

If you are considering one of these policies you should remember that you might have more clients than you think. Each director will be a separate client, assuming you act for him personally, and each subsidiary company is a separate client. The same applies to partnerships; typically a husband and wife partnership would be three clients, i.e. the partnership, the husband and the wife.

The author would advise you to read the actual policy wording very carefully indeed; some have promotional material that is frequently misinterpreted, so there is no substitute for going to the master policy and considering every clause carefully.

You are likely to find that self-assessment enquiries are not covered until it is clear that a full investigation is taking place. More importantly, clauses that the author has come across exclude claims if the client has failed to keep good records. Faults with bookkeeping are however a feature of most, if not all, investigations and so the insurer can often refuse to pay. Likewise any technical failure could invalidate the policy e.g. delivering a return a few days late.

It could be argued that the policy wording is such that the insurers could exclude most claims if they had a mind to. Insurers the author has discussed this with say the strict wording is needed to protect the underwriter from those who ask to be investigated, and in practice they interpret the wording in a sensible and reasonable manner. This may sometimes be the case but the author would prefer to have a policy that worked rather than relying on the goodwill of the underwriter, such goodwill being influenced by the claims experience from your practice.

9.17 These comments are made from the author's experience of a few schemes in practice. One scheme rarely agreed to pay out the full costs, but in their defence usually offered a contribution as a goodwill gesture. Another always paid in full but only if the administration of the policy was in order. They demanded that no costs be incurred until they confirmed cover, but took a long time to do this. In the meantime the inspector was starting to warn of the consequences of non-co-operation. They would then authorise a fee limit that did not cover the costs of the first meeting with the inspector.

The author's firm struggles to recall any case in which they were not paid the full fees during the years before they used insurers, nor since they decided not to continue with a policy. It is however true that they lost fees under the insurance schemes. To put the side for the insurers, they did not blanket cover the entire client base but asked each client to decide if they wanted to buy cover i.e. a 'client decide' scheme. The problem with this type of cover is that the statistical spread is weakened and it is those clients who believe themselves to be at risk who take out the policy, thereby increasing the risk to the insurer. Those who cover their entire client base seem to have a better claims experience than the author's firm but there are still familiar complaints.

John Newth echoed the above experiences in Taxation magazine in an article on the subject of fee insurance (10 June 1999). John then went on to consider the policy wording changes being introduced by the leading companies in response to the sort of criticism outlined above, which, if implemented, should make for a more satisfactory product.

By all means consider insurance; for those who are currently doing the work at undervalue or for nothing at all it probably makes good sense, but please do read the policy wording very carefully and perhaps follow the advice John Newth gave in that Taxation article.

9.18 You may be fortunate enough to claim your fees from the Revenue. If the Revenue has behaved in an appalling manner or the Inspector has caused costs to be incurred unnecessarily then the Revenue will consider claims.

On the subject of fees the Revenue will allow tax relief on these if their investigation resulted in no fraudulent or negligent conduct being established, otherwise they will be disallowed (see *Tax Bulletin* October 1998).

Main points

1. Accounts must always be prepared on a technically correct basis.
2. Commercial accounts provide the starting point for tax liability.
3. The negligence of an accountant is attributed to his client and he incurs penalties.
4. Involvement in avoidance schemes can bring unwelcome problems.
5. If a scheme relies upon the Revenue not knowing all the facts it obviously does not work.
6. Offshore tax avoidance is complex; ensure you are fully competent in this area or take independent advice.
7. Answer any questions truthfully.
8. The modern tax return demands a series of 'yes or no' answers. Do not merely assume answers on behalf of clients, ask them.

9. Ensure you know the money laundering reporting rules.
10. Agree fees and perhaps consider one of the fee indemnity insurance schemes.
11. If considering an insurance scheme read the policy wording and exclusions very carefully before deciding to proceed.

Chapter 10

Voluntary Disclosure

Summary of chapter

10.1 This is a short chapter devoted to the problem of disclosing errors and problems to the Inland Revenue. It highlights the difficult decisions accountants may have to make but gives advice on how to make these for the benefit of clients and the accountant himself. Guidance is given on how to decide on levels of culpability and the circumstances under which expert help should be called in.

Introduction

10.2 There comes a point in every practitioner's life when moral dilemmas arise.

- You discover an error in previous tax returns or accounts.
- You discover that your client has overlooked telling you about some source of income.
- You stumble across evidence that your client is deliberately falsifying his accounts.
- Occasionally a client comes and tells you that his tax affairs are not in order.

What should you do in such circumstances? There can be a great temptation to ignore the past and get it right for the future but this would be wrong for many reasons.

10.3 Quite rightly, your client instructs you to sort matters out for him with the Revenue authorities. How do you do this? It seems easy but you could encounter problems.

The Inland Revenue are currently more aggressive than they have ever been. New powers are added to their armoury on quite a regular basis and they seek more and more. Prosecutions, or at least the potential for them, arise more frequently and they are not reserved for the largest of cases such as on the scale of Nissan or Allen. There have been prosecutions when tax of as little as £28,000 is involved. Special Compliance Office inspectors regularly litter their conversations with references to 'CP' ('CP' standing for criminal prosecution).

Finance Act 2000 introduced legislation to enable the Revenue to prosecute in the magistrates' court, so making the prosecution process simpler and quicker. A declared aim of this legislation is to prosecute the long-term tax evader. In the words of the Paymaster General (Inland Revenue Press Release, 27 June 2000):

> 'The new statutory offence will be just one in a package of measures aimed at cracking down on the informal economy. Our message is simple – get the confidential advice and help offered by the Inland Revenue to help join the legitimate world of work, or face the consequences in six months' time.'

The Revenue have said that most cases will still be settled by way of a monetary offer.

> 'But the Inland Revenue operates a policy of taking criminal proceedings in a number of serious cases across the range of tax offences to bolster its enforcement strategy. The new offence will enable serious but smaller cases to be prosecuted in greater numbers, and up to 50 extra staff will be allocated to this work.' (Inland Revenue Press Release, 27 June 2000.)

10.4 Since then, however, there has been the Revenue Press Release of 18th January 2001. This announced the successful prosecution of Frank Moran but the release contained the following announcement by the Revenue:

'4. The Inland Revenue is also committed to ensuring that people pay the right amount of tax at the right time. Anyone who has used offshore bank accounts, in a similar way to Moran, or understated their profits or income by any other means, should make an early voluntary disclosure to the Inland Revenue.

5. Taxpayers who make a voluntary disclosure by coming forward before the Inland Revenue starts an investigation can normally expect to settle with the Inland Revenue for tax, interest and penalties.

6. The amount that has to be paid by someone who comes forward voluntarily is usually considerably less than would be payable under a confiscation order, which is normally sought in prosecution cases. Additionally, the matter is dealt confidence and there would be no criminal record against the individual concerned.'

This makes it quite clear that voluntary disclosures will not be prosecuted so in the vast majority of cases there will be nothing to fear but it would just be as well to be sure your client has adequate protections in place under the Code of Practice the Inspector is working under.

This gives a great measure of comfort but it would still be sensible to proceed with some caution until the Revenue confirm it will be a civil investigation.

Making voluntary disclosures

10.5 So what should you do if you discover a problem? The question of what has to be done is very easily resolved. For those who are members of professional bodies there will usually be a Code of Conduct ordered or recommended by their ethics committee and this will be well set out in the Members Handbook (see, for example, ICAEW Members Handbook, 'Professional Conduct in Relation to Taxation' para 5.1 et seq). For those who are not members of a professional body or are members of a body that has not formulated a Code of Conduct in this particular area, they will be well advised to follow the practice of, for example, the Institute of Chartered Accountants.

10.6 In essence, you should advise your client of the problem and the possible outcomes and advise him that he must put right his errors or misdemeanours.

The client is of course free to completely ignore your advice and instruct you not to disclose understatements of income on previous returns. Faced with such a client you should, after making every effort to persuade him that a disclosure should be made, resign from acting for that client. Easier said than done perhaps if this is a major client, the loss of whom would seriously affect the well being of your practice, but nevertheless professionalism must prevail and you should resign. The Institute say it is acceptable to have regard to materiality in deciding if this is appropriate but point out that the concept for tax differs from that in relation to the conduct of an audit, and that the Revenue do not recognise the concept of materiality (Members Handbook, para 2.23 et seq). There is therefore a conflict that is left for you to decide on.

It is at this point where it becomes clear that the agent only really ends up with problems when he is reluctant to follow the ethical guidelines laid down by the Institute. Follow those and decisions are relatively easy although possibly hard on fee income.

Perhaps unfortunately, the guidelines then go on to say that simply resigning is insufficient. If you have assisted your client to prepare returns that you now discover are incorrect, and that will of course include incorrect accounts, then you should also write to the Revenue authorities advising them that you have resigned and that they can no longer rely upon returns or accounts that have been submitted in the past (Members Handbook, para 5.22).

It does not of course take a genius to work out what the Revenue's next step will be. Your now ex-client will inevitably face an investigation and you yourself could expect to receive a request for third party information under *TMA 1970, s 20(3)*. You should therefore draw your client's attention to the fact that you must proceed in this way when he refuses to accept your advice to sort out his history.

10.7 The matter does not quite end there either. There is now a professional reason why another accountant should refuse to accept instructions to act in the future. So having been advised of an approach by a potential new agent, you respond saying there is a professional reason not to accept the appointment. Unless this potential new client advises him of the problem and instructs him to put it right then the new agent should decline the appointment. In theory therefore the errant client cannot find professional representation until he decides to cleanse his fiscal sins (Members Handbook, para 5.23).

When advising the Revenue of your resignation and advising the prospective new agent that there is a professional reason why he should not accept the appointment, you must go no further than those simple statements. You should not advise the Revenue of the nature of any problem nor should you advise the prospective new agent of this either. Doing so would breach your duty of confidentiality and place you at risk of an action by your client (Members Handbook, para 5.24).

Problems in this area could be avoided by ensuring engagement letters contain an authority for you to advise the Revenue of all facts relating to tax liabilities.

10.8 So if your client takes your advice, he will instruct you to approach the Revenue and have his affairs sorted out. You must first assess the nature of the problem. If it is a minor error and indeed that is what it is, an error, then really all that is needed is a letter to the local tax office briefly explaining what has happened and providing the necessary figures to have the matter settled. You should bear in mind that it is possible to 'repair' the previously submitted self-assessment return within the appropriate time limits. The Revenue do however say that even if a return is repaired the submission of the original incorrect one could give rise to a penalty (see EH 665: 'penalties can still apply if it can be shown that the original return was submitted fraudulently or negligently').

If the figures involved have some substance to them but culpability is not an issue, then, again, the matter is quite straightforward and the local tax office should be approached to explain the nature of the problem and how it arose. Be alert, however, when considering how to present the issue to the inspector that he is likely to allege neglect and seek a penalty i.e. culpability may become an issue.

Culpability

10.9 The borderlines of neglect can be difficult to determine. It could be argued that every mistake is neglect because mistakes only arise if insufficient care and attention has been given to the matter in hand. We all make mistakes however and we all make errors of judgement and not all of these can amount to an act of neglect.

There is a difference between misunderstanding a complex piece of new legislation after having read it or even taken advice on it, and not bothering to read up the correct rules and simply going with whatever you think you would prefer the answer to be. Bear in mind that tax counsel are not infallible and occasionally give opinions with which the Revenue do not agree and with which the courts do not agree. Judges in the High Court, indeed in the Court of Appeal, get the answers wrong also, otherwise there would be no need for the Higher Courts of the Court of Appeal and the House of Lords. The House of Lords members do not always agree with each other. There is many a case that is won on a majority of 3:2 with two of the Law Lords giving a dissenting judgement. Had the taxpayers in those cases completed their tax returns on the basis that they believed was correct, would they be guilty of neglect? Of course not, but many inspectors of taxes will argue that they are, and that of course must be resisted.

Of great value in these situations is the case of *Olin Energy Systems Ltd v Scorer 1985 58 TC 592*. That case concerned a company that had losses from a trade that had ceased. In the computations submitted to the Revenue they had carried these losses forward and set these against profits of a different trade. The inspector issued an amended assessment reflecting this computation and so determined an appeal by agreement. A different inspector later decided that this was incorrect and issued assessments to correct the position by withdrawing the losses.

The company appealed and eventually the House of Lords agreed that they were protected by *TMA 1970, s 54(1)* (determination of appeals by agreement) saying that the computations were sufficient to alert a competent inspector to the fact that the loss claim was incorrect. The question to be asked was would a reasonable man have concluded that the inspector had decided to admit the claim having regard to the material in his possession. In this case they concluded that he would. So provided an error is there to be seen in a return, the Revenue are stopped from reopening that earlier year.

Apart from such arguments about neglect coming from inspectors there should be little problem when disclosing errors from the past.

10.10 This happy situation does however change when there is culpability. It is as well to be aware of the varying levels of culpability and in particular of the Inland Revenue's prosecution policy which is set out in detail in Chapter 13. But do stop and consider if you are dealing with a case of fraud as opposed to neglect. If fraud is not present, you are on reasonably safe ground in making an early approach to the Revenue.

If you think that some degree of fraud is involved, then the wisest course may be to consult a solicitor or tax investigation specialist before making any approach to the inspector. The tactic has to be the obtaining of 'Hansard' for the client under the Code of Practice 9 procedure.

If your client has had a previous investigation and the current disclosure involves the period of that previous investigation or, if not, but your client has repeated his offence and it is one that amounts to fraud then there is no decision to be made: the lawyer or specialist must be called in.

10.11 If after giving the matter considerable thought and after discussion with your client you decide to proceed with a disclosure to the Revenue, you must now decide whether the disclosure should be to the Special Compliance Office or to the local district. These are realms where the help of the investigation specialist is needed. If the matter involves a significant amount of tax, say in excess of £100,000, it is likely that the district would refer it to the Special Compliance Office. You, however, need to maintain an element of control over what is to happen. In short, if the case is to be worked by Special Compliance Office, you want 'Hansard' (this is explained and discussed in detail in Chapter 13) or to be more precise in the modern day, Code of Practice 9. If the Revenue refuse to open the case under Code of Practice 9, proceed no further but consult a specialist. The Institute of Chartered Accountants tells its members to ensure that at each meeting with Special Compliance Office 'the client is represented by a professional adviser experienced in that type of investigation' (Members Handbook, para 5.12).

If the approach, as in most cases, is to the local tax office, it is recommended that there is an initial, informal, meeting between you and the inspector without your client being present. Advise the inspector in general terms of the nature of the problem and the amounts involved and ask him to advise under which Code of Practice he will now proceed. If he declines to issue a Code of Practice at this stage, then proceed no further without specialist help.

10.12 If Code of Practice 9 is offered, or even Code of Practice 8, the Revenue will be expecting a full disclosure and a disclosure report. Such reports are discussed in Chapter 13 and again specialist help should be obtained.

Protecting yourself

10.13 Seemingly friendly and loyal clients become amazingly aggressive when tax problems arise, and human nature being what it is, rarely accept the blame for what is happening themselves. Even in the more minor cases of PAYE errors, they frequently seek to blame their accountant.

It is on these occasions that you may begin to regret having turned a blind eye to something your client was doing. Potentially more embarrassing is when the client turns round and says it was you who put him up to it, for example over his wife's wages.

There may sometimes be a temptation to take the blame to try and deflect the inspector's wrath away from your client in the hope that the penalty will be less and your client will be eternally grateful for what you have done for him. At worst the Revenue may take it into their heads that you are the problem and must be stopped from acting in a professional capacity for other people. At best it gives your client every opportunity to commence an action against you to recover any loss that he incurs. Do not be tempted, act professionally at all times and sleepless nights will be something for others to be concerned with.

Main points

1. Agents cannot ignore problems they discover in relation to their clients' affairs.
2. As the Revenue have had prosecution made easier for them and are expecting to take more cases to court, we must decide on the best approach for a voluntary disclosure with that in mind to protect our clients.
3. Have regard to the Revenue press release of 18 January 2001 relating to voluntary disclosure and prosecution.
4. Following the ethical guidelines of a professional body will ensure that problems for the accountant are avoidable.
5. Consider the extent of culpability when deciding how best to make a disclosure.
6. Call in a specialist if there is a previous investigation history or it appears fraud is involved.
7. Consider inserting a clause in engagement letters to permit you to make disclosures to the Revenue and so avoid possible litigation for disclosing something without authority.
8. Do not be tempted to try and deflect blame from your client and on to yourself.

Chapter 11

Interaction with VAT

Summary of chapter

11.1 This book is about Inland Revenue investigations but these do mesh with VAT so it is useful to have some knowledge of how Customs go about their investigations. This chapter also looks at:

- the adjustment of the figures agreed with the Revenue to take account of VAT;
- the differing penalty systems and time limits.

Exchange of information with Customs

11.2 In the course of a very long argument with an inspector of taxes concerning the level of profits and how certain events have happened, it is all too easy simply to focus on the direct tax effect of what you are arguing. This can cause problems if care is not taken because one must consider how other taxes may interact in any given situation.

Once the inspector of taxes has finished, it is likely that he will advise his colleagues at H M Customs & Excise. He is permitted to do this by *FA 1972, s 127* (see also IH 6506). Even if he does not tip off the VAT man, you would in any event have to consider advising your client to make a disclosure to Customs & Excise and follow the ethical guidelines if your client refuses to do anything about it (see Chapter 10 above).

It follows that additional sales for Inland Revenue purposes will result in additions to sales for VAT purposes, as may adjustments to purchases.

It does not follow that the VAT man will simply accept the figures that have been agreed by the inspector and so you may want to take some steps in ensuring that your client does not face another investigation on the same problem for the same years immediately after the Inland Revenue have finished. This could be done by trying to co-ordinate Customs & Excise and the Inland Revenue at the same time. There is now close working between the two departments and, on rare occasions, the joint working of a case has been seen. There are however marked differences in various areas as to how closely they do work together and to what extent they exchange information.

11.3 As soon as it is clear that sales have been understated, you may wish to consider approaching Customs & Excise and advising them of the investigation under way with the Inland Revenue and inviting them to participate in it so that figures eventually agreed are acceptable to both departments. In doing this, you should have regard to protecting your client by ensuring that Leaflet 730 is supplied by Customs to confirm that they will deal with the case as a civil offence.

It is believed that there is an understanding between the two departments that they will follow whatever the other has decided. If therefore the Inland Revenue investigate on a civil basis and the disclosure is made then Customs will also deal with the matter on a civil basis and vice versa. Unfortunately this is merely a belief and each department clearly reserves the right to make its own decision.

11.4 There can be some very marked differences in the treatment of something for direct taxation and VAT purposes. For example Customs are quite happy if you explain away missing sales as thefts of cash by employees. This is because the VAT liability point arises when goods or services are sold and most certainly when money is received. This being so, the VAT point has been triggered and there is liability whether or not the VAT proceeds have been stolen. For Inland Revenue purposes, however, the theft may be a legitimate deduction from profits should the original sale be recorded. If, however, the employee had stolen stock, not cash, and then proceeded to sell the stock for his own purposes, then the VAT point has not been triggered and no additional VAT liability arises. The practical effect for direct taxation purposes does not change whether it is goods or cash. This is just one example of how it is important to carefully think through the effect of an argument or proposal you may be about to accept. A more careful analysis of events may provide the basis for an argument that goods have been stolen, not cash, thereby securing substantial VAT advantages.

You should therefore carefully consider the effects of either tax and if necessary consult a VAT practitioner before proceeding to present a case to the Revenue.

VAT effect on the settlement

11.5 When it comes to the settlement don't forget that your client should be paying tax on sales after VAT has been deducted. It is all too easy to agree a settlement based on the gross figures with a resulting higher liability to interest and penalties and then sort out the VAT later down the line. It is far more efficient to deal with the VAT at the time of the settlement with the Revenue and not afterwards. Although inspectors are instructed in their manual to 'always consider whether there are any VAT implications for the proposed additions to profits' (IH 6507) the author has occasionally come across inspectors who do not.

The actual adjustment does however depend on how figures have been arrived at.

(*a*) Accounts are usually prepared on a VAT exclusive basis and so if the figures arrived at include VAT they should be adjusted before the calculation of income tax or corporation tax is made. This is because VAT is deemed to be included in the consideration for a supply, it is not something added to consideration. [*VATA 1994, s 19(2)*].

For example, a sum of £10,000 has been diverted into your client's pocket. Had he recorded this you would have sales in the accounts of £8,511 i.e.

Takings	10,000
VAT @ 7/47	(1,489)
Sales	8,511

If your client is a company and the director is liable to repay this £10,000 to the company then the debit to his loan account is £10,000. It can be easy to work on the figure of £8,511 and so give your client a low estimate of his liabilities. Clients get upset when they are told they will have to pay more than has been estimated.

(*b*) If accounts are prepared on a VAT inclusive basis the VAT payable will be an allowable deduction. The Revenue accept that the adjustment can be made when calculating the tax lost (IH 6508).

(c) The Revenue take the view that additions calculated by using a business economics exercise (e.g. gross profit calculation) are after VAT and so no adjustments are needed (IH 6511). Customs do not appear to fully agree with the Revenue on this and will frequently treat all figures reported by the Revenue as VAT inclusive. The author's view is that Customs are right on this one, unless the inspector has done his calculations on a VAT exclusive basis and in his experience this is not always the case.

To prove the point consider this example:

A gross profit calculation is carried out on a business. The inspector will typically look at the prices being charged and compare these with the cost price. Unless he adjusts these for VAT the wrong result is obtained i.e.

Sales (ex VAT)	10,000
Cost (ex VAT)	(5,000)
Profit	5,000 (GPR 50%)

or

Sales (inc VAT)	11,750	VAT	1750
Cost (inc VAT)	(5,875)	VAT	(875)
Profit	5,875 (GPR 50%)	Net	875

Quite clearly the Revenue's advice to their inspectors is misleading (see IH 6509) so you must carefully consider VAT matters yourself and not assume the inspector will be right.

Customs investigations

11.6 This book is about Inland Revenue investigations, those carried out by Customs are a completely different subject. It is however useful to be aware of the differences, especially as the Revenue investigation may follow one initiated by Customs.

You will frequently see assessments for additional VAT following a VAT visit to (what they call) a trader and this may follow on from a long debate with you over figures that mirror the sort of thing you do in a Revenue investigation. Customs do not however regard these as investigations; penalties may apply but these may arise simply because there has been a 'misdeclaration' on a VAT return when the adjustment exceeds certain limits (these limits are 30 per cent of the VAT or £1 million; see Customs leaflet 700/45/93). With these cases the assessing time limit is only three years, a point to bear in mind.

Customs are not very subtle when it comes to what they call investigation work. Local investigation teams are referred to as 'fraud units' and their officers use the word 'fraud' liberally. Their head office unit is called the National Investigation Service (NIS) but is responsible for all areas of investigation work undertaken by Customs e.g. drug smuggling, bootlegging as well as serious VAT fraud. They are much more geared up to prosecute than the Inland Revenue and are more likely to work a case with a view to prosecution from the outset. Like the Revenue, they can accept a monetary settlement however. If NIS are involved it is vital to call in some expert help.

11.7 The local investigation unit is more likely to work the case under the civil procedures. In this they will start a case with an interview, usually taped (but note not under caution), and give your client Notice 730. This tells your client that the case is one of 'conduct involving dishonesty', what the penalties are, and the policy on mitigation for disclosure and co-operation. Your client is then expected to disclose the VAT due by providing a schedule of arrears.

In this respect it works a little like the Revenue's Hansard procedure, so be prepared to do the work yourself. Be aware that it will also form the basis of a report for the Revenue.

11.8 The courts tend to be harsher on VAT offenders than on those who commit direct tax offences. This is because VAT is paid over to a trader in trust for him to hand on to Customs; the Revenue has a similar attitude themselves over PAYE offences. One judge has said 'a cheat on the public revenue involving VAT is a theft of money and far more serious than a cheat on the public revenue involving the Inland Revenue' (Judge Owen Stable as quoted in the Tax Journal, 29 May 1993).

One thing to be aware of, however, is that there is no offence of 'neglect' as far as VAT is concerned. There is either some form of dishonesty (and this may be sufficient for criminal proceedings or for the lesser civil penalty for conduct involving dishonesty) or not. If there is no dishonesty then there is no offence and the only worry may be the misdeclaration penalty. Something that attracts a penalty from the Revenue therefore may not from Customs.

Main points

1. The Inland Revenue and Customs & Excise exchange information.
2. There can be differences in treatment between the taxes e.g. a theft of goods by an employee is not VATable but a theft of money is.
3. VAT must be adjusted for before agreeing tax lost with the Revenue.
4. Customs are more likely to prosecute if the NIS are involved.
5. Local offices are more likely to use the civil procedures for 'conduct involving dishonesty' and hand over form 730.
6. Interviews by Customs are likely to be taped.
7. There is no offence of neglect in VAT so unless there has been dishonesty Customs can only assess for the previous three years.

Chapter 12

Company Investigations

Summary of chapter

12.1 This chapter considers some of the issues affecting companies which are not covered elsewhere in the book. In particular it discusses:

- the liability that arises under *section 419* following the rewriting of the loan account;
- the potential liability of the directors; and
- the risks of putting a company into liquidation.

A fully worked example of the typical adjustments that need to be made following a settlement with the Revenue is provided.

Introduction

12.2 Throughout this book company liability has been dealt with alongside that of individuals but some matters are specific to companies. The techniques for investigating companies and unincorporated businesses, particularly partnerships, have material differences; unincorporated businesses tend to have simpler accounting systems and fewer participants in the business and so are generally technically simpler to perform.

Some companies are little more than incorporated corner shops, but generally speaking limited companies have larger turnovers, more staff, more transactions and more participators in the business. An investigation of a limited company therefore demands more in resources and in co-ordination. To effectively investigate a limited company the affairs of its directors also need investigating simultaneously.

As a result, if an enquiry is commenced into a limited company, one can expect enquiries also to be commenced into the directors of that company (see IH 2945 and EH 441). This means that there are several open enquiries covering one investigation but this does not prevent one party making an application to the Appeal Commissioners for an order to close his enquiry.

Companies create complex technical issues. Accounting policy and standards play a greater part. There are issues concerning loans to participators, benefits in kind and PAYE/NIC, as well as who is liable – the directors or the company.

Section 419

12.3 *ICTA 1988, s 419* features because, typically, directors will have diverted cash sales away from the company and into their own pockets.

Precedents have it that this is money not lawfully due to them and is therefore a debt incurred to the company by the director who has taken the money. (The Revenue rely upon *Curtis v J & G Oldfield Ltd 2 TC 319*, *Erddig Motors Ltd v McGregor 1961 40 TC 95*, *Frederick Lack Ltd v Doggett 1970 46 TC 524*, *Bamford v ATA Advertising Ltd 48 TC 359*, and *Fen Farming Co Ltd v Dunsford 1974 49 TC 246*; see IH 2995.) Such a debt gives rise to a *section 419* liability and so the inspector of taxes will tax the same amount twice.

Example

12.4 Assume that a director has taken £10,000 in one year from the company.

The accounts have to be rewritten to show the correct figure of profit for that year and thus tax is due on an extra £10,000 plus interest and penalties.

In addition, the director has incurred a debt to the company of £10,000 and so a liability under *section 419* on £10,000 plus interest and penalties also arises. The liability may typically work out as follows:

(*a*) In year to 31 March 1999 director/participator took £10,000 of cash by diverting sales to himself. Assume no VAT liability arises.

Profits for year ended 31 March 1999 understated by £10,000

Corporation tax	
£10,000 @ 20% =	£2,000
Interest (assume settlement 1 April 2001)	£185
Penalty (say 35%)	£700
Sub total	£2,885

Because the £10,000 was not voted as remuneration, nor as a dividend, the participator owes this to the company (*ICTA 1988, s 419*) and so additional liability arises as follows:

Section 419 liability	
£10,000 @ 25% =	£2,500
Interest (assume settlement 1 April 2001)	£250
Penalty (assume 35%)	£875
Sub total	£3,625

Total settlement:	
Corporation tax	£2,885
Section 419	£3,625
Total	£6,510

The tax liability under *section 419* will be refunded after the participator has repaid the debt. [*ICTA 1988, s 419(4)*]. You should ensure the settlement offer indicates that a repayment will be made. Note that only the tax will be repaid, not the interest and penalty. All liability falls upon the company.

(*b*) If VAT is due the figures work out as follows:

VAT	
£10,000 @ 7⁄47	£1,489
Corporation tax	
£10,000 – £1,489 = £8,511 @ 20%	£1,702
Interest	£170
Penalty	£744
Sub total	£2,616
Section 419	
£10,000 @ 25%	£2,500
Interest	£250
Penalty	£875
Sub total	£3,625
Total settlement:	
Corporation tax	£2,616
s 419	£3,625
Total	£6,241
+ VAT settlement	
VAT	£1,489
Interest (say)	£300
Penalty (say 20%)	£298
Total	£2,087
Total settlements	£8,328

12.5 It may follow that the director also has a personal income tax liability on the £10,000 being an interest-free loan or advance. [*ICTA 1988, s 160*]. It is the Revenue view that there would be such a liability but they will only pursue it if it is clear that the company is not going to pay its settlement for some reason (IH 2980).

This, however, may not be the case because the wording of *section 419* differs from that of *section 160*. *Section 419* applies to any debt whatsoever whereas *section 160* only applies to loans or advances and it can be argued that money taken without legal authority is not a loan or an advance and so liability under *section 160* is avoided. This may not however always be the case and it is therefore necessary to check out the facts. The wording of the Revenue's guidance does appear to indicate that they are not as confident of their view as they would like, as it says 'it is arguable' and gives no authority for their view (IH 2980).

If *section 160* does apply then the company could be in further trouble. It is likely that it failed to submit a correctly completed form P11D (the form that returns benefits and expenses paid to directors and employees).

12.6 Although the Revenue quote case law as authority for their view that a settlement should be on the company and not on the director who extracted funds the position is not that clear cut. In 1969 there was a non-tax case that decided directors were not liable to repay remuneration not properly voted to them (*Re Duomatic Ltd [1969] 2 Ch 365*; the court held that it was still remuneration even though it was not formally voted). The Revenue do not accept this case because it did not involve any concealment of money and PAYE had been operated. This, however, contradicts the Revenue argument that *section 419* applies because concealed moneys have not been authorised!

It does seem odd if all the directors are also the shareholders that there is a pretence that the company did not authorise the extractions. It would seem to the author that they were authorised but such authorisation was not committed to writing. The *Re Duomatic* case would appear to support such a view.

Nevertheless, the Revenue have succeeded for many years in maintaining their view and have not been seriously challenged. From time to time they do take the director route by raising Schedule E assessments and have succeeded in having these supported by the courts also (see *Hudson v Humbles 1965 42 TC 380, Frowd v Whalley 1965 42 TC 599*).

It therefore seems that either view is correct and so it is difficult to convince an Appeal Tribunal to discharge the Revenue's assessment. The author believes it is open to doubt, and when the facts permit you should not be too ready to agree with the Revenue that *section 419* should apply.

12.7 It may be decided to agree with the Revenue for the purpose of reaching a settlement but refuse to rewrite the accounts to reflect the debt allegedly due from the director. It could be that the company does not see the money as something that is due to it; if so it must be wrong to produce accounts that show an asset that the company does not acknowledge. If the money was taken with the knowledge of the company (because all shareholders knew of it) would they be successful if they sued for return of it in the courts?

The Revenue will treat such conflicts of opinion with them as a write-off of the loan account and apply the liability attaching to such write-offs. [*ICTA 1988, s 421*, see IH 2985(c)].

12.8 The Revenue normally only take the Schedule E option if a company has gone into liquidation or they think they will not be paid by the company. Some advisors may now argue that the director client should therefore have nothing to pay because it was a company responsibility to operate PAYE on the extra, undeclared salary and so the Revenue must return to the company to seek redress.

There is something in this argument and it can be successfully used in some situations. In an investigation situation where there has clearly been default and especially if the director has failed to declare his full income on his own tax returns then the argument is usually futile.

The Revenue turn to *reg 46* of the *Income Tax (Employments) Regulations 1993 (SI 1993 No 744)* and direct that the individual director should be held responsible for the PAYE that the company failed to deduct. They can do this if the Revenue are of the opinion that the director received his remuneration knowing that the company wilfully failed to deduct tax.

If a director is in a position where he can divert sales receipts to himself and ensure that this avoids being recorded in the company's books and records, he usually knows that he has received money without deduction of tax. It is of course possible to pursue an individual director for the non-payment of national insurance contributions and so there really is no hiding place.

Phoenixism

12.9 It is in the field of company investigations that the 'phoenix' situation arises. This is the practice of forming a company, stripping it of its resources, having failed to hand over VAT and PAYE but having paid all other creditors. The company then ceases to trade, leaving the Revenue authorities struggling to collect their cash.

The Revenue then see the very same directors recommence trading with the same customers and suppliers but under the auspices of a new company and they do the same again. The Revenue have now had some successful prosecutions in this area and so, as well as being morally questionable, the practice can amount to fraud or cheating and lead to a prison sentence.

This is also an area where the company advisor could find himself in trouble because an advisor is frequently asked if a company should cease trading and a new one be formed during the course of a tax investigation.

The client is of course looking to see if he can completely get away without paying the Revenue anything or minimising his exposure to pay the full amount that he fears he may have to find. Apart from having to have regard to the insolvency rules, for which the advice of a licensed insolvency practitioner should be obtained, it is necessary to pay attention to all the armoury at the Revenue's disposal because it may make such a plan completely inoperative in a practical way.

The issue is not without some merit however. If the directors are aware of a big tax liability, which the company is going to be in some difficulty meeting as it arises, then the question of insolvency arises and ceasing to trade may be the correct and proper thing to do in order to protect other creditors. Once again the early advice of an insolvency practitioner could be highly desirable and appropriate.

Simply putting a company into liquidation to avoid a tax liability without any commercial merit in doing so is however a potentially risky thing to do. In the extreme the Revenue may take the view that phoenixism is taking place and refer the case to the criminal prosecution unit at the Special Compliance Office. In any event they will look to shift the liability on to the individual directors and, although the arithmetic may be different, there will be no escaping liability. The attempt to avoid paying up will affect the inspector's thinking on the penalty loading for co-operation.

Settlements

12.10 Settlements in investigations related to companies are often more complex than those involving individuals. Frequently there are various different liabilities. There is usually corporation tax, together with *section 419* liabilities and often PAYE-type liabilities relating to payment of expenses or other items. It is also likely that some element of benefits-in-kind are present and the Revenue may seek settlement by the company rather than approach each individual for payment of tax on the benefits they have not declared personally on their tax returns.

The payment of the settlement can be complex when *section 419* is involved. If the now overdrawn directors' loan account has been repaid there is of course relief under *section 419(4)* available but there may be questions of the timing of this relief. There may be an undertaking by the directors to correct their loan account position within a relatively short period of time, say 30 or 60 days. In these circumstances the inspector may frequently agree that *section 419* liability need not be paid over but could be treated as met by the *section 419(4)* relief that would become available upon repayment of the loan account. This does however again raise timing questions following the *Finance Act 1996* but inspectors can frequently be flexible in the wording of the offer. This does of course achieve the result that the tax under *section 419* need not be paid to the Revenue and then have to be reclaimed at a later date, but the liability to interest on *section 419* and to penalties does of course remain.

It will occasionally be the case that the inspector will require the directors to join in a corporate settlement. This will be particularly so when extensive *section 419* liabilities arise and the company's ability to pay the settlement rests upon the directors reimbursing the company at an early date. The question also arises when there may be significant individual liabilities that the company is agreeing to meet for administrative convenience.

An important point to remember is that the inspector cannot dictate a settlement offer to you or your client. He may recommend, he may suggest but he cannot insist. An offer is freely made without duress. It is of course open to the Revenue to reject any offer and commence formal proceedings to collect tax, interest and penalties and you will have to consider each case on its own merit given the usual desire by your client to have the matter settled and the fact that it is usually a cheaper alternative to make an offer and inspectors are usually reasonable in taking a broad brush approach to matters at settlement negotiation stage.

Accounts adjustments

12.11 Following settlement on traditional lines it will be necessary to reflect the position in the accounts. This subject is covered in detail in *Tolley's Accounting Principles for Tax Purposes* and the relevant section is reproduced at Appendix N with the consent of its author, Mike Cochrane.

Main points

1. A company investigation will involve an investigation of its directors.
2. Typically directors will have diverted money away from the company into their own pockets. The Revenue view is that this is money owed to the company and so *section 419* will apply to it.
3. If the Revenue think the company is unlikely to be able to pay they may treat the amounts taken by directors as chargeable on them under Schedule E.
4. The Revenue view on the application of *section 419* is not free from doubt.
5. Putting companies into liquidation can be risky and will not enable the directors to escape personal liability.
6. Company settlements result in accounts having to be rewritten.

Chapter 13

Special Compliance Office

Summary of chapter

13.1 It would be irresponsible to suggest that one could handle an investigation by the Special Compliance Office (SCO) after reading a book on the subject. That would be akin to saying that you could learn to swim, or drive a car simply by reading a good book. It is a specialist area and an expert should be consulted if SCO are involved.

The aim is therefore to introduce you to this unit and explain what it does and the sort of case that will end up there. The chapter will:

- enable you to identify the risk areas and seek expert help before it all goes wrong. By calling in an expert and working alongside him you may gain the experience needed to deal with these cases yourself;
- identify the prosecution risk cases and give tips on spotting these;
- explain the 'Hansard' procedures and what will happen in the early stages of these;
- reveal the possible consequences of involving non-resident friends or relatives in explanations to the Revenue.

Introduction

13.2 The Revenue have several offices and agencies under their control. These range from the local tax office, located in most large towns and cities, the Valuation Office, Capital Taxes Office and the National Insurance Contributions Office. They also have some elite investigation units. Special Investigation Division deals with complex and major avoidance schemes but the one agents may come into contact with at some stage in their careers is the Special Compliance Office (see IH 400).

This is in effect the Inland Revenue's serious fraud office and deals with the most serious of cases in which prosecution may not be very far away. Special Compliance Office (SCO) inspectors are specially selected from the office network after showing considerable talent for investigation work; these talents are improved once within the SCO units.

There are a number of these units in key cities in the UK namely Birmingham, Bristol, Edinburgh, Leeds, Liverpool, London, Manchester and Nottingham.

13.3 SCO is split into three units.

- *The prosecution group.* As it implies, this unit seeks out and conducts investigations leading to a criminal prosecution. This group will take an interest in cases referred to SCO that justify working to criminal prosecution standards, although not all such cases proceed to court.
- *The Hansard group.* This group deals with cases when a prosecution is not intended and work them with the intention of bringing the case to a monetary settlement to include tax, interest and penalties. They work within the Revenue Code of Practice 9, more commonly known as 'Hansard'.
- *The avoidance group.* This group looks into cases which prima facie do not appear to be a case of serious fraud but where something appears wrong with someone's tax affairs due to involvement in some attempt to avoid tax; the attempt may not work or be technically deficient. They work under the Revenue's Code of Practice 8.

Other operational matters dealt with by SCO include (see IH 403):

- Foreign entertainers
- Agricultural compliance
- Computer investigations
- Internal fraud
- Exchange of information with foreign tax authorities.

Prosecutions

13.4 Prosecution work, and protecting clients who are under threat of prosecution, is not something for accountants to do. Experienced, and specialist, solicitors should be engaged when a risk of prosecution is present. The signals, and forgive me if some of these are so obvious, might be:

- Your client is arrested.
- Your client's premises are searched.
- Your premises are searched relating to the affairs of a particular client.
- You are served with a statutory order to produce documents under the *TMA 1970 Section 20(BA)* procedures.
- Your client is interviewed under caution (i.e. prior to questions being asked the officer says 'You are not obliged to say anything . . .').
- Officers of the Special Compliance Office wish to interview your client but have not issued Code of Practice 8 or Code of Practice 9.

In any of the above situations a solicitor, or tax investigation specialist, should be consulted immediately. They may be able to persuade the Revenue to change their minds on a possible prosecution and have the case worked under the Hansard procedure with a monetary settlement in mind.

13.5 The Revenue have a selective prosecution policy but the following are high risk (IH 451):

- deliberate false accounting
- false claims for allowances and reliefs
- documents which have been forged or altered
- an accountant or solicitor is involved
- there is conspiracy with a third party to commit fraud
- previous certificate of disclosure is false
- previous statement of assets is false
- offshore trusts or companies are involved.

The Hansard group

13.6 Most cases dealt with by the Special Compliance Office are dealt with under Code of Practice 8 or Code of Practice 9. Code of Practice 9 is more commonly referred to as 'Hansard'.

This is because at the opening of a case the inspector will acquaint your client with the Inland Revenue's policy relating to tax fraud. This is set out in the answer given to a parliamentary question and is therefore recorded in the parliamentary minutes known as Hansard.

In essence the Hansard statement says that the Board of Inland Revenue reserve the right to prosecute in all cases of tax fraud but in deciding whether they prosecute or not, are influenced by the extent of an individual's disclosure and if there is co-operation in calculating the tax lost and settling this with the Inland Revenue.

In other words they are very much influenced by a full confession on challenge and a full and frank disclosure of all tax irregularities.

13.7 Amongst tax investigation professionals the phrase 'under the protection of Hansard' is often used. It is generally thought that if the Revenue have given Hansard under Code of Practice 9 then there will be no prosecution, provided that the client makes a full disclosure. Indeed, many Revenue prosecutions relate to cases in which a taxpayer failed to make a full disclosure under the Hansard procedure.

Whilst in general day-to-day life the 'protection of Hansard' is probably valid, it could be that something arises that the Revenue regard as far too serious to overlook and they may decide that a prosecution should proceed.

13.8 In 1998, however, there was a case that appeared to upset this. A Court of Appeal ruling in the case of *R v Werner & Clarke* (commonly referred to as *R v W & Another [1998] STC 550*) caused quite a stir amongst investigation professionals. The Revenue had negotiated a monetary settlement in a case involving a tax avoidance scheme. The Crown Prosecution Service were however also prosecuting the same individuals on charges of false accounting and conspiracy to defraud. The defence argued that a prosecution could not proceed because the Revenue had accepted a cash settlement. The court however ruled that the acceptance by the Revenue of a tax settlement did not prevent the Crown Prosecution Service from continuing with its case.

This raised the possibility that a settlement may be made with the Revenue yet another agency may come along and prosecute for a similar offence. This may be:

- Serious Fraud Office
- H M Customs & Excise
- Crown Prosecution Service
- Department of Trade and Industry
- Health and Safety Executive
- Department of Health and Social Security
- Environment Agency
- Ministry of Agriculture Fisheries and Food
- Intervention Board
- Bank of England.

It must therefore be realised that making one's peace with the Revenue would not necessarily prevent a prosecution taking place if the offences committed come within the areas covered by these other agencies.

A major risk in tax cases must therefore be H M Customs & Excise because VAT will usually be involved if there is a fraud on the Inland Revenue. There does however appear to be some sort of understanding between the Revenue and H M Customs & Excise that each will follow the other's lead.

In a Hansard case it is therefore necessary to consider what other agencies may become involved, having regard to what your client has done, and perhaps take good legal advice to identify the offences and the agencies that may be interested. A co-ordinated approach may therefore become necessary.

13.9 The case of *R v W & Another* was in danger of throwing the Revenue's monetary settlement procedures into chaos. For a period of time some investigation specialists were refusing to have their clients interviewed even under the Hansard procedures. This prompted a statement in the Commons by the Attorney General on 8 April 1998 who said that:

> 'This ruling accorded with the existing understanding of the Crown Prosecution Service and Inland Revenue as to their respective roles in relation to criminal investigation and prosecution, and does not require any change of policy or practice on the part of either. Nor does it affect the position of those individuals who co-operate with the Inland Revenue on what is commonly referred to as the "Hansard practice" or otherwise. Primary responsibility for investigation and prosecution in relation to alleged tax evasion rests with the Inland Revenue; proceedings brought by the Crown Prosecution Service will ordinarily encompass charges relating to tax evasion only in circumstances where that evasion is incidental to allegations of non-fiscal criminal conduct.'

This followed the signing of a 'Convention Between Prosecuting Authorities' on 11 February 1998 which tries to establish a structure to ensure there is co-ordination between agencies in cases when more than one may be interested.

In the author's view nothing was really changed by *R v W & Another,* other than better communication between the various authorities to avoid one being played off against another. The case did not, in fact, involve the Hansard procedure; it was worked by the Revenue under Code of Practice 8 and so was not identified as a potential serious fraud case by the Revenue when their investigation commenced. Such a case can always move into prosecution or to Hansard as facts emerge.

This was an unusual case that caused a stir for a while. The message to clients is therefore that the Revenue are unlikely to prosecute if Hansard is offered but it does not mean that someone else may not if the misdeeds offend their area of policing.

Refusing Hansard means throwing away the opportunity to be almost certain of avoiding prosecution, and the maximum mitigation of penalties. The tiny risk that it may all go wrong must be taken.

13.10 Hansard is an important procedure and a very serious one and clients should grasp their opportunity under Hansard if it is granted to them. The usual procedure after the Hansard extract has been read by the taxpayer is to ask him several questions. Typically these are as follows:

1. Have any transactions been omitted from or incorrectly recorded in the books of any business or company in which you are or have been concerned either as proprietor or director?
2. Are the accounts which have been sent to the Inland Revenue for the companies and businesses mentioned in question 1 correct and complete to the best of your knowledge and belief?
3. Are all your personal tax returns as submitted to the Inland Revenue correct and complete to the best of your knowledge and belief?
4. Are all tax returns submitted to the Revenue by the companies and businesses mentioned in question 1 correct and complete to the best of your knowledge and belief?

5. Are you prepared to permit an examination of the books, bank books and other records of the companies and businesses mentioned in question 1 and of your bank books and records?

The inspector will point out that the questions are not limited in time.

If in answering these questions your client effectively makes a disclosure by saying that the tax returns are not correct, he will be invited to have a report prepared setting out what is wrong with these tax returns and quantifying the extent to which they are incorrect.

The disclosure report

13.11 Such a report is very important and is often best prepared by a specialist experienced in doing these. The Institute of Chartered Accountants advises its members to engage a specialist to deal with SCO (ICAEW Members Handbook, para 5.12). The report can be expensive to prepare and indeed is very intensive and time-consuming. It is vital to realise that this is your client's disclosure report. If anything is wrong with it, your client faces a serious risk of prosecution and imprisonment.

Each report is individual because each case is different and its format must, therefore, be tailored to the needs of that case. A good report should place itself in the mind of the inspector and cover everything that he would if he was conducting an investigation himself.

Preparing a report will take time and use up your resources so you must consider if you can properly undertake it.

In preparing the report you will have regard to your client's disclosure and prove that it is full and complete. This means that you must carry out an investigation of your client's affairs, which can often be done more effectively by an independent third party who does not have to protect an ongoing business relationship with the client.

It may mean a re-audit of certain areas. Audits do not cover every conceivable transaction, so it may therefore be thought desirable to look at new areas or revisit others in the light of a client's disclosure or a request by the Revenue. A re-audit may be appropriate if there was some problem during an audit that was not pursued because it was not considered material.

A full analysis of all bank accounts is necessary with supporting evidence to establish precisely, and without doubt, what all deposits and withdrawals related to.

It may involve making third party enquiries and obtaining statements.

It must address the relevant legislation, which may be up to 20 years old. In recent times the author has had to have regard to stock relief, investment income surcharge and close company apportionment. It may involve the complex world of offshore trusts and companies with all the anti-avoidance legislation that goes with it.

This must all be collated in a report and be submitted with all supporting evidence. Once received the inspector will examine the report and test it out.

Remember that this is your client's disclosure report. It is not a defensive document of the sort that may be a letter during a local district investigation. It is important to be impartial but at the same time defend your client's position, robustly putting forward and arguing all points in his favour.

13.12 The inspector will want the report adopted by your client by the signing of a certificate. This adoption certificate acknowledges the Hansard procedure, confirms it is understood and confirms that the report has been read, is fully understood and is the client's full disclosure under the terms of Hansard.

Some additional forms are required that do not generally appear in district investigation work.

Statements of assets will be required but in addition a list of bank accounts operated during the period covered by the report will be demanded. It is, of course, vitally important when preparing a report to ensure that all accounts have been identified and copy statements seen, but over a lengthy period of time it is always possible that a client has opened and closed an account that he has completely forgotten about and it is therefore vital that all leads are followed up.

It can, sometimes, be surprising how clients' memories fade. It has been known for clients to forget they had Swiss bank accounts containing hundreds of thousands of pounds some 12 to 15 years previously. The inspector can take quite some convincing that such accounts are genuinely overlooked and forgotten about; the risk is that some day a jury may also not be convinced that there could be such forgetfulness.

The usual certificates of disclosure will be required.

13.13 Once the report is with the inspector he will test it to satisfy himself that it is a complete disclosure, that he can proceed to settlement on the figures it contains, and on the technical basis put forward in the report.

If so, the case will then proceed to settlement in a manner that is very similar to district cases, with agreement of tax liabilities for each year, agreement of the interest charge and debate on the mitigation of penalties. The penalty mitigation factors remain the same as with district cases. Your client will then be invited to make an offer in the same way as set out in Chapter 8.

The avoidance group

13.14 The avoidance group will commence a case by issuing Code of Practice 8. This will say that it relates to cases not involved in serious fraud. This means that the client isn't given the Hansard procedure and such cases therefore fall into something of a 'no man's land'. The case is not being worked as a prosecution nor is it being worked as something that is serious but will lead to a cash settlement with the client not having been warned of the dangers of prosecution and invited to make a disclosure and co-operate.

Indeed, the Revenue at this stage appears to think that any tax offence would be one of neglect, or if fraud, certainly not of a serious variety.

Code of Practice 8 is often seen when the Revenue come across some offshore activity, especially if trusts or offshore companies are involved. They may believe the structure has been put together for the purpose of avoiding tax rather than evading it. Most taxpayers and, arguably, their non-specialist advisors could, perhaps, be forgiven for having lost track of anti-avoidance legislation and court decisions and so the Revenue want to explore the structures and establish if any UK taxation should be applied.

Unfortunately it is frequently the case that a client has deliberately put together an offshore structure to evade tax and he may blurt this out to the inspector during the course of an interview without being 'under the protection of Hansard'.

If your client is offered Code of Practice 8 prior to a meeting with SCO, it is very important to have a long, serious and frank discussion with him to establish if there is any possibility of the Revenue changing their view about any possible offence and the case becoming one that they view as serious fraud. If so, attempts must be made to obtain Code of Practice 9 (i.e. Hansard). If there is difficulty getting the Revenue to agree to Code of Practice 9, and you think your client has committed serious fraud then any invitations to attend an interview should be declined and specialist advice taken to ensure that your client is protected as far as possible.

The comments made at 13.8 and 13.9 above apply also to COP 8 cases.

13.15 Tax offices are urged to report the following types of case to the avoidance group (IH 441):

- company residence
- non-domiciled individuals
- transfer of assets abroad
- sportsmen and entertainers
- phoenixism.

General

13.16 Special Compliance Office also gets involved in some spin-off activities. Their accountants will become involved in cases that have a strong technical accountancy feature to them and they will also be seen when the Revenue suspect the honesty or competency of an accountant.

They also adopt the role of postbox for the receipt of and distribution of information coming from and going to foreign tax authorities as mentioned in Chapter 11.

13.17 If your client tries to explain away his source of money as coming from a rich friend or relative in some far off land and that distant relative is even prepared to supply written testimony to this fact then it is likely that SCO will advise the tax authorities in the relative's country of residence of the fact and he or she may then be faced with having to explain to those tax authorities where this money came from.

This could lead to difficulties if tax offences have been committed in that country. At this point, it may be worth remembering that not all countries are as lenient as the UK when it comes to punishing tax offences. Whilst the UK takes a dim view of tax offences and imposes stiff penalties, most are concluded with a monetary payment and there is not even any publicity. Although Ireland has a similar system, the names of such offenders are published once a settlement has been agreed. Some countries, however, for example China, execute tax dodgers!

Conclusion

13.18 Quite clearly dealing with the offences covered by the Special Compliance Office, even under the Hansard procedure, requires an experience, knowledge and skill that can rarely be found in most accountants' offices simply because most accountants do not come across the Special Compliance Office or if they do it is very infrequently. This is far too important a matter to use a client as a learning experience and it would be much better to obtain that experience by working alongside a specialist in this field.

Chapter 14

PAYE and National Insurance

Summary of Chapter

14.1 PAYE is a stand-alone subject and has its own audit systems by the Revenue, totally separate from investigations into accounts and returns. It is briefly included in this book because it does impact on full investigations and all large investigations usually include a full review of PAYE compliance. A PAYE failure can lead to a full accounts investigation and so it is essential that something more than a passing regard is had to PAYE. Do not forget with this duty Revenue officials are out in the field visiting employer's premises and inspecting records, they feed information back to the accounts Inspector.

This chapter therefore looks at:

- what PAYE is and how it operates;
- the Revenue's powers to inspect documents; and
- the Revenue's awesome powers linked to their new role in administering NIC.
- the advise to be given to a client about to undergo a PAYE/NIC inspection

Introduction

14.2 Pay As You Earn (PAYE) and National Insurance (NIC) both became the responsibility of the Inland Revenue from April 1999. On balance this is better because employers are no longer faced with the prospect of visits from two separate agencies effectively looking at similar things.

The rules relating to liability to PAYE and NIC are broadly similar but with some differences, e.g. genuine expenses payments are not earnings for National Insurance purposes but are emoluments for PAYE purposes. These differences are slowly being eroded, for example we now have NIC liability on benefits in kind, but it cannot be assumed that both duties will apply to any payment.

In their determined fight against those who do not comply with the many and complex regulations the Revenue find the policing of the PAYE system produces good results. The Revenue has put resources into PAYE compliance and inspections.

14.3 A Revenue PAYE inspection usually leads to tax, interest and penalties being paid over to the Revenue, but additionally the Revenue can, and do, use it as a platform to launch a full investigation.

They have found a relationship between failure to comply with the PAYE regulations and a failure to comply with other tax regulations, including the submission of correct accounts and tax returns. This is not really surprising. Those who have a responsible attitude to PAYE and make every effort to get it right are also likely to be the ones who have a responsible attitude to other aspects of their tax affairs. On the other hand those who have a cavalier attitude to PAYE compliance generally have this attitude to their overall tax affairs.

Spotting the person with incorrect accounts is not, however, an exact science; a PAYE inspection is however, usually quick, relatively inexpensive and gets the Revenue inside an organisation.

14.4 A typical PAYE inspection will involve a lower grade Revenue official (i.e. not an inspector) making a visit to the employer's premises to inspect the relevant payroll records. Rarely will there be any professional representation in attendance at the time of the visit and the Revenue official is likely to be placed in the care of a relatively junior employee in the employer's organisation. The Revenue officers are usually given all that they ask for and their questions are usually answered openly, and honestly, by the employer's staff.

It is not surprising that with this scenario the Revenue find evidence of lax bookkeeping systems and poor payroll practices and so a report is made to the Accounts Inspector in the local tax office who may decide that there is sufficient evidence to justify a full investigation. The Inspector in this case already knows that there may be some tax to be obtained from the efforts of his PAYE colleague. He also knows from the outset that there are weaknesses in the record keeping system and so much of the early groundwork that he would seek to do has already been done.

Payroll is becoming an increasingly complex subject. It goes beyond simply operating tax codes against wages. The Revenue now has responsibility for working family tax credits, statutory sick pay, statutory maternity pay and student loans. In the best-run organisations, with professional payroll staff and sophisticated software, it is difficult to get it 100% right. Smaller employers are at greater risk, this is therefore an area in which they would be well advised to have regular reviews and so an opportunity for accountants to generate fee income.

PAYE inspections

14.5 The general scheme of PAYE is set out at *ICTA 1988, s 203*. Basically when any employee is paid, tax is deducted and handed over to the Revenue. Pay includes expenses, indeed virtually anything that is given to the employee.

Additional regulations provide for returns to be made of anything that has been given to an employee from which tax cannot be deducted i.e. benefits in kind like company cars. At the end of each tax year ending on 5 April, the employer must make returns to his local tax office giving details of each employee and the tax that has been deducted from their pay together with a return of any expenses and benefits that relate to each employee. Failure to provide these returns on time or correctly attracts penalties.

The detailed legislation on PAYE operation is contained in Regulations made by the Board of Inland Revenue (*The Income Tax (Employment) Regulations 1993, SI 1993 No 744*).

14.6 Not surprisingly the legislation does not leave everything to the entire honesty of the individual employer but grants the Revenue the right to check that this system is being applied correctly.

The Revenue has the right to inspect an employer's records (*Reg. 55*). It obliges every employer to produce records for inspection at such time as the Revenue Inspector may reasonably require and at a prescribed place.

The process will start with a notice of an intended visit and enclosing the relevant Code of Practice. If the time and date is not convenient the Revenue will be co-operative in agreeing one that is mutually acceptable.

Clients should be encouraged to alert you to the visit. This will enable you to brief him on the process, the Revenue's rights and the documents that need to be ready for the visit. Some advisers seem to favour a pre-inspection audit to check if there are any problems. Whether doing this is worthwhile and represents value for money as far as your client is concerned is probably something that needs to be decided on a client-by-client basis. It could be argued that it is 'shutting the door' after the event and so the only potential value will be to obtain every advantage from a disclosure at the commencement of the visit. Potential difficulties that a pre-inspection audit could create include some ethical ones.

What would you do if your audit discovered, say ten, problem areas all giving rise to a loss of tax. Your client takes the view that the Revenue inspection may not catch all of these, and his prediction proves to be correct; the Revenue have missed, say five, of the problems. You however, are aware of these but your client refuses to disclose them; what should you do? It has created a difficult client relationship problem for you.

Your client would appreciate support during the visit. You could suggest that you attend for the duration of the inspection. In the author's experience you will spend a day or so watching the Revenue turn over pieces of paper. It may be better to ensure that you keep your diary free for the duration of the visit and are easily contactable by telephone so that you may attend your client if the need arises and be present for any interviews that may be conducted.

Your advice should also extend to:

- The facilities made available to the inspector.

  Revenue staff are humans and will appreciate being treated reasonably. Ensure their working area is comfortable. If possible provide a separate room, this helps to prevent them 'snooping' around unnoticed. Ensure drinks are provided, or made available.

- Copying facilities

  It is to be preferred that they have to hand documents to your client for copying. In this way an extra copy can be taken for you and you will know what they have.

- Provision of assistance

  A member of your client's staff should be assigned to managing the visit. They should provide the documents requested by the inspector (within the legislative requirements of course) and be able to answer any straightforward questions on the payroll system and operation.

- Interviews

  You are likely to be absent and so there is risk that simple questions become an interview. Ideally you should be called to any such meeting but advise your client on the correct behaviour at interviews.

- Agreements

  Tell your client to listen to any points put forward by the inspector but not to agree anything. Ask the inspector to put the points in writing so they can be considered.

14.7 The two phrases, 'reasonably require' and 'prescribed place', deserve some attention.

'Prescribed place' is easy because the regulations dictate that place. It is a place in the United Kingdom on which the Revenue's inspector and the employer mutually agree. So, if the inspector and the employer mutually agree that the records can be inspected in the car park at Watford Gap Services on the M1 then that is the prescribed place in accordance with *Reg. 55*.

The person who drafted this legislation did however have the foresight to think that the Inspector and the employer may not always agree and so it follows that if there is no such agreement it will be the place, within the United Kingdom, at which the records are normally kept. If there is no such place within the United Kingdom, or the records are not normally kept in one place, then the prescribed place will be the employer's principal place of business within the United Kingdom.

Most visits will therefore be to the employer's premises unless all the relevant records are kept elsewhere.

This gives rise to an interesting question on whether a PAYE inspector has a general right of entry to business premises. The legislation certainly does not give him this right, as it does for a VAT Inspector or even an NIC Inspector, but *Reg. 55* certainly does require an employer to produce records to an Inspector at his business premises if called upon to do so. It must therefore follow that he must be allowed access to carry out his task.

14.8 The regulation refers to such time as the officer may 'reasonably require'. That must be interpreted as during the normal working day; for the Revenue to demand that premises are opened up at 02:00 am for the purposes of inspection of the PAYE records would be regarded as unreasonable.

Equally, the Revenue may regard the employer as being unreasonable if he told the inspector to call at 04:50 pm on a Friday evening to carry out his inspection. He may retort by advising that they are coming at 09:00 am that morning and the Courts would probably regard that as at such time as the officer may reasonably require.

14.9 PAYE inspectors are not granted unfettered rights to inspect every single document that may exist on an employer's premises. The regulations set out the records that may be inspected and covers what would be expected i.e. wage sheets, deduction working sheets and any documents or records related to the calculation and payment of wages and relating to the calculation of the deduction of tax from such wages, but it also goes on to say that the employer should produce other documents and records as may be specified by the Inspector (*Reg. 55(2)*).

It must be argued that any such document or record has to be relevant to the PAYE regulations. Thus inspection of stock records and purchase invoices will not usually be relevant but the inspector would typically ask to see petty cash records. Revenue officers usually have success with petty cash records because it is from here that they see round sum expenses being paid out or other ad hoc payments being made to staff and it would be difficult to deny access to such a document.

14.10 The inspection of such records frequently gives rise to problems for the employer because areas such as round sum expenses, suspect subsistence allowances, provision of cars or fuel to family members, occupation of holiday villas abroad, or home telephone bills being paid comes to light. Usually there is an accurate record of these items, which enables the Revenue inspector simply to extract these items from the company records and provide a computation of the tax that is due.

Clients may frequently find their agents apparently impotent because so often there is little to argue against. Either something has been paid to an individual or it has not. If it has it is a matter of fact. If there is no dispute on the amount that has been paid, there is little room to negotiate what needs to be taxed and so the agent's room to manoeuvre can be very limited.

Revenue inspectors are, however, usually reasonable and will not seek to tax those items that would usually be allowable in the hands of the employee; but when it comes to considering whether to deny the Revenue their tax and go to appeal, it may often be found that there is little to appeal against other than to plead for the application of some common sense. Thankfully Revenue inspectors frequently apply common sense.

This underlines the advantage of periodic health-checks.

14.11 The author does not wish to be over pessimistic in relation to PAYE investigations because more often than not some item can be found to be not taxable or, if strictly subject to PAYE, is an item which should be relievable upon a claim by an employee.. A detailed knowledge of Schedule E and the PAYE mechanism is required and that is a subject beyond the scope of this book.

Frequently the Revenue's calculations will fall into two categories.

1. Tax that should have been deducted from cash payments to an employee e.g. relating to expenses payments that are not allowable. This is a liability of the employer because of his failure to operate PAYE in the first instance; and
2. Tax on benefits in kind that the employer had failed to report on forms P9D and P11D. It usually follows that the employee has also failed to declare these items on his own personal tax return. As it is not usually the employer's responsibility to collect the tax and pay it over to the Revenue the tax settlement is the responsibility of the individual employee. The employer may find himself facing penalties for incorrect forms P11D etc. but nevertheless he has no liability to tax.

The Revenue usually prefers to have a negotiated global settlement with the employer rather than knocking on the door of various individual employees and negotiating separate settlements with them. Equally, employers frequently do not wish their employees to be upset and troubled by the Revenue seeking tax on some benefit in kind that may have been a reward for good work. They may believe that doing so could be a de-motivating factor.

It is therefore to the benefit of both the Revenue and the employer that such a global settlement is reached and that the employer meets the tax that would have been paid by the employee. Certainly, however, the employer should not be agreeing to pay penalties on this unless it relates to a penalty for an incorrect return.

14.12 There are penalties for failing to make returns on time and also for incorrect returns. Incorrect returns bring a tax related penalty which is 100% of the difference between the tax declared and the tax that should have been declared had a return been correct, provided of course the incorrect return was the result of fraud or neglect [*TMA 1970, s 98A*].

The penalty for late returns is dependent on the number of employees.

Incorrect forms P11D can attract a penalty under *TMA 1970, s 98* of a maximum of £3,000 per form, provided it has been provided fraudulently or negligently.

14.13 A similar set of rules applies to the sub-contractor tax deduction scheme as regards the keeping of records and the Revenue's right to inspect these.

National Insurance Contributions

14.14 National Insurance Contributions are payable both by employees and employers on earnings and are also paid by self-employed individuals under Class 2 and Class 4.

Class 4 is generally speaking a percentage of profits declared for tax within a certain band and any additions to profits will give rise to extra Class 4 National Insurance Contributions also.

It is therefore only necessary to concentrate on the Class 1 National Insurance Contributions i.e. those paid by employees and their employers on their earnings.

14.15 The powers of National Insurance Inspectors are draconian [*SSAA 1992, s 110*]. The legislation provides that the Secretary of State for the purposes of Social Security may appoint Inspectors. Such Inspectors have the following powers:

(*a*) to enter at all reasonable time any premises liable to inspection;

(*b*) to make such examinations and enquiry as may be necessary; for ascertaining the provisions of the *Social Security Acts* are being or have been complied with in any such premises;

(*c*) to examine, either alone or in the presence of any other person, as he thinks fit, in relation to any matters on the *Acts* on which he may reasonably require information, every person he finds in any such premises or whom he has reasonable cause to believe could be or to have been a person liable to pay and to require every such person to be so examined; and

(*d*) to exercise such other powers as may be necessary for carrying the *Acts* into effect.

Before considering these powers in some detail it must be noted that from 1 April 1999 the Inland Revenue took responsibility for National Insurance Contributions and so there is new legislation which provides that the Inland Revenue will authorise any of their officers to exercise the powers conferred by this section, that section provides similar powers as those described above. [*SSAA 1992, s 110ZA*].

14.16 The premises liable for inspection are those that an officer has reasonable grounds for believing that:

(*a*) any persons are employed there;

(*b*) any trade or business is being carried on in there;

(*c*) any records relating to a trade or business are kept there; or

(*d*) a personal or occupational pension scheme is being administered from there.

A private dwelling house is not liable to inspection unless the officer has reasonable grounds for believing that a trade or business is being carried on from that house and that that trade or business is not also being carried on from premises other than a dwelling house.

This is the wording from the new Revenue power at *SSAA 1992, s 110ZA* and differs from the old National Insurance inspector power at *SSAA 1992, s 110*. The Revenue appear to have managed to sneak in some extra powers for themselves when taking over responsibility for National Insurance Contributions. The old legislation in *section 110* made no reference to a trade or business being carried on at premises, it referred only to premises where someone was employed.

14.17 It would therefore seem that an Inland Revenue officer now has the right to enter any premises provided he can show that he has reasonable grounds for believing that a trade is carried on there, the only limits being that this power is only relevant for the purposes of establishing liability to National Insurance Contributions and he can only enter a dwelling house if that is the only place from which the trade is conducted.

It is questionable whether there is sufficient oversight of this awesome power. Given that National Insurance Contributions are, in some way or other, payable by everybody then it would seem that the Inland Revenue have managed to obtain a general right to enter business premises, provided it is for the purposes of establishing National Insurance Contribution liability. It is, however a small leap from National Insurance to income tax liability as one frequently gives rise to the other.

14.18 The awesome power of this section does not end there.

Once on the premises the inspector can examine (i.e. interview), alone, any person he thinks fit to examine whom he finds on the premises and he reasonably thinks to be a person who is liable, or has been liable to pay National Insurance Contributions. So the section gives the inspector the right to interview anyone he finds on the premises and gives him the right to interview that person alone.

The concern continues however. The legislation requires any such person the inspector finds on the premises to submit to such examination (i.e.

questioning). In other words it appears that there is no right to remain silent and no right to be represented when being questioned.

It is questionable whether these power would survive a challenge under the Human Rights legislation if the associated penalties are to be treated as criminal in nature.

There is one difference between *sections 110* and *110ZA* and that is that *section 110* provided a further power to its inspectors and that was to exercise such powers as may be necessary for carrying the Acts into effect. In other words, a Social Security Inspector could do anything he wished provided he could show that it was necessary for establishing liability to National Insurance Contributions.

The Inland Revenue have not been given that general power within *section 110ZA*. It could be that they are happy with the terms of *section 110ZA(2)(b)* which provides that their officer may make such examination or enquiry, as may be necessary, for checking whether the National Insurance Contributions legislation has been complied with.

14.19 It would seem that force cannot be used to enter premises. If the inspector's entry to the premises is barred he may not force his way past, but anyone barring the inspector's progress may be committing an offence. The legislation provides that intentionally delaying or obstructing an inspector is an offence liable to a criminal conviction with a maximum fine of £1,000 [*SSAA 1992, s 111*]. It may however be comforting to note that the Inland Revenue powers, under *section 110ZA*, are deliberately excluded from this.

Section 111 also punishes anybody who refuses or neglects to answer any questions or furnish any information when required to do so. It therefore seems that if a Social Security inspector calls then being uncooperative with him and obstructing him could lead to a criminal conviction but if it is one of the Inland Revenue's men, the civil penalty codes under *TMA 1970, s 98* will apply.

Breaches of the National Insurance regulations can give rise to civil penalties similar to the ones we are familiar with for Income Tax.

14.20 A National Insurance inspection is very much similar to a PAYE inspection and tends to give rise to the same sort of problems and arguments. The agent must be alert to the fact that not all items carry the same liability as for income tax and must take care that, especially, Inland Revenue staff, are not trying to impose National Insurance liability where none is due. Extensive advice on liability to National Insurance Contributions and the various offences, powers and remedies can be found in Tolley's National Insurance Contributions.

Main points

1. There is a relationship between PAYE failures and cases being taken up for full investigation.

2. Revenue officials are frequently given free access to books and records and allowed to interview employees without oversight and they report back to the accounts inspector.
3. For the purposes of checking PAYE compliance the Revenue can inspect records at the place they are kept unless you agree on another venue, at any reasonable time.
4. There can be argument over what records the Revenue can see. They are allowed those necessary for the purpose of checking the PAYE system, no others. Some of the records requested can have doubtful links to the PAYE system.
5. The Revenue are usually reasonable in negotiation of liabilities for PAYE failures but a thorough knowledge of the system and the regulations is needed to get the best out of this.
6. Often it is the employees who are strictly liable but the Revenue may ask the employer to pay because it is easier for them. This usually arises out of a failure to disclose benefits on a form P11D. Such settlements are acceptable but penalties should be negotiated.
7. The scheme for deducting tax from sub-contractors has similar record inspection powers to PAYE.
8. Don't forget that if there has been a failure to deduct tax under the sub-contractor scheme liability is forgiven if it can be shown that the recipient has declared the payment in his accounts.
9. NIC is now administered by the Inland Revenue and operates alongside PAYE with mainly similar rules.
10. An NIC inspector has the power to enter any premises if people are employed there and interview anyone found there, alone if necessary. They may also do anything they consider necessary for the purpose of the NIC legislation.
11. The Revenue have adopted similar powers to allow them to check NIC but they go a stage further and specify premises liable for entry as any at which a business is being carried on if there are employees there, there always will be if a company is involved.
12. It is an offence to obstruct an officer but they cannot use force to enter.

Chapter 15

Penalties and Interest

Summary of chapter

15.1 This chapter contains:

- a very brief outline of the main penalty provisions;
- a discussion on the mitigation of penalties; and
- a brief referral to interest provisions.

Penalties

15.2 The *Taxes Act* demands that certain things be done. If there is default it provides penalties for such failure.

Failure to make an income tax or capital gains tax return [*TMA 1970, s 93*]

15.3 An individual or a trustee must make a return if required to do so and do this within certain time limits. Essentially this is usually 31 January following the end of the tax year concerned but this may be extended if a tax return has been issued for completion after 31 October. Failure to comply with these time limits results in an automatic penalty of £100, rising by a further £100 if the return is still outstanding six months later.

The Revenue do, however, have the option of not seeking the extra £100 arising because of the further six months delay but instead applying to the Appeal Commissioners for a daily penalty not exceeding £60 for each day on which the failure continues after the taxpayer being notified of the Commissioners' direction. This daily penalty cannot be imposed if the failure has been remedied.

If the return is very late i.e. a year after the filing date (filing dates are dealt with at Chapter 3) then the penalty is tax geared. It is a maximum of the tax due on the late return.

Any late filing penalty cannot exceed the tax due. So if a return is late but the only tax due on it is say £25 then the late filing penalty cannot exceed £25.

Note however that this does not apply to partnership tax returns.

These penalties can be appealed on the basis that there is a reasonable excuse for the failure. It is far too early in the life of the self-assessment procedures to come to any conclusions on the sorts of reasonable excuse that the Appeal Commissioners, or the Revenue, may accept. We have experience of the same concept for VAT purposes, however, and there is every reason to think the same sort of approach may be applied.

15.4 The VAT experience is that H M Customs & Excise take a very harsh line, with the Appeal Tribunal generally supporting Customs but with a slightly softer edge.

With VAT one is usually trying to rescue a penalty situation following the late submission of a quarterly VAT return. The reasonable excuses that are accepted tend to relate to something sudden and unpredictable that has happened which prevents timely completion of the forms, and also prevents alternative procedures being applied to ensure that there is compliance with its statutory requirements. Given the length of time there is to complete a tax return i.e. the best part of ten months, one could expect the Appeal Commissioners to have less sympathy with someone who, for example, only looks to commence preparation with a couple of weeks to go and then finds that information has to be obtained from elsewhere to assist him.

The sudden onset of illness close to the deadline may be acceptable in some circumstances, but the absence of accurate figures may not be. The Revenue have published a Code of Practice on using estimates when accurate information is not available to ensure that returns are in on time.

15.5 It is probably unlikely that a great body of case law will be built up on the subject of reasonable excuse for the lateness of tax returns. The maximum penalty that will most commonly be incurred is £200 and it is not therefore economic to pursue appeals except on a point of principle. With VAT the penalty is a percentage of the VAT shown on the return and this could obviously amount to a significant figure in some cases, hence the motivation to appeal together with the fact that costs are frequently awarded to the taxpayer if there is a successful appeal.

15.6 If tax is paid late it attracts a surcharge [*TMA 1970, s 59C*] for income tax and capital gains tax under the self-assessment rules. There may of course be a tax-related penalty for late submission of the return. The rule is however that there cannot be a surcharge and a tax-geared penalty on the same liability. The Revenue can choose which they impose and will undoubtedly pick the one that gives them the most.

Example

A surcharge has been imposed on £10,000 as follows;

After 28 days	5% on £10,000 = £500
After 6 months	5% on £10,000 = £500
Interest on surcharge say	£50
Total surcharge + interest	£1,050
Mitigated penalty say 20% of £10,000	£2,000

The inspector can only take the surcharge plus interest of £1,050 or the penalty of £2,000, he cannot take both.

Late returns for corporation tax purposes [*FA 1998, Sch 18, paras 17–19*]

15.7 Failing to make a return for corporation tax purposes on time attracts very similar penalties to those attracted by individuals and partners as described above. The time limit for companies is however a little tighter. There is a penalty of £100 for lateness rising by a further £100 after a further three months. It is worth noting that for corporation tax purposes, a tax return includes a company's accounts, statements and reports.

Persistent defaulters are punished by an increase in these penalty amounts. If a penalty has been imposed for two consecutive accounting periods for a late return, the third period attracts a £500 penalty rising to £1,000 after a further three months.

Those who are extraordinarily late in making a return, attract a tax-geared penalty. 18 months after the accounting date attracts a 10 per cent penalty based upon the tax outstanding at that 18-month point. At the 24-month point that tax-geared penalty rises to 20 per cent.

Unlike income tax there is no restriction of penalties to the amount of tax due.

Incorrect accounts or returns

15.8 If incorrect returns, or accounts, are delivered to the Revenue, penalties apply depending upon the taxpayer's status as an individual, a trustee, a partner [*TMA 1970, ss 95–95A*] or a company. [*FA 1998, Sch 18, para 20*].

The penalty is a maximum of 100 per cent of the difference in tax payable between that declared and what it would have been if a correct return had been submitted.

Of course, some returns may not be correct for a legitimate reason. A penalty can only be applied if the return, accounts etc. have been fraudulently or negligently delivered to the Revenue. Neglect was discussed in Chapter 10. It is difficult to persuade the Revenue that an innocent error has occurred but it is quite clear that the incorrect return penalty applies whether a return was deliberately incorrect or not.

Deliberately submitting an incorrect return or accounts may amount to fraud. Neglect is nowhere as serious as fraud and is clearly something that happens without prior deliberation. Laziness in writing up books and records to the extent that correct and accurate information cannot be remembered will amount to neglect.

If you come across an incorrect return or accounts you may conclude that it is because of an innocent error. This would avoid the penalty described above but only if the error is remedied with sufficient haste; unless an error is remedied without 'unreasonable delay' then the matter will be treated as negligence. [*TMA 1970, s 97*].

15.9 Clients will often argue that accounts that are incorrect have nothing to do with them. They left all that to their accountants, they don't understand accounts, they don't know when looking at a set of accounts whether they are correct or not, they rely on the professionals to get it right, that is why they pay them. Unfortunately for these clients the legislation deems that accounts submitted on behalf of any person are deemed to be submitted by him unless he can prove that they were submitted without his consent, or connivance. [*TMA 1970, s 97(2)*].

Connivance signifies something sinister, the getting together of two people to agree that incorrect accounts are submitted. This in itself could give rise to some very serious offences and a risk of prosecution. Rarely would it be suggested that the accountant and his client connived to submit a set of incorrect accounts but it would usually be difficult to argue that they were submitted without his consent.

Accountants should adopt the good practice of seeking the client's consent before using the accounts to prepare self-assessment tax returns and so avoid difficulties for themselves if a client claims he has problems.

Whilst on this point, it is worth mentioning the submission of tax returns. Clients frequently sign a blank return and send it to their accountant for him to complete the details and submit to the Revenue without bothering him any further. This is not good practice either for the accountant or his client. The client must accept responsibility for the tax return; it is his return. The accountant will be depending upon information provided by his client to correctly complete the return on his behalf. It is all too easy to omit something or make some glaring error that is obvious to the client when he sees the return. Clients should therefore have the opportunity to check the return and be happy that it is correct before signing and authorising its submission to the Revenue.

Inspectors of taxes will have little sympathy with those who claim they haven't seen a return before it was submitted and will probably argue that this is evidence of neglect because the client clearly had no interest in the return and didn't care what figures were entered on it and so must amount to negligence.

Failure to produce documents etc.

15.10 There are two separate penalty regimes for failing to supply information, documents or other sorts of special returns that may be required under the numerous provisions of the *Taxes Acts*.

The simple one is the failure to produce documents when ordered to do so under *TMA 1970, s 19A* (the requirement to produce documents relating to enquiries into self-assessment returns). Failure to comply with an order gives rise to a penalty of £50, followed by a daily penalty for each day on which the failure continues after the £50 penalty was imposed. [*TMA 1970, s 97AA*]. This daily amount is £30 if the penalty is determined by the Revenue themselves but can be as high as £150 per day if the penalty is determined by the Appeal Commissioners. The Revenue may decide to commence proceedings before the Appeal Commissioners for the higher penalty rather than determine the lower penalty themselves. The penalty is appealable.

15.11 If the failure relates to an order under the *section 20* family of *TMA 1970* then the case is different. These penalties are also applied if there is a failure to submit a special return or provide information under other legislation. The legislation is detailed in the table to *TMA 1970, s 98* but the commonest forms of special return would be returns of commissions paid, and under the anti-avoidance sections of *ICTA 1988*.

The penalty for such a failure is a maximum of £300 with a further penalty of a maximum of £60 per day for continuing failure after the initial penalty has been imposed.

A word of caution; if the failure relates to reporting requirements relating to the migration of companies the initial penalty is as much as £3,000 and the continuing daily penalty £600. [*ICTA 1988, s 765A*].

If incorrect documents, information, particulars are given fraudulently or negligently, a penalty not exceeding £3,000 can be imposed. [*TMA 1970, s 98(2)*].

Assisting in the preparation of incorrect returns or accounts

15.12 The wording of *TMA 1970, s 99* is wonderfully simple and understandable and is as follows:

> 'Any person who assists in or induces the preparation or delivery of any information, return, accounts or documents which:
>
> (*a*) he knows will be, or is or likely to be, used for any purpose of tax; and
>
> (*b*) he knows to be incorrect;
>
> shall be liable to a penalty not exceeding £3,000.'

Agents should also remember that incurring a penalty under *section 99* permits *TMA 1970, s 20A* to kick in and under that section the Revenue might access all of your client's records (see Chapter 7).

The determination of penalties

15.13 For most penalties the Revenue themselves may determine the amount of the penalty and effectively make an assessment for it. There is, as would be expected, an appeal procedure for those who feel aggrieved. The appeal may be made to the Appeal Commissioners and they, on hearing the case, may set aside the penalty, or if they think the amount determined is incorrect they may reduce it or even increase it. If unhappy with the Commissioners' decision an appeal may be made to the High Court. [*TMA 1970, s 98(2)*].

If the penalty is one which the inspector himself cannot determine then proceedings must be taken before the Appeal Commissioners, who upon hearing the inspector's complaint and considering any mitigating pleas from the appellant, will impose a penalty they feel appropriate in the circumstances.

Once again there is provision for appeal to the High Court if aggrieved by the Appeal Commissioners' decision, but once again both the Appeal Commissioners and indeed the High Court may set aside and reduce or increase any penalty. [*TMA 1970, ss 100C, 100D*].

Mitigation of penalties

15.14 The Revenue have a general power to mitigate any penalty. This also applies after a penalty has been imposed by the Appeal Commissioners or the courts. [*TMA 1970, s 102*].

Throughout the penalty sections of *TMA 1970* the wording changes. Some provisions say that penalties shall not exceed a certain figure, others say there shall be a penalty of £x and this would seem to signify that, for example, a late tax return will receive a penalty of £100 whereas the penalty for incorrect accounts is a maximum of 100 per cent of the tax lost and so it is clear that the amount could vary. Despite these differences of wording, *section 102* provides that the Board of Inland Revenue may in their discretion mitigate any penalty and so it would seem that all penalties can be mitigated no matter what the specific wording of the particular provision under which the penalty is imposed.

The Revenue set out their policy on mitigating penalties for tax offences relating to incorrect returns or accounts in their leaflet relating to settlements of tax liabilities at the conclusion of a tax investigation (IR 73).

The mitigating factors for tax-geared penalties take account of the following:

Disclosure	giving up to 20% off (30% in some cases).
Co-operation	giving up to 40% off.
Size and gravity	giving up to 40% off.

Disclosure

15.15 The Revenue view a disclosure as a full explanation of all irregularities whether or not they can be quantified when it is made. Disclosure also involves describing the manner in which the irregularities have occurred, not merely that they have occurred and the amount of them. It means a voluntary and useful contribution to the Revenue's knowledge of the taxpayer's affairs.

There can therefore be certain extremes. These range from the taxpayer who makes a complete voluntary disclosure without being under investigation at that point in time, nor fearing that his wrongdoing may be uncovered in the near future. For these 'prodigal sons' the Revenue are prepared to extend the normal mitigation of a maximum of 20 per cent up to a maximum of 30 per cent.

The other extreme is the taxpayer who makes no admission, continues to deny throughout the investigation and continues his denial after he has lost his case before the Appeal Commissioners. Such a taxpayer cannot expect to receive mitigation for a disclosure.

Between these extremes are various degrees of disclosure (see IH 5530).

15.16 When considering penalty loading it is therefore necessary to step back from the case, to consider how it commenced and what contribution your client has made to the inspector's knowledge and at what stage during the process of the investigation. The various degrees of disclosure may be as follows:

- A complete and voluntary disclosure by someone who has no reason to fear early discovery.
- The complete and voluntary disclosure by someone who feared early discovery.
- A full disclosure as soon as the Revenue mount an enquiry or investigation.
- A disclosure that is voluntary but was not a full and complete one.
- A disclosure once the Revenue announced their investigation but again only a partial one and restricted to what your client thought the inspector may know.
- A complete denial that anything is wrong with accounts or returns at the commencement of an investigation but a disclosure is made by your client later down the line.

The author would suggest that the first item qualifies for the 30 per cent mitigation, the next two 20 per cent and then each one comes down by 5 per cent leading to zero for the person who makes absolutely no disclosure whatsoever.

It must be emphasised that this is the author's personal view but it is supported by the comments made by the Revenue in their Investigation Handbook (IH 5530).

Someone who has failed to notify his or her liability to tax need only spontaneously advise the Revenue to have a good case for the full 30 per cent mitigation.

Someone who is known to the Revenue and has already been served a tax return, completes it with the correct figures and sends it in would probably attract 20 per cent because he could argue that he feared no early discovery.

Co-operation

15.17 A substantial 40 per cent is available to be mitigated for co-operation and it can clearly be seen how the conduct of a case can massively reduce the ultimate settlement, or conversely substantially increase it.

Co-operation effectively means working with the inspector to arrive at the likely amount of tax that is due. The agent is deemed to be the taxpayer in the Revenue's eyes so an unco-operative agent could cost his client dearly.

The inspector is willing to take account of the information supplied, the speed within which it was supplied, and help with understanding what has happened and indeed the openness of the agent and the taxpayer during the course of his enquiry.

Delaying tactics could attract a black mark and it goes without saying that refusal to explain things and telling lies could never be seen as co-operation (IH 5535).

If the inspector has to resort to using formal powers to obtain information, mitigation for co-operation will be reduced. The Revenue also cite the necessity to have liability determined by the Appeal Commissioners or persisting in 'unacceptable stories' relating to gifts, cash hoards, or betting wins as affecting the degree of mitigation for co-operation.

It is the author's view that the Revenue is being unreasonable in this area. If a client has a genuine cash hoard or a genuine betting win then it is right that he should persist with that explanation even if the inspector is programmed to reject it.

Equally, one must be careful not to confuse co-operation with agreement. This can frequently be the case. An inspector may regard those who agree with the Revenue's views as being very co-operative with him but those that question some of his actions and disagree with his conclusions as being awkward and unco-operative.

15.18 When considering the level of mitigation for co-operation, you must not fall into the same trap but carefully evaluate the case and how it has been worked.

Did you provide the inspector with all the information he requested within the time he asked for it? If not, was there good reason for a delay or for refusal to provide certain documents and information?

If the Revenue complained that co-operation was poor because of the agent's actions, did the inspector draw this to the taxpayer's attention during the course of the enquiry and explain that it now effects his penalty mitigation, or did the inspector permit the agent to carry on without warning the taxpayer of the possible consequences?

Refusing to allow the Revenue access to information that Parliament has decided they have no right to, must not lead to a client being punished under the penalty mitigation policy.

It would be hoped that all those who have read this book and conducted investigations following its guidance would have attracted the full 40 per cent mitigation for co-operation. Refusal to provide any information except on formal order, challenging all the formal orders in the face of legislation, precedents and common sense, forcing the Revenue to seek determinations of figures before the Appeal Commissioners will surely attract no mitigation of penalty for co-operation.

Within the extremes it is a matter of judgement but much can be earned by ensuring that the Revenue's correspondence is attended to promptly and if there is likely to be any delay that the inspector is advised immediately of the reasons and given a likely time of response.

Size and gravity

15.19 The final area of abatement is described as size and gravity by the Revenue and 40 per cent is available. Quite frankly this is the one area in which little can be done to influence the abatement.

The gravity of the offence committed by your client is dictated by what he did when he did it; in other words it is the degree of culpability ranging from negligence to serious fraud.

Size is both relative to the case and an absolute concept. Someone who is earning £20,000 per annum and omits £10,000 from his return, omits a very significant sum relative to his total income and must have known that his accounts were incorrect. £10,000 per annum omitted by a successful businessman returning profits of £¼ million per annum is still a significant amount but he may not notice £10,000 in the same way as most others would.

In this regard, note should be taken of the comments of Rowlatt J in the case of *Attorney General v Johnstone 1926 10 TC 763*:

> 'This is a very bad case. Here is a man who says he put down £300 bona fide, when he was making £1,500 and had been making it for years.
>
> Do you tell me that a man who can conduct a successful business – he says he does it all himself – making £1,500 a year does not know at the end of the year what his books show? His banking account will tell him; his household expenses will tell him; what he has got in his pocket will tell him. He would know if he made £300 or £1,500. It is no use putting up this argument to me or to anybody else who knows anything of human affairs.'

15.20 The Revenue's guidance seems to relate more towards the gravity of the offence rather than the size of it with size being an indicator of the gravity of the offence. They advise their inspectors always to mitigate by at least 15 per cent unless the case involves a very serious fraud, in which case the Special Compliance Office would be involved (IH 5540). It would appear that cases of serious fraud should expect no mitigation under this heading at all but that then triggers a debate on what is meant by serious fraud and its various degrees of culpability.

The Revenue will always wish to take some penalty to reflect the fact that there has been wrongdoing and so it is unlikely that anything more than 35 per cent mitigation could ever be obtained unless there are some extraordinary mitigating circumstances, and the Revenue cite cases of persons who are aged or infirm as perhaps deserving of special consideration.

The penalty loading

15.21 The Revenue assist their inspectors in considering the various degrees of mitigation and the amount that is to be applied by giving a variety of examples. These can be found at IH 5545 and are very well worth studying by the novice to investigation settlements and also by experienced practitioners because it does serve as a reminder of the thought process of the inspector on this subject.

Once you have considered all the areas of mitigation and carefully and honestly reached a conclusion on what you believe the mitigating factors are and how they should be applied, then you should approach the inspector of taxes to present these mitigating factors.

It is much easier to influence a decision than it is to have one changed. Once the inspector has considered his case of penalties and arrived at a conclusion, he will discuss this with his superiors and obtain their agreement to his views and will be far more reluctant to agree with you in respect of any area of difference.

As in many differing areas with the Revenue you are likely to be very unsuccessful in your presentation if you simply go for the extremes of full mitigation in each and every case you argue. The inspector will simply come to regard you as someone not to be taken seriously, will ignore all that you say and will reach his own conclusions upon which he will be difficult to budge.

Those who reach honest conclusions based on the facts of the case are the ones who receive the best results.

Interest

15.22 Tax that is paid late attracts an interest charge; the Revenue see this as commercial restitution and not a penalty. The current legislation is much more straightforward than that existing for 1995 to 1996 and earlier. It is now under one section for income and capital gains tax and another for corporation tax. [*TMA 1970, ss 86, 87A*].

The old legislation distinguished between simple late paid tax and tax paid late due to default and had differing dates from which interest was calculated. There were also some awkward technical problems for the Revenue from time to time.

Now it is simple. Interest runs from the date the tax should have been paid until the date it is paid.

The Revenue will not easily mitigate an interest charge but do say that if they have contributed to any delays they will consider some relief. The delay would usually have to exceed six months. They will also consider mitigation if there is a serious means problem (IH 4408, 4423).

Payments on account during the course of an investigation will reduce the interest charge and will also show goodwill and so help to obtain penalty mitigation.

It is likely that the inspector will raise the issue of a payment on account from time to time and generally speaking clients should be encouraged to make these.

Main points

1. Failure to comply with any requirement of the *Taxes Acts* will result in a penalty.
2. Penalties can be appealed on the basis of reasonable excuse.
3. The penalty for incorrect accounts can be 100 per cent of the tax evaded.
4. Penalties are mitigated for disclosure (20 per cent), co-operation (40 per cent) and gravity (40 per cent).
5. Inspectors can sometimes confuse co-operation with agreement.
6. Anything done by an agent is deemed to be done by the taxpayer
7. Interest is charged on tax paid late.

Chapter 16

Human Rights

Introduction

16.1 This Chapter introduces the reader to the human rights legislation and the impact it may have on tax investigation issues. This is a very new area as far as the UK is concerned and cases examining the issues are working their way through the Court system. It has therefore been kept very brief until the issues and precedents form a clear pattern.

16.2 The *Human Rights Act 1998* came into force in the UK on 2 October 2000, following which we can now take human rights issues before our domestic Courts. We have been able do enforce such rights before the European Court for many years as the UK was signed up to the European Convention on Human Rights from 1951 but only now can we take such issues to our own Courts.

Having been subject to human rights legislation since 1951 it may be thought that there is nothing new and the issues by now well settled in the European Court, however it seems not.

This is new and its impact on taxation issues will develop as the years go by but we have already seen how it becomes an issue during investigations.

The legislation that may be relevant during an investigation is as follows:

16.3 Article 1

This provides for the peaceful enjoyment of property and the right not to be deprived of it.

This may therefore affect demands for documents or seizure of goods by Customs. There is however a let out for taxation matters and so it appears unlikely that this could be successfully used. The European Court of Human Rights considered the application of Article 1 in respect of taxation in the case of *Georgiou and Another (t/a Mario's Chippery) v United Kingdom [2001] STC 80* confirming that the right to protection of property cannot prevent the enforcement of tax laws.

16.4 Article 6

The right to a fair and public hearing within a reasonable time by an independent tribunal; the presumption of innocence until proved guilty; the provision of free legal assistance if required; to be informed of the nature of the accusation and its causes.

This is probably the big one as far as investigation work is concerned.

It does not, however, apply to the assessment of tax. This was decided in 1983 in a French case (*X v France No 9908/82 32 DR 266 (1983)*. 'Article 6 does not apply to proceedings relating to tax assessments')

It does therefore seem that the burden of proof will still be on the taxpayer when appealing against a tax assessment; even in an investigation situation. This however changes when penalty proceedings apply.

It has been decided in the UK Courts that penalties for tax offences are criminal in nature for the purposes of Article 6 (*Han and Yau v Customs and Excise Comrs [2000] V&DR 312 and King v Walden [2001] STC 822*). This means that the tax authorities must prove the dishonesty necessary to impose a penalty. There is however a difference between VAT cases and direct taxation in that VAT penalties are for 'conduct involving dishonesty' whereas direct tax ones can be for 'neglect' which involve no deliberate wrongdoing. Whether this difference will work in favour of the Inland Revenue is yet to be seen.

The question is raised of who can impose the penalty. Should this be by the independent tribunal following a public trial or is the current practice of imposition by the taxman with a right of appeal sufficient?

Customs and Excise have tackled the issue following the review of their procedures in the *Han and Yau* case. They now state that there will be no prosecution and that the penalty will not exceed 20%. The amount of the penalty is significant because it was a factor in the conclusion that such penalties are criminal in nature, one under 20% appears to be thought to fall the right side of the line on this point. Customs have also announced the availability of legal aid for VAT penalties, this is however very limited and does not mean that state funding is now available to defend clients during tax investigations.

The Inland Revenue have, so far, not changed any of their procedures but it is difficult to agree that they are unaffected and so it does seem that they must change, especially their 'Hansard' procedures.

16.5 Article 8

The right for respect of private and family life, home and correspondence.

It is often said that this may be used to prevent the Revenue obtaining documents, such as private bank statements. It could be that we may see it as effective in some cases but the precedents are not good.

In *X v Belgium No 9804/82* it was argued that information demanded by the tax authorities would disclose information about his private life and so was protected but the court thought otherwise. Also the case of *R v CIR ex parte Banque International a Luxembourg SA [2000] STC 708* considered demands by the Revenue for third party information. The court agreed that Article 8 was relevant but did not apply because there was justification for the order.

So we know that this article is relevant when we have requests for information and the Revenue will have to demonstrate that they have sufficient justification for asking for a particular document.

Searches not requiring prior judicial approval have been held to be an infringement. Revenue searches require judicial approval so would appear to be in order. One may however wonder about the powers enjoyed by National Insurance inspectors as examined in Chapter 14.

Appendix A

Pre-Interview Advice

See Chapter 5.

1. Keep your answers concise and to the point.
2. If a question is not understood, say so, do not guess at what you think the question is.
3. Do not guess at the answer to a question. If the full and correct answer is not known, say so and explain that the answer will be researched and the inspector informed as quickly as possible.
4. Above everything else do not lie or tell an untruth. It is best to stay silent. If it is difficult to answer a question, tell your adviser and seek his advice.

Appendix B

The Hansard Extract

See Chapter 13.

In reply to a Parliamentary Question on 18 October 1990, the Chancellor of the Exchequer gave the following answer regarding tax fraud:

> 'The practice of the Board of Inland Revenue in cases of tax fraud is as follows:
>
> 1. The Board may accept a monetary settlement instead of instituting criminal proceedings in respect of fraud alleged to have been committed by a taxpayer.
> 2. They can give no undertaking that they will accept a monetary settlement and refrain from instituting criminal proceedings even if the case is one in which the taxpayer has made full confession and has given full facilities for investigation of the facts. They reserve to themselves full discretion in all cases as to the course they pursue.
> 3. But in considering whether to accept a monetary settlement or to institute criminal proceedings, it is their practice to be influenced by the fact that the taxpayer has made a full confession and has given full facilities for investigation into his affairs and for examination of such books, papers, documents or information as the Board may consider necessary.'

The above statement of practice should be regarded as replacing the one given by the then Chancellor of the Exchequer on 5 October 1944.

Appendix C

Business Ratios

See Chapter 2.

Gross profit rate

This is a much used ratio by the Inland Revenue when selecting small cases and arrived at by the formula:

$$\frac{\text{Gross profit}}{\text{Sales}} \times 100$$

E.g.:

Sales	75,000
Cost of sales (purchases)	(50,000)
Gross Profit	25,000

Gross profit ratio is :

$$\frac{25{,}000 \times 100}{75{,}000} = 33.33\%$$

This is sometimes converted to a mark-up, and indeed this is what most business men understand i.e. what do they add to the cost of purchases to make a profit.

Mark-up formula is:

$$\frac{\text{Gross profit}}{\text{Cost of sales}} \times 100$$

In the above example mark-up would be:

$$\frac{25{,}000 \times 100}{50{,}000} = 50\%$$

Net profitability

Gross profit calculations give the inspector a clue that evasion is present but variations may not be as marked as in the net profitability ratio because this takes a smaller figure than gross profit and so can show up evasion linked to the business expenses as well as sales or purchases.

If dealing with a company, directors' remuneration should be added back before performing the calculation.

The formula is:

$$\frac{\text{Net profit}}{\text{Turnover}} \times 100$$

E.g.:

Turnover		120,000
Cost of sales		20,000
Gross profit		100,000
Wages	15,000	
Rent	1,000	
Motor expenses	3,500	
Directors' remuneration	50,000	69,500
Net profit		30,500

So:

Net profit	30,500
Add directors' remuneration	50,000
	80,500

$$\frac{80{,}500}{120{,}000} \times 100 = 67.08\%$$

Stock

Businesses, especially unincorporated ones that do not require an audit, frequently fail to value stock at the balance sheet date. This means introducing an estimate that may then be inaccurate.

Accounting convention matches costs with sales to arrive at profit. No tax relief is therefore obtained on goods bought but not sold before the year end and so the taxpayer has to wait another year to obtain relief. This upsets some people so they undervalue stock, or omit some from the valuation, in order to accelerate their tax relief.

It has also been known for accountants to change their clients' stock figure to one that produces a 'more sensible' gross profit rate to prevent the Revenue from selecting their client for investigation.

There is also a practice of suppressing purchases to avoid the fact that not all sales are recorded showing up in the gross profit ratio or the net profitability ratio.

The Revenue try to spot these cases by trying to test the validity of the stock value. They will apply the following formula:

$$\text{Stock ratio} = \frac{\text{Stock}}{\text{Purchases}} \times 365$$

This gives the number of days purchases on hand at the balance sheet date. Does this look credible having regard to the business and taking into account seasonal variations?

To take a couple of extreme examples as illustration:

A toy shop showing 10 days' worth of purchases on hand in November would seem odd given that they should be stocked up for the Christmas period.

A seasonal shop in Brighton selling 'rock' to tourists would hardly be expected to have 100 days' worth of purchases on hand in October.

$$\text{Stock turnover} = \frac{\text{Purchases}}{\text{Average of opening and closing stock}}$$

From this we can tell the number of times stock is turned over in the year so if we are looking at a greengrocer we would expect this to be high because of the perishable nature of his stock but if we are looking at a retailer of antiques we would expect it to be lower.

Debtors

Debtor days are important to businesses.The longer money is outstanding the higher the overdraft and so the higher interest charges are. It is also possible for a business to be forced to close simply because it was starved of cash.

The Revenue equate lower debtor days with a well run business and vice versa. The formula for this is:

$$\text{Debtor days} = \frac{\text{Closing debtors}}{\text{Annual credit sales}} \times 365$$

So if debtors at balance sheet date are £45,000 and annual sales on credit terms are £190,000 debtor days will be:

$$\frac{45{,}000}{190{,}000} \times 365 = 87 \text{ days}$$

In other words it takes, on average, 87 days to get paid.

If other businesses in the same category are being paid in say 35 days then something looks amiss with this business and it may also indicate lax attention to record-keeping because the business is poorly run.

It may however indicate that credit sales have been omitted from the accounts. In the above example the debtor days would be 66 if the credit sales were really £250,000.

Liquidity

The Revenue use these ratios for two main purposes.

A business that has liquidity problems year in year out alerts an inspector to the possibility that, if the proprietor is doing nothing about it, it is known that profits are greater than disclosed in the accounts.

If there are loans from banks, or elsewhere, and apparently insufficient assets for security it could be that the directors, or proprietors, have put up private assets as security.This can bring to light previously undisclosed assets.

Three ratios are used:

Current ratio

The current ratio includes current assets such as cash, bank deposits, realisable investments, stock and debtors, and is compared with current liabilities such as overdrafts, and payments due in the short term e.g. creditors payable within a year.

The formula is:

$$\frac{\text{Current assets}}{\text{Current liabilities}} = \text{Current ratio}$$

So if the balance sheet shows:

Cash on hand	750	
Stock	1,500	
Debtors	2,000	4,250
Overdraft	1,900	
Current creditors	1,250	3,150

The current ratio would be:

$$\frac{4{,}250}{3{,}150} = 1.3$$

Quick ratio

The quick ratio is the same as the current one but excludes stock as follows:

$$\frac{\text{Very liquid current assets}}{\text{Current liabilities}} = \text{Quick ratio}$$

So in the above example it would be:

$$\frac{2{,}750}{3{,}150} = 0.87$$

A ratio of less than 1 means that the business cannot meet its immediate liabilities. A little over 1 means there is cause for concern because it may only need a bad debt to cause a crisis.

Borrowing ratio

This third borrowing ratio uses the formula:

$$\frac{\text{Outstanding loans}}{\text{Net assets}} = \text{Borrowing ratio}$$

The Revenue think bank managers may be given better-looking accounts than are given to them in order to obtain loan finance and so will question any case that looks worthy of enquiry.

Return on capital

A businessman has a choice. He can take his money and invest it, perhaps in the building society or on the stock market, or he can acquire some assets and use them for the purposes of a business. If already running a business he could sell his assets and invest the money.

The Revenue therefore look to see what return is being achieved. They may wonder why someone persists with a business when the return is poor, why does he not sell, invest the proceeds and get a salaried job?

The answer may be that the return is better than the Revenue see and so the case is considered for investigation.

The formula for this is:

$$\frac{\text{Operating profit}}{\text{Capital employed}} \times 100 = \text{Return}$$

'Operating profit' is that per the accounts but with any interest paid being added back to it.

'Capital employed' is the net assets per the balance sheet less current liabilities.

So if operating profit is £60,000 and the net assets employed are £450,000 the return on capital would be:

$$\frac{60,000}{450,000} \times 100 = 13\%$$

One of the problems of using this ratio as a comparison with other businesses is the question of valuations. Not all businesses re-value their assets on a regular basis nor do they use the same method if they do.

The return may look good but it has to be compared against a return after the proprietor's wages are taken and care has to be taken that this is a fair market rate for the job done.

Wages

Are employees fully occupied? The inspector may explore this at an interview or come to a judgement following casual observation of the business premises over a period of time.

If ratio tests on the accounts show something different he may start to believe that sales are suppressed. Inspectors are always suspicious if the proprietor's drawings are less than wages paid to an employee.

The Revenue may do one of two tests.

1. Sales per employee $= \dfrac{\text{Sales}}{\text{No of employees}}$
2. The other simply compares wages to sales and will be used if the number of employees is not known.

Appendix D

Certificates of Full Disclosure

See Chapter 8.

When an investigation is near completion and it has been found there is extra tax to pay the inspector will ask for a certificate of full disclosure. This assures the Revenue that they now know all facts relevant to assessing liability. The Revenue take a very serious view of false certificates and a high risk of prosecution is present in such cases. The Revenue issue a warning to everyone they invite to sign a certificate which is usually reproduced on the reverse of their form, but if not will be issued separately. It reads as follows.

Tax offences

Certificates of full disclosure

Where it has been established that you have understated your income, profits, or gains, or failed to notify your chargeability to tax, the inspector will normally ask you to certify that you have made a complete disclosure of all facts about your tax affairs for the period under review.

This will give you the chance to consider the statements you have made to the inspector. If at some later date it is found that the statements were *materially* incorrect, the Board of Inland Revenue will take a serious view of the false completion of the certificate and any loss of tax which may have arisen as a result.

Before you complete the certificate please consider the wording most carefully. If you consider there are any facts relating to your tax affairs or any assets held that you have not given details of, then inform the inspector of these *before* you sign the certificate.

False statements can result in prosecution.

Board of Inland Revenue

Appendix D

Certificate 1

For use in simple small cases in which no penalties are being levied. E.g. an employee who has not declared a few tips.

To HM Inspector of Taxes

I have read the statement overleaf and I hereby certify that to the best of my knowledge and belief I have made a complete disclosure to you of all

(*a*) sources of my income (including tips, gratuities and casual earnings);

(*b*) amounts derived from each source;

(*c*) facts bearing upon my liability to Income Tax, Capital Gains Tax and any other duties to which I am, or have been, liable for the period

from .... to .... inclusive;

Signature ....

Address ....
....
....

Date ....

Certificate 2

For use in cases not involving a company

To HM Inspector of Taxes

I have read the statement overleaf and I hereby certify that to the best of my knowledge and belief I have made a complete disclosure to you of all –

(*a*) (i) banking accounts, whether current or deposit, business or private;

(ii) savings and loan accounts, deposit receipts, Building Society and Co-Operative Society accounts;

(iii) investments, including Savings Certificates and Premium Bonds, and loans (whether interest bearing or not);

(iv) other assets of whatsoever nature, including cash, life assurance policies, jewellery, furnishings and other valuables;

which I now possess, or possessed, or which I have or have had any interest in or power to operate or control, jointly or solely, now or at any time during the period

from .... to .... inclusive;

(*b*) gifts, whether in cash or in any other form, made by me to any person (including my spouse or domestic partner, or my children) during the period

from .... to .... inclusive;

(*c*) sources of income, whether or not specified above, and of all income derived therefrom by me and of all facts bearing on my liability to Income Tax, Capital Gains Tax and other duties to which I am or have been liable for the period

from .... to .... inclusive;

Signature ....

Address ....
....
....

Date ....

Appendix D

Certificate 3

For use in cases not involving a company that are reasonably simple and uninvolved

To HM Inspector of Taxes

I have read the statement overleaf and I hereby certify that to the best of my knowledge and belief I have made a complete disclosure to you of all –

(*a*) banking accounts, whether current or deposit, business or private, and all Building Society and Co-Operative Society accounts, in my own name, or in any other name, in which I have been interested or on which I have, or have had, power to operate, jointly or solely, and which are in existence now or which have existed at any time during the period

from .... to .... inclusive;

(*b*) assets including deposit receipts, which I possess, or have possessed during the period

from .... to .... inclusive;

(*c*) sources of income, and all facts bearing on my liability to Income Tax, Capital Gains Tax and other duties to which I am or have been liable for the period

from .... to .... inclusive;

Signature ....

Address ....
....
....

Date ....

Certificate 4

Used in cases involving a company but in which no penalties are being levied

To HM Inspector of Taxes

We . . . .

Being directors of . . . . Ltd have read the statement overleaf and hereby certify that to the best of our knowledge and belief we have made a complete disclosure to you of all –

(*a*) the sources of the company's income and amounts thereof;

(*b*) the facts bearing on the company's liability to Corporation Tax and other duties to which the company is, or has been, liable in the period

from . . . . to . . . . inclusive;

Signature . . . .

Address . . . .
. . . .
. . . .

Date . . . .

Signature . . . .

Address . . . .
. . . .
. . . .

Date . . . .

Signature . . . .

Address . . . .
. . . .
. . . .

Date . . . .

Certificate 5

For use in a full case involving a company

To HM Inspector of Taxes

I . . . .

Of . . . .
have read the statement overleaf and I hereby certify that to the best of my knowledge and belief I have made a complete disclosure to you of all –

(*a*) banking accounts, whether current or deposit, business or private, savings and loan accounts, deposit receipts, Building Society and Co-Operative Society accounts

(i) which stand, or at any time stood, in my name or in the name of any business with which I have been concerned, or

(ii) in which I am, or have been, interested or on which I have had power to operate or control, jointly or solely,

which are in existence now, or which have existed at any time during the period

from . . . . to . . . . inclusive;

(*b*) assets of whatever description and wherever kept, including Savings Certificates, Premium Bonds, life insurance policies, cash in hand, jewellery, furnishings and other valuables which I, or any business with which I have been concerned, now possess or have possessed, at any time during the period

from . . . . to . . . . inclusive;

(*c*) gifts, whether in cash or in any other form, made by me to any person (including my spouse or domestic partner, or my children) during the period

from . . . . to . . . . inclusive;

(*d*) sources of income not indicated in (*a*) and (*b*) above and the amounts of income derived therefrom and the facts bearing upon my liability to Income Tax, Capital Gains Tax and other duties in the period

from . . . . to . . . . inclusive;

(*e*) facts bearing upon the liability of . . . . Ltd and any other businesses with which I have been concerned to Corporation Tax and other duties in the period

from . . . . to . . . . inclusive;

Signature . . . .

Date . . . .

Appendix E

Letters of offer

See Chapter 8.

1. For an individual.

This will be suitably amended to fit the case e.g. Class 4 National Insurance contributions will be deleted if they do not apply.

To the Commissioners of Inland Revenue

In consideration of no proceedings being taken against me in respect of the duties and the Class 4 National Insurance contributions set out in the Statements below, which I acknowledge and agree to be unpaid by reason, wholly or in part, of my default, or in respect of the penalties and interest to which I may thereby have become liable under the Taxes Acts, I . . . . of . . . . hereby offer in respect of the said duties, contributions, penalties and interest, the sum of £. . . . . ('the said sum') of which I have already paid £. . . . . on account, to be paid within . . . . days of the date of the letter notifying acceptance of this offer by you. If the said sum has not been paid by the date specified herein then interest shall be payable upon any unpaid balance of the said sum at the rate applicable from time to time for the purposes of section 86 of the Taxes Management Act 1970 or any amendment or re-enactment thereof, from that day. Any such interest shall be paid without deduction of Income Tax.

If this offer is accepted it shall be without prejudice to the assessment and collection of any additional tax and Class 4 National Insurance contributions which may become due for any year included in this offer under the provisions of section 63 of the Income and Corporation Taxes Act 1988.

Date . . . .   Signed . . . .

Statement of duties unpaid by me

Year	Nature of duty	Amount

2. For a partnership other than in Scotland.

Under self-assessment joint and several liability does not apply so it is more likely that the offer will be that applicable to individuals.

To the Commissioners of Inland Revenue

In consideration of no proceedings being taken against us in respect of the duties and the Class 4 National Insurance contributions set out in the Statements below, which we acknowledge and agree to be unpaid by reason, wholly or in part, of our default, or in respect of the penalties and interest to which we may thereby have become liable under the Taxes Acts, we .... of .... partners in the firm of .... hereby jointly and severally offer in respect of the said duties, contributions, penalties and interest, the sum of £.......... ('the said sum') of which we have already paid £.......... on account, to be paid within .... days of the date of the letter notifying acceptance of this offer by you. If the said sum has not been paid by the date specified herein then interest shall be payable upon any unpaid balance of the said sum at the rate applicable from time to time for the purposes of section 86 of the Taxes Management Act 1970 or any amendment or re-enactment thereof, from that day. Any such interest shall be paid without deduction of Income Tax.

If this offer is accepted it shall be without prejudice to the assessment and collection of any additional tax and Class 4 National Insurance contributions which may become due for any year included in this offer under the provisions of section 63 of the Income and Corporation Taxes Act 1988.

Date ....   Signed ....

Statement of duties unpaid by us

Year	Nature of duty	Amount

3. For a partnership in Scotland

To the Commissioners of Inland Revenue

In consideration of no proceedings being taken against us in respect of the duties and the Class 4 National Insurance contributions set out in the Statements below, which we acknowledge and agree to be unpaid by reason, wholly or in part, of our default, or in respect of the penalties and interest to which we may thereby have become liable under the Taxes Acts, we the partnership firm of .... and .... the whole partners thereof as such partners and individuals, the partnership name being adhibited hereto by me ...., the precedent acting partner hereby jointly and severally offer in respect of the said duties, contributions, penalties and interest, the sum of £.......... ('the said sum') of which we have already paid £.......... on account, to be paid within .... days of the date of the letter notifying acceptance of this offer by you. If the said sum has not been paid by the date specified herein then interest shall be payable upon any unpaid balance of the said sum at the rate applicable from time to time for the purposes of section 86 of the Taxes Management Act 1970 or any amendment or re-enactment thereof, from that day. Any such interest shall be paid without deduction of Income Tax.

If this offer is accepted it shall be without prejudice to the assessment and collection of any additional tax and Class 4 National Insurance contributions which may become due for any year included in this offer under the provisions of section 63 of the Income and Corporation Taxes Act 1988.

Date	Signed	
	Partnership	....
	Individual Partners	....
		....
		....

Statement of duties unpaid by us

Year	Nature of duty	Amount

4. A company but with no section 419 liability excluding Scotland

To the Commissioners of Inland Revenue

In consideration of no proceedings being taken against .... Ltd of .... (hereinafter called 'the Company') in respect of the duties set out in the Statement below, which the Company acknowledges and agrees to be unpaid by reason, wholly or in part, of its default, or in respect of the penalties and interest to which the Company may thereby have become liable under the Taxes Acts, the Company hereby offers in respect of the said duties, contributions, penalties and interest, the sum of £.......... ('the said sum') of which £.......... has already been paid on account, to be paid within .... days of the date of the letter notifying acceptance of this offer by you. If the said sum has not been paid by the date specified herein then interest shall be payable upon any unpaid balance of the said sum at the rate applicable from time to time for the purposes of section 86 of the Taxes Management Act 1970 or any amendment or re-enactment thereof, from that day. Any such interest shall be paid without deduction of Income Tax.

Statement of duties unpaid by the Company

Year or Accounting period	Duty	Amount

Signed on behalf of the Company this .... day of 2000

Director ....

Director or Company Secretary ....

5. Company offer in Scotland not involving section 419

To the Commissioners of Inland Revenue

In consideration of no proceedings being taken against .... Ltd of .... (hereinafter called 'the Company') in respect of the duties set out in the Statement below, which the Company acknowledges and agrees to be unpaid by reason, wholly or in part, of its default, or in respect of the penalties and interest to which the Company may thereby have become liable under the Taxes Acts, the Company hereby offers in respect of the said duties, contributions, penalties and interest, the sum of £.......... ('the said sum') of which £.......... has already been paid on account, to be paid within .... days of the date of the letter notifying acceptance of this offer by you. If the said sum has not been paid by the date specified herein then interest shall be payable upon any unpaid balance of the said sum at the rate applicable from time to time for the purposes of section 86 of the Taxes Management Act 1970 or any amendment or re-enactment thereof, from that day. Any such interest shall be paid without deduction of Income Tax.

Statement of duties unpaid by the Company

Year or Accounting period	Duty	Amount

In witness whereof these presents are subscribed on behalf of the Company by .... and .... at .... on ....

....
....

6. For companies with section 419 liability

To the Commissioners of Inland Revenue

Whereas

A .... Ltd of .... (hereinafter called 'the Company') acknowledges and agrees that the duties set out in the Statement below are unpaid by reason, wholly or in part, of its default.

B .... of .... is a participator in the Company and has received amounts diverted from the Company and has repaid the total sum of £.......... being a reimbursement of amounts diverted from the Company.

The Company and the said .... in consideration of no proceedings being taken against the Company in respect of the said duties, or in respect of the penalties and interest to which the Company may have become liable under the Taxes Acts by reason of that default, hereby jointly and severally offer in respect of the said duties, penalties and interest the sum of £.......... ('the said sum') subject to deduction of £.......... in full settlement of any claim to relief under section 419(4) of the Income and Corporation Taxes Act 1988 arising from the said repayment, leaving the sum of £.......... of which £.......... has already been paid on account, to be paid within .... days of the date of the letter notifying acceptance of this offer by you. If the said sum has not been paid by the date specified herein then interest shall be payable upon any unpaid balance of the said sum at the rate applicable from time to time for the purposes of section 86 of the Taxes Management Act 1970 or any amendment or re-enactment thereof, from that day. Any such interest shall be paid without deduction of Income Tax.

Statement of duties unpaid by the Company

Year or Accounting period	Duty	Amount

Signed on behalf of the Company this .... day of 2000

Director ....

Director or Company Secretary ....

[In Scotland the signatories change as shown in Example 5]

Appendix F

Tax Rates from 1980/81 to 2001/02

Income Tax (Individuals)

2001/02

	Rate	*On taxable income*	*Cumulative tax*
Starting rate	10%	0–£1,880	£188
Basic rate	22%	£1,881–£29,400	£6,242.40
Higher rate	40%	Over £29,400	

2000/01

	Rate	*On taxable income*	*Cumulative tax*
Starting rate	10%	0–£1,520	£152
Basic rate	22%	£1,521–£28,400	£6,065.60
Higher rate	40%	Over £28,400	

Non-dividend savings income within the basic rate band is taxable at the lower rate of 20%. Dividend etc. income within the basic rate band is taxable at the Schedule F ordinary rate of 10%; such income is taxable at the Schedule F upper rate of 32.5% where (if treated as the top slice of income) it exceeds the basic rate limit.

1999/2000

	Rate	*On taxable income*	*Cumulative tax*
Starting rate	10%	0–£1,500	£150
Basic rate	23%	£1,501–£28,000	£6,245
Higher rate	40%	Over £28,000	

Non-dividend savings income within the basic rate band is taxable at the lower rate of 20%. Dividend etc. income within the basic rate band is taxable at the Schedule F ordinary rate of 10%; such income is taxable at the Schedule F upper rate of 32.5% where (if treated as the top slice of income) it exceeds the basic rate limit.

1998/99

	Rate	*On taxable income*	*Cumulative tax*
Lower rate	20%	0–£4,300	£860
Basic rate	23%	£4,301–£27,100	£6,104
Higher rate	40%	Over £27,100	

Savings income (including dividends etc.) within the basic rate band is taxable at the lower rate of 20%.

1997/98

	Rate	*On taxable income*	*Cumulative tax*
Lower rate	20%	0–£4,100	£820
Basic rate	23%	£4,101–£26,100	£5,880
Higher rate	40%	Over £26,100	

Savings income (including dividends etc.) within the basic rate band is taxable at the lower rate of 20%.

1996/97

	Rate	*On taxable income*	*Cumulative tax*
Lower rate	20%	0–£3,900	£780
Basic rate	24%	£3,901–£25,500	£5,964
Higher rate	40%	Over £25,500	

Savings income (including dividends etc.) within the basic rate band is taxable at the lower rate of 20%.

1995/96

	Rate	*On taxable income*	*Cumulative tax*
Lower rate	20%	0–£3,200	£640
Basic rate	25%	£3,201–£24,300	£5,915
Higher rate	40%	Over £24,300	

Dividend etc. income within the basic rate band is taxable at the lower rate of 20%.

1994/95

	Rate	*On taxable income*	*Cumulative tax*
Lower rate	20%	0–£3,000	£600
Basic rate	25%	£3,001–£23,700	£5,775
Higher rate	40%	Over £23,700	

Dividend etc. income within the basic rate band is taxable at the lower rate of 20%.

1993/94

	Rate	*On taxable income*	*Cumulative tax*
Lower rate	20%	0–£2,500	£500
Basic rate	25%	£2,501–£23,700	£5,800
Higher rate	40%	Over £23,700	

Dividend etc. income within the basic rate band is taxable at the lower rate of 20%.

1992/93

	Rate	*On taxable income*	*Cumulative tax*
Lower rate	20%	0–£2,000	£400
Basic rate	25%	£2,001–£23,700	£5,825
Higher rate	40%	Over £23,700	

1991/92

	Rate	*On taxable income*	*Cumulative tax*
Basic rate	25%	0–£23,700	£5,925
Higher rate	40%	Over £23,700	

1989/90 and 1990/91

	Rate	*On taxable income*	*Cumulative tax*
Basic rate	25%	0–£20,700	£5,175
Higher rate	40%	Over £20,700	

1988/89

	Rate	*On taxable income*	*Cumulative tax*
Basic rate	25%	0–£19,300	£4,825
Higher rate	40%	Over £19,300	

1987/88

	Rate	*On taxable income*	*Cumulative tax*
Basic rate	27%	0–£17,900	£4,833
Higher rates			
Next £2,500	40%	£17,901–£20,400	£5,833
Next £5,000	45%	£20,401–£25,400	£8,083
Next £7,900	50%	£25,401–£33,300	£12,033
Next £7,900	55%	£33,301–£41,200	£16,378
Above £41,200	60%		

1986/87

	Rate	*On taxable income*	*Cumulative tax*
Basic rate	29%	0–£17,200	£4,860
Higher rates			
Next £3,000	40%	£17,201–£20,200	£6,188
Next £5,200	45%	£20,201–£25,400	£8,528
Next £7,900	50%	£25,401–£33,300	£12,478
Next £7,900	55%	£33,301–£41,200	£16,823
Above £41,200	60%		

1985/86

	Rate	*On taxable income*	*Cumulative tax*
Basic rate	30%	0–£16,200	£4,860
Higher rates			
Next £3,000	40%	£16,201–£19,200	£6,060
Next £5,200	45%	£19,201–£24,400	£8,400
Next £7,900	50%	£24,401–£32,300	£12,350
Next £7,900	55%	£32,301–£40,200	£16,695
Above £40,200	60%		

1984/85

	Rate	*On taxable income*	*Cumulative tax*
Basic rate	30%	0–£15,400	£4,620
Higher rates			
Next £2,800	40%	£15,401–£18,200	£5,740
Next £4,900	45%	£18,201–£23,100	£7,945

Next £7,500	50%	£23,101–£30,600	£11,695
Next £7,500	55%	£30,601–£38,100	£15,820
Above £38,100	60%		

1983/84

	Rate	*On taxable income*	*Cumulative tax*
Basic Rate	30%	0–£14,600	£4,380
Higher Rates			
Next £2,600	40%	£14,601–£17,200	£5,420
Next £4,600	45%	£17,201–£21,800	£7,490
Next £7,100	50%	£21,801–£28,900	£11,040
Next £7,100	55%	£28,901–£36,000	£14,945
Above £36,000	60%		

Investment income surcharge

0–£7,100	Nil
Above £7,100	15%

1982/83

	Rate	*On taxable income*	*Cumulative tax*
Basic Rate	30%	0–£12,800	£3,840
Higher Rates			
Next £2,300	40%	£12,801–£15,100	£4,760
Next £4,000	45%	£15,101–£19,100	£6,560
Next £6,200	50%	£19,101–£25,300	£9,660
Next £6,200	55%	£25,301–£31,500	£13,070
Above £31,500	60%		

Investment income surcharge

0–£6,250	Nil
Above £6,250	15%

1980/81 and 1981/82

	Rate	*On taxable income*	*Cumulative tax*
Basic Rate	30%	0–£11,250	£3,375
Higher Rates			
Next £2,000	40%	£11,251–£13,250	£4,175
Next £3,500	45%	£13,251–£16,750	£5,750
Next £5,500	50%	£16,751–£22,250	£8,500
Next £5,500	55%	£22,251–£27,750	£11,525
Above £27,750	60%		

Investment income surcharge

0–£5,500	Nil
Above £5,500	15%

Capital Gains Tax (Individuals)

2001/02
As per 2000/01

2000/01
Gains taxed as top slice of income: 10% to starting rate limit, 20% to basic rate limit, 40% above.

1999/2000
Gains taxed as top slice of income: 20% to basic rate limit, 40% above.

1988/89 to 1998/99
Gains taxed as top slice of income at income tax rates.

1980/81 to 1987/88: 30%

Annual exemption

2001/02	£7,500
2000/01	£7,200
1999/2000	£7,100
1998/99	£6,800
1997/98	£6,500
1996/97	£6,300
1995/96	£6,000
1994/95	£5,800
1993/94	£5,800
1992/93	£5,800
1991/92	£5,500
1990/91	£5,000
1989/90	£5,000
1988/89	£5,000
1987/88	£6,600
1986/87	£6,300
1985/86	£5,900
1984/85	£5,600
1983/84	£5,300
1982/83	£5,000
1981/82	£3.000
1980/81	£3,000

Corporation Tax

Financial year 2001

Full rate	30%
Small companies rate	20%
lower relevant amount	£300,000
upper relevant amount	£1,500,000
marginal relief fraction	1/40

Starting rate	10%
first relevant amount	£10,000
second relevant amount	£50,000
marginal relief fraction	1/40

Financial year 2000

Full rate	30%
Small companies rate	20%
lower relevant amount	£300,000
upper relevant amount	£1,500,000
marginal relief fraction	1/40
Starting rate	10%
first relevant amount	£10,000
second relevant amount	£50,000
marginal relief fraction	1/40

Financial year 1999

Full rate	30%
Small companies rate	20%
lower relevant amount	£300,000
upper relevant amount	£1,500,000
marginal relief fraction	1/40

Financial years 1997 and 1998

Full rate	31%
Small companies rate	21%
lower relevant amount	£300,000
upper relevant amount	£1,500,000
marginal relief fraction	1/40

Financial year 1996

Full rate	33%
Small companies rate	24%
lower relevant amount	£300,000
upper relevant amount	£1,500,000
marginal relief fraction	9/400

Financial years 1994 and 1995

Full rate	33%
Small companies rate	25%
lower relevant amount	£300,000
upper relevant amount	£1,500,000
marginal relief fraction	1/50

Financial years 1991 to 1993

Full rate	33%
Small companies rate	25%
lower relevant amount	£250,000
upper relevant amount	£1,250,000
marginal relief fraction	1/50

Financial year 1990

Full rate	34%
Small companies rate	25%
lower relevant amount	£200,000
upper relevant amount	£1,000,000
marginal relief fraction	9/400

Financial year 1989

Full rate	35%
Small companies rate	25%
lower relevant amount	£150,000
upper relevant amount	£750,000
marginal relief fraction	1/40

Financial year 1988

Full rate	35%
Small companies rate	25%
lower relevant amount	£100,000
upper relevant amount	£500,000
marginal relief fraction	1/40

Financial year 1987

Full rate	35%
Small companies rate	27%
lower relevant amount	£100,000
upper relevant amount	£500,000
marginal relief fraction	1/50

Financial year 1986

Full rate	35%
Small companies rate	29%
lower relevant amount	£100,000
upper relevant amount	£500,000
marginal relief fraction	3/200

Financial year 1985

Full rate	40%
Small companies rate	30%
lower relevant amount	£100,000
upper relevant amount	£500,000
marginal relief fraction	1/40

Financial year 1984

Full rate	45%
Small companies rate	30%
lower relevant amount	£100,000
upper relevant amount	£500,000
marginal relief fraction	3/80

Financial year 1983	
Full rate	50%
Small companies rate	30%
lower relevant amount	£100,000
upper relevant amount	£500,000
marginal relief fraction	1/20
Financial year 1982	
Full rate	52%
Small companies rate	38%
lower relevant amount	£100,000
upper relevant amount	£500,000
marginal relief fraction	7/200
Financial year 1981	
Full rate	52%
Small companies rate	40%
lower relevant amount	£90,000
upper relevant amount	£225,000
marginal relief fraction	2/25
Financial year 1980	
Full rate	52%
Small companies rate	40%
lower relevant amount	£80,000
upper relevant amount	£200,000
marginal relief fraction	2/25

Corporation tax on chargeable gains

For accounting periods beginning after *16 March 1987*, the whole of the chargeable gains (less allowable losses) is included in the profits chargeable to corporation tax. The rate of corporation tax applicable will either be the full rate or the starting or small companies rate (with marginal relief as appropriate).

For accounting periods ending before 17 March 1987, corporation tax on chargeable gains is levied at the full rate of corporation tax, but those gains are reduced for tax purposes by the following fractions:

Financial year 1986	1/7
Financial year 1985	1/4
Financial year 1984	1/3
Financial year 1983	2/5
Financial years 1979 to 1982	11/26

For accounting periods beginning before 17 March 1987 and ending after 16 March 1987, there are transitional provisions whereby, broadly, the accounting period is split into two notional accounting periods. The first period is deemed to end immediately before 17 March 1987 and is treated as for accounting periods ending before 17 March 1987. The second period is deemed to commence on 17 March 1987 and is treated as for accounting periods beginning after 16 March 1987.

Advance Corporation Tax

1 April 1994–5 April 1999	1/4th	(i.e. 20% of dividend etc. plus ACT)
1 April 1993–31 March 1994	9/31sts	(i.e. 22.5% of dividend etc. plus ACT)
1 April 1988–31 March 1993	1/3rd	(i.e. 25% of dividend etc. plus ACT)
1 April 1987–31 March 1988	27/73rds	(i.e. 27% of dividend etc. plus ACT)
1 April 1986–31 March 1987	29/71sts	(i.e. 29% of dividend etc. plus ACT)
1 April 1979–31 March 1986	3/7ths	(i.e. 30% of dividend etc. plus ACT)

Appendix G

Interest rates on overdue tax 1979/80 to 2000/01

Income tax and capital gains tax

7.50% p.a. from 6 May 2001
8.50% p.a. from 6 February 2000
7.50% p.a. from 6 March 1999 to 5 February 2000
8.50% p.a. from 6 January 1999 to 5 March 1999
9.50% p.a. from 6 August 1997 to 5 January 1999
8.50% p.a. from 31 January 1997 to 5 August 1997
6.25% p.a. from 6 February 1996 to 30 January 1997
7.00% p.a. from 6 March 1995 to 5 February 1996
6.25% p.a. from 6 October 1994 to 5 March 1995
5.50% p.a. from 6 January 1994 to 5 October 1994
6.25% p.a. from 6 March 1993 to 5 January 1994
7.00% p.a. from 6 December 1992 to 5 March 1993
7.75% p.a. from 6 November 1992 to 5 December 1992
9.25% p.a. from 6 October 1991 to 5 November 1992
10.00% p.a. from 6 July 1991 to 5 October 1991
10.75% p.a. from 6 May 1991 to 5 July 1991
11.50% p.a. from 6 March 1991 to 5 May 1991
12.25% p.a. from 6 November 1990 to 5 March 1991
13.00% p.a. from 6 November 1989 to 5 November 1990
12.25% p.a. from 6 July 1989 to 5 November 1989
11.50% p.a. from 6 January 1989 to 5 July 1989
10.50% p.a. from 6 October 1988 to 5 January 1989
9.75% p.a. from 6 August 1988 to 5 October 1988
7.75% p.a. from 6 May 1988 to 5 August 1988
8.25% p.a. from 6 December 1987 to 5 May 1988
9.00% p.a. from 6 September 1987 to 5 December 1987
8.25% p.a. from 6 June 1987 to 5 September 1987
9.00% p.a. from 6 April 1987 to 5 June 1987
9.50% p.a. from 6 November 1986 to 5 April 1987
8.50% p.a. from 6 August 1986 to 5 November 1986
11.00% p.a. from 1 May 1985 to 5 August 1986
8.00% p.a. from 1 December 1982 to 30 April 1985
12.00% p.a. from 1 January 1980 to 30 November 1982
9.00% p.a. from 1 July 1974 to 31 December 1979

Companies — accounting periods ending after 30 June 1999 (self-assessment) (other than instalment payments for large companies)

7.50% p.a. from 6 May 2001
8.50% p.a. from 6 February 2000 to 5 May 2001
7.50% p.a. from 6 March 1999 to 5 February 2000
8.50% p.a. from 7 January 1999 to 5 March 1999

Companies — accounting periods ending after 30 September 1993 and before 1 July 1999 (Pay and File)

6% p.a. from 6 May 2001
6.75% p.a. from 6 February 2000 to 5 May 2001
5.75% p.a. from 6 March 1999 to 5 February 2000
6.50% p.a. from 6 January 1999 to 5 March 1999
7.50% p.a. from 6 August 1997 to 5 January 1999
6.25% p.a. from 6 February 1996 to 5 August 1997
7.00% p.a. from 6 March 1995 to 5 February 1996
6.25% p.a. from 6 October 1994 to 5 March 1995
5.50% p.a. from 6 January 1994 to 5 October 1994
6.25% p.a. from 1 October 1993 to 5 January 1994

Companies — accounting periods ending before 1 October 1993

5.75% p.a. from 6 May 2001
6.50% p.a. from 6 February 2000 to 5 May 2001
5.75% p.a. from 6 March 1999 to 5 February 2000
6.50% p.a. from 6 January 1999 to 5 March 1999
7.25% p.a. from 6 August 1997 to 5 January 1999
6.25% p.a. from 6 February 1996 to 5 August 1997
7.00% p.a. from 6 March 1995 to 5 February 1996
6.25% p.a. from 6 October 1994 to 5 March 1995
5.50% p.a. from 6 January 1994 to 5 October 1994
6.25% p.a. from 6 March 1993 to 5 January 1994
7.00% p.a. from 6 December 1992 to 5 March 1993
7.75% p.a. from 6 November 1992 to 5 December 1992
9.25% p.a. from 6 October 1991 to 5 November 1992
10.00% p.a. from 6 July 1991 to 5 October 1991
10.75% p.a. from 6 May 1991 to 5 July 1991
11.50% p.a. from 6 March 1991 to 5 May 1991
12.25% p.a. from 6 November 1990 to 5 March 1991
13.00% p.a. from 6 November 1989 to 5 November 1990
12.25% p.a. from 6 July 1989 to 5 November 1989
11.50% p.a. from 6 January 1989 to 5 July 1989
10.75% p.a. from 6 October 1988 to 5 January 1989

9.75% p.a. from 6 August 1988 to 5 October 1988
7.75% p.a. from 6 May 1988 to 5 August 1988
8.25% p.a. from 6 December 1987 to 5 May 1988
9.00% p.a. from 6 September 1987 to 5 December 1987
8.25% p.a. from 6 June 1987 to 5 September 1987
9.00% p.a. from 6 April 1987 to 5 June 1987
9.50% p.a. from 6 November 1986 to 5 April 1987
8.50% p.a. from 6 August 1986 to 5 November 1986
11.00% p.a. from 1 May 1985 to 5 August 1986
8.00% p.a. from 1 December 1982 to 30 April 1985
12.00% p.a. from 1 January 1980 to 30 November 1982
9.00% p.a. from 1 July 1974 to 31 December 1979

Appendix H

Retail Price Index 1980 to 2001

In January 1987 the index was reset to 100.This table has converted the pre-1987 index to reflect this.

In investigation work you will rarely, if ever, need to go back 20 years but if you do this table will help in estimating profits for those back years. For the purpose of such estimation the month-by-month index is not really necessary but you may find it useful for capital gains tax indexation so it has been reproduced in full from March 1982.

Should you need extra detail this can be obtained from the Central Office for Statistics but if in an investigation situation you may find the Inspector helpful.

	1980	1981	1982	1983	1984	1985	1986	1987	1988	1989	1990	1991
January				82.61	86.84	91.20	96.25	100.0	103.3	111.0	119.5	130.2
February				82.97	87.20	91.94	96.60	100.4	103.7	111.8	120.2	130.9
March			79.44	83.12	87.48	92.80	96.73	100.6	104.1	112.3	121.4	131.4
April			81.04	84.28	88.64	94.78	97.67	101.8	105.8	114.3	125.1	133.1
May			81.62	84.64	88.97	95.21	97.85	101.9	106.2	115.0	126.2	133.5
June			81.85	84.84	89.20	95.41	97.79	101.9	106.6	115.4	126.7	134.1
July			81.88	85.30	89.10	95.23	97.52	101.8	106.7	115.5	126.8	133.8
August			81.9	85.68	89.94	95.49	97.82	102.1	107.9	115.8	128.1	134.1
September			81.85	86.06	90.11	95.44	98.30	102.4	108.4	116.6	129.3	134.6
October			82.26	86.36	90.67	95.59	98.45	102.9	109.5	117.5	130.3	135.1
November			82.66	86.67	90.95	95.92	99.29	103.4	110.0	118.5	130.0	135.6
December	69.86	78.27	82.51	86.89	90.87	96.05	99.62	103.3	110.3	118.8	129.9	135.7

	1992	1993	1994	1995	1996	1997	1998	1999	2000	2001
January	135.6	137.9	141.3	146.0	150.2	154.4	159.5	163.4	166.6	171.7
February	136.3	138.8	142.1	146.9	150.9	155.0	160.3	163.7	166.5	172.0
March	136.7	139.3	142.5	147.5	151.5	155.4	160.8	164.1	168.4	172.2
April	138.8	140.6	144.2	149.0	152.6	156.3	162.6	165.2	170.1	173.1
May	139.3	141.1	144.7	149.6	152.9	156.9	163.5	165.6	170.7	174.2
June	139.3	141.0	144.7	149.8	153.0	157.5	163.4	165.6	171.1	
July	139.8	140.7	144.0	149.1	152.4	157.5	163.0	165.1	170.5	
August	138.9	141.3	144.7	149.9	153.1	158.5	163.7	165.5	170.5	
September	139.4	141.9	145.0	150.6	153.8	159.3	164.4	166.2	171.7	
October	139.9	141.8	145.2	149.8	153.8	159.5	164.5	166.5	171.6	
November	139.7	141.6	145.3	149.8	153.9	159.6	164.4	166.7	172.1	
December	139.2	141.9	146.0	150.7	154.4	160.0	164.4	167.3	172.2	

Appendix I

Bank base rates 1980 to 2000

The following table shows the main retail base rates at high street banks. Not all banks change their rates at the same time so there may be a day or two difference between banks. This is not really critical for using the table in a tax investigation situation where it might be used to reconstruct possible investment returns.

The data has been compiled from information supplied by the Bank of England.

Date	Rate (%)	Date	Rate (%)	Date	Rate (%)
4 July 1980	16.00	29 July 1985	11.50	8 Feb 1994	5.25
25 Nov 1980	14.00	9 Jan 1986	12.50	12 Sept 1994	5.75
11 Mar 1981	12.00	19 Mar 1986	11.50	7 Dec 1994	6.25
16 Sept 1981	14.00	8 Apr 1986	11.00	3 Feb 1995	6.75
1 Oct 1981	16.00	21 Apr 1986	10.50	13 Dec 1995	6.50
14 Oct 1981	15.50	23 May 1986	10.00	18 Jun 1996	6.25
9 Nov 1981	15.00	14 Oct 1986	11.00	8 Mar 1996	6.00
4 Dec 1981	14.50	10 Mar 1987	10.50	6 Jun 1996	5.75
25 Jan 1982	14.00	18 Mar 1987	10.00	31 Oct 1996	6.00
25 Feb 1982	13.50	28 Apr 1987	9.50	6 May 1997	6.25
12 Mar 1982	13.00	11 May 1987	9.00	9 Jun 1997	6.50
8 Jun 1982	12.50	7 Aug 1987	10.00	10 July 1997	6.75
14 July 1982	12.00	23 Oct 1987	9.50	7 Aug 1997	7.00
2 Aug 1982	11.50	4 Nov 1987	9.00	6 Nov 1997	7.25
18 Aug 1982	11.00	4 Dec 1987	8.50	4 Jun 1998	7.50
31 Aug 1982	10.50	2 Feb 1988	9.00	8 Oct 1998	7.25
7 Oct 1982	10.00	18 Mar 1988	8.50	5 Nov 1998	6.75
14 Oct 1982	9.50	11 Apr 1988	8.00	10 Dec 1998	6.25
5 Nov 1982	9.00	18 May 1988	7.50	7 Jan 1999	6.00
26 Nov 1982	10.00	3 Jun 1988	8.00	4 Feb 1999	5.50
29 Nov 1982	10.25	7 Jun 1988	8.50	8 Apr 1999	5.25
12 Jan 1983	11.00	23 Jun 1988	9.00	10 Jun 1999	5.00
15 Mar 1983	10.50	29 Jun 1988	9.50	10 Sept 1999	5.25
15 Apr 1983	10.00	5 July 1988	10.00	4 Nov 1999	5.50
15 June 1983	9.50	19 July 1988	10.50	13 Jan 2000	5.75
4 Oct 1983	9.00	9 Aug 1988	11.00	10 Feb 2000	6.00
7 Mar 1984	8.75	26 Aug 1988	12.00	8 Feb 2001	5.75
15 Mar 1984	8.50	25 Nov 1988	13.00	4 Apr 2001	5.50
10 May 1984	9.00	24 May 1989	14.00	9 May 2001	5.25
27 Jun 1984	9.25	5 Oct 1989	15.00		
6 July 1984	10.00	8 Oct 1990	14.00		
11 July 1984	12.00	13 Feb 1991	13.50		
9 Aug 1984	11.50	27 Feb 1991	13.00		
10 Aug 1984	11.00	22 Mar 1991	12.50		
20 Aug 1984	10.50	12 Apr 1991	12.00		
7 Nov 1984	10.00	24 May 1991	11.50		
20 Nov 1984	9.75	12 July 1991	11.00		
23 Nov 1984	9.50	4 Sept 1991	10.50		
11 Jan 1985	10.50	5 May 1992	10.00		
14 Jan 1985	12.00	16 Sept 1992	12.00		
28 Jan 1985	14.00	17 Sept 1992	10.00		
20 Mar 1985	13.50	22 Sept 1992	9.00		
29 Mar 1985	13.00	19 Oct 1992	8.00		
12 Apr 1985	12.75	13 Nov 1992	7.00		
19 Apr 1985	12.50	26 Jan 1993	6.00		
15 July 1985	12.00	23 Nov 1993	5.50		

Appendix J

Vehicle running costs

In some trades a car is the essential tool, and in others may represent a major expense. In an investigation situation you may have to estimate these costs. The following tables will help. The Revenue no longer accept these AA figures for expenses purposes, but these do provide a basis for some figures. Tables have been provided for the last 10 years, it will be a rare case that goes beyond this.

1990 – Petrol cars

	Engine capacity (cc)				
	Up to 1000	1001 to 1400	1401 to 2000	2001 to 3000	3001 to 4500
Standing charges per annum (£)					
(a) Road Fund	100.00	100.00	100.00	100.00	100.00
(b) Insurance	449.44	550.88	647.79	1,045.98	1,176.33
(c) Depreciation (based on 10,000 miles per annum)	771.06	1,118.44	1,441.02	2,818.44	3,771.12
(d) Subscription	51.00	51.00	51.00	51.00	51.00
£	1,371.50	1,820.32	2,239.81	4,015.42	5,098.45
Cost per mile (in pence)					
5,000	27.430	36.406	44.796	80.308	101.968
10,000	13.715	18.203	22.398	40.154	50.984
15,000	10.171	13.627	16.853	30.527	39.018
20,000	9.171	12.457	15.522	28.532	36.806
25,000	8.570	11.755	14.723	27.335	35.478
30,000	7.142	9.796	12.269	22.779	29.565
Running costs per mile (in pence)					
Petrol*	4.600	5.257	6.134	8.364	9.200
Oil	0.457	0.457	0.487	0.537	0.878
Tyres	0.467	0.600	0.725	1.403	1.819
Servicing	0.969	0.969	0.969	1.264	1.887
Repairs and replacements	4.946	5.236	6.119	9.259	11.507
Pence	11.439	12.519	14.434	20.827	25.291
*unleaded at 40.5 p per litre. For every penny more or less add or subtract	0.025	0.028	0.033	0.045	0.050
Total of standing and running costs based on annual mileages of (in pence)					
5,000	38.869	48.925	59.230	101.135	127.259
10,000	25.154	30.722	36.832	60.981	76.275
15,000	21.610	26.146	31.287	51.534	64.309
20,000	20.610	24.976	29.956	49.359	62.097
25,000	20.009	24.274	29.157	48.162	60.769
30,000	18.581	22.315	26.703	43.606	54.856

1990 – Diesel cars

Engine capacity (cc)

	Up to 2000	Over 2000cc	
		A	B
Standing charges per annum (£)			
(a) Road Fund	100.00	100.00	100.00
(b) Insurance	599.33	647.79	1,045.98
(c) Depreciation (based on 10,000 miles per annum)	1,148.19	1,505.52	2,471.48
(d) Subscription	51.00	51.00	51.00
£	1,898.52	2,304.31	3,668.46
Cost per mile (in pence)			
5,000	37.970	46.086	73.370
10,000	18.985	23.043	36.685
15,000	14.188	17.369	27.752
20,000	10.641	13.027	20.814
25,000	10.350	12.830	20.605
30,000	8.625	10.692	17.171
Running costs per mile (in pence)			
Diesel*	3.956	5.086	5.934
Oil	0.623	0.686	0.686
Tyres	0.662	0.725	1.403
Servicing	0.934	1.006	1.006
Repairs and replacements	5.678	6.119	9.259
Pence	11.853	13.622	18.288
* at 39.2 p per litre. For every penny more or less add or subtract	0.022	0.028	0.033
Total of standing and running costs based on annual mileages of (in pence)			
5,000	49.823	59.708	91.658
10,000	30.838	36.665	54.973
15,000	26.041	30.991	46.040
20,000	22.494	26.649	39.102
25,000	22.203	26.452	38.893
30,000	20.478	24.314	35.459

A cars in excess of 2000cc and a new purchase price less than £14,000.
B cars in excess of 2000cc and a new purchase price more than £14,000.

1991 – Petrol cars

Engine capacity (cc)

	Up to 1000	1001 to 1400	1401 to 2000	2001 to 3000	3001 to 4500
Standing charges per annum (£)					
(a) Road Fund	100.00	100.00	100.00	100.00	100.00
(b) Insurance	499.71	615.71	725.52	1,185.00	1,325.76
(c) Depreciation (based on 10,000 miles per annum)	866.85	1,223.42	1,624.06	3,061.25	3,949.87
(d) Subscription	56.25	56.25	56.25	56.25	56.25
£	1,522.81	1,995.38	2,505.83	4,402.50	5,431.88
Cost per mile (in pence)					
5,000	30.456	39.613	50.117	88.050	108.638
10,000	15.228	19.956	25.058	44.025	54.318
15,000	11.308	14.935	18.871	33.432	41.479
20,000	10.215	13.648	17.401	31.196	39.009
25,000	9.558	12.876	16.519	29.855	37.527
30,000	7.965	10.730	13.766	24.879	31.272
Running costs per mile (in pence)					
Petrol*	5.227	5.974	6.970	9.504	10.455
Oil	0.527	0.527	0.561	0.618	1.011
Tyres	0.528	0.689	0.834	1.605	2.068
Servicing	1.189	1.189	1.189	1.420	2.121
Repairs and replacements	4.995	5.288	6.180	9.351	11.622
Pence	12.466	13.667	15.734	22.498	27.277
*unleaded at 46.91 p per litre. For every penny more or less add or subtract	0.025	0.028	0.033	0.045	0.050
Total of standing and running costs based on annual mileages of (in pence)					
5,000	42.822	53.480	65.751	110.548	135.915
10,000	27.594	33.523	40.692	66.523	81.595
15,000	23.674	28.502	34.505	55.930	68.756
20,000	22.581	27.215	33.035	53.694	66.286
25,000	21.924	26.443	32.153	52.353	64.804
30,000	20.331	24.297	29.400	47.377	58.549

1991 – Diesel cars

Engine capacity (cc)

	Up to 2000	Over 2000cc	
		A	B
Standing charges per annum (£)			
(a) Road Fund	100.00	100.00	100.00
(b) Insurance	670.75	725.52	1,185.00
(c) Depreciation (based on 10,000 miles per annum)	1,251.53	1,641.02	2,693.91
(d) Subscription	56.25	56.25	56.25
£	2,078.53	2,522.79	4,035.16
Cost per mile (in pence)			
5,000	41.570	50.455	80.703
10,000	20.785	25.228	40.351
15,000	15.525	19.006	30.493
20,000	11.644	14.225	22.869
25,000	11.317	14.029	22.606
30,000	9.431	11.691	18.838
Running costs per mile (in pence)			
Diesel*	4.555	5.857	6.833
Oil	0.718	0.790	0.790
Tyres	0.761	0.833	1.605
Servicing	1.049	1.131	1.131
Repairs and replacements	5.735	6.180	9.351
Pence	12.818	14.791	19.710
* at 44.93 p per litre. For every penny more or less add or subtract	0.022	0.028	0.033
Total of standing and running costs based on annual mileages of (in pence)			
5,000	54.388	65.246	100.413
10,000	33.603	40.019	60.061
15,000	28.343	33.797	50.203
20,000	24.462	29.046	42.579
25,000	24.135	28.820	42.316
30,000	22.249	26.482	38.548

A cars in excess of 2000cc and a new purchase price less than £14,000.
B cars in excess of 2000cc and a new purchase price more than £14,000.

1992 – Petrol cars

Engine capacity (cc)

	Up to 1000	1001 to 1400	1401 to 2000	2001 to 3000	3001 to 4500
Standing charges per annum (£)					
(a) Road Fund	110.00	110.00	110.00	110.00	110.00
(b) Insurance	565.90	729.50	880.02	1,359.19	1,404.12
(c) Depreciation (based on 10,000 miles per annum)	817.00	1,224.87	1,675.62	3,168.75	4,180.37
(d) Subscription	60.00	60.00	60.00	60.00	60.00
£	1,552.90	2,124.37	2,725.64	4,697.94	5,754.49
Cost per mile (in pence)					
5,000	31.058	42.487	54.513	93.959	115.089
10,000	15.529	21.244	27.256	46.979	57.449
15,000	11.442	15.796	20.405	35.545	43.937
20,000	10.215	14.296	18.655	32.996	41.314
25,000	9.479	13.397	17.605	31.467	39.739
30,000	7.899	11.164	14.671	26.222	33.116
Running costs per mile (in pence)					
Petrol*	5.325	6.086	7.100	9.682	10.650
Oil	0.527	0.527	0.561	0.618	1.011
Tyres	0.573	0.747	0.905	1.741	2.244
Servicing	1.198	1.198	1.198	1.562	2.333
Repairs and replacements	4.995	5.288	6.180	9.351	11.622
Pence	12.618	13.846	15.944	22.954	27.860
*unleaded at 46.91 p per litre. For every penny more or less add or subtract	0.025	0.028	0.033	0.045	0.050
Total of standing and running costs based on annual mileages of (in pence)					
5,000	43.675	56.904	71.124	117.822	143.949
10,000	28.147	35.661	43.867	70.842	86.309
15,000	24.060	30.213	37.016	59.408	72.797
20,000	22.833	28.713	35.266	56.859	70.174
25,000	22.097	27.814	34.216	55.330	68.599
30,000	20.517	25.581	31.282	50.085	61.976

1992 – Diesel cars

Engine Capacity (cc)

	Up to 2000	Over 2000cc	
		A	B
Standing charges per annum (£)			
(a) Road Fund	110.00	110.00	110.00
(b) Insurance	804.76	880.02	1,359.19
(c) Depreciation (based on 10,000 miles per annum)	1,293.37	1,696.27	2,783.78
(d) Subscription	60.00	60.00	60.00
£	2,268.13	2,746.29	4,312.97
Cost per mile (in pence)			
5,000	45.362	54.926	86.259
10,000	22.681	27.463	43.130
15,000	16.845	20.570	32.465
20,000	12.634	15.428	24.349
25,000	12.177	15.056	23.933
30,000	10.147	12.547	19.944
Running costs per mile (in pence)			
Diesel*	4.534	5.828	6.800
Oil	0.718	0.790	0.790
Tyres	0.826	0.905	1.741
Servicing	1.154	1.244	1.244
Repairs and replacements	5.735	6.180	9.351
Pence	12.967	14.947	19.926
* at 44.93 p per litre. For every penny more or less add or subtract	0.022	0.028	0.033
Total of standing and running costs based on annual mileages of (in pence)			
5,000	58.329	69.873	106.185
10,000	35.648	42.410	63.056
15,000	29.812	35.517	52.391
20,000	25.601	30.375	44.275
25,000	25.144	30.003	43.859
30,000	23.114	27.494	39.870

A cars in excess of 2000cc and a new purchase price less than £14,000.
B cars in excess of 2000cc and a new purchase price more than £14,000.

1993 – Petrol cars

	Engine capacity (cc)				
	Up to 1000	1001 to 1400	1401 to 2000	2001 to 3000	3001 to 4500
Standing charges per annum (£)					
(a) Road Fund	125.00	125.00	125.00	125.00	125.00
(b) Insurance	622.49	802.45	968.00	1,495.10	1,544.53
(c) Depreciation (based on 10,000 miles per annum)	833.50	1,253.13	1,253.13	3,288.88	4,287.00
(d) Subscription	64.00	64.00	64.00	64.00	64.00
£	1,644.99	2,244.58	2,410.13	4,972.98	6,020.53
Cost per mile (in pence)					
5,000	32.90	44.89	58.18	99.46	120.41
10,000	16.45	22.45	29.09	49.73	60.21
15,000	12.08	16.63	21.73	37.54	45.85
20,000	10.73	14.98	19.80	34.73	42.96
25,000	9.91	13.99	18.64	33.05	41.23
30,000	8.26	11.66	15.54	27.54	34.36
Running costs per mile (in pence)					
Petrol*	5.69	6.50	7.58	10.34	11.37
Oil	0.53	0.53	0.57	0.63	1.03
Tyres	0.61	0.80	0.97	1.86	2.40
Servicing	1.20	1.20	1.20	1.62	2.43
Repairs and replacements	5.00	5.29	6.18	9.35	11.62
Pence	13.03	14.32	16.50	23.80	28.85
*unleaded at 0.50 p per litre. For every penny more or less add or subtract	0.11	0.13	0.15	0.21	0.23
Total of standing and running costs based on annual mileages of (in pence)					
5,000	45.93	59.21	74.68	123.26	149.26
10,000	29.48	36.77	45.59	73.53	89.06
15,000	25.11	30.95	38.23	61.34	74.70
20,000	23.76	29.30	36.30	58.53	71.81
25,000	22.94	28.31	35.14	56.85	70.08
30,000	21.29	25.98	32.04	51.34	63.21

1993 – Diesel cars

	New purchase price (£)		
	Up to £10,000	£10,001 to £15,000	Over £15,001
Standing charges per annum (£)			
(a) Road Fund	125.00	125.00	125.00
(b) Insurance	885.24	968.00	1,495.10
(c) Depreciation (based on 10,000 miles per annum)	1,096.28	1,581.34	2,651.06
(d) Subscription	64.00	64.00	64.00
£	2,170.52	2,738.34	4,335.16
Cost per mile (in pence)			
5,000	43.41	54.77	86.70
10,000	21.71	27.38	43.35
15,000	15.93	20.36	32.44
20,000	11.95	15.27	24.33
25,000	11.31	14.75	23.70
30,000	9.43	12.29	19.75
Running costs per mile (in pence)			
Diesel*	5.05	5.99	7.58
Oil	0.74	0.82	0.82
Tyres	0.88	0.97	1.86
Servicing	1.20	1.20	1.29
Repairs and replacements	5.74	6.18	9.35
Pence	13.61	15.16	20.90
* at 0.50 p per litre. For every penny more or less add or subtract	0.10	0.12	0.15
Total of standing and running costs based on annual mileages of (in pence)			
5,000	57.02	69.63	107.60
10,000	35.32	42.54	64.25
15,000	29.54	35.52	53.34
20,000	25.56	30.43	45.23
25,000	24.92	29.91	44.60
30,000	23.04	27.45	40.65

It is felt that engine size does not properly reflect the class of car due to the use of turbo chargers. New purchase price is now used for classification.

1994 – Petrol cars

	Engine capacity (cc)				
	Up to 1100	1101 to 1400	1401 to 2000	2001 to 3000	3001 to 4500
Standing charges per annum (£)					
(a) Road Fund	130.00	130.00	130.00	130.00	130.00
(b) Insurance	252.73	325.79	393.00	578.00	627.00
(c) Depreciation (based on 10,000 miles per annum)	866.87	1,276.87	1,805.47	3,327.29	4,479.15
(d) Subscription	62.00	62.00	62.00	62.00	62.00
£	1,311.60	1,794.66	2,390.47	4,097.29	5,298.15
Cost per mile (in pence)					
5,000	26.24	35.90	47.80	81.94	105.96
10,000	13.12	17.95	23.90	40.97	52.98
15,000	9.90	13.67	18.34	31.75	41.29
20,000	9.16	12.80	17.37	30.47	39.93
25,000	8.71	12.29	16.78	29.70	39.10
30,000	7.26	10.24	13.99	24.75	32.59
Running costs per mile (in pence)					
Petrol*	5.79	6.62	7.72	10.53	11.59
Oil	0.26	0.27	0.28	0.34	0.55
Tyres	0.66	0.86	1.05	2.01	2.59
Servicing	0.76	0.76	0.76	1.19	1.68
Repairs and replacements	2.80	3.18	3.26	5.00	5.14
Pence	10.27	11.69	13.07	19.07	21.55
*unleaded at 0.51 p per litre. For every penny more or less add or subtract	0.11	0.13	0.15	0.21	0.23
Total of standing and running costs based on annual mileages of (in pence)					
5,000	36.51	47.59	60.87	101.01	127.51
10,000	23.39	29.64	36.97	60.04	74.53
15,000	20.17	25.36	31.41	50.82	62.84
20,000	19.43	24.49	30.44	49.54	61.48
25,000	18.98	23.98	29.85	48.77	60.65
30,000	17.53	21.93	27.06	43.82	54.14

1994 – Diesel cars

New purchase price (£)

	Up to £10,000	£10,001 to £15,000	Over £15,001
Standing charges per annum (£)			
(a) Road Fund	130.00	130.00	130.00
(b) Insurance	359.39	393.00	578.00
(c) Depreciation (based on 10,000 miles per annum)	1,129.16	1,628.78	2,730.59
(d) Subscription	62.00	62.00	62.00
£	1,680.55	2,213.78	3,500.59
Cost per mile (in pence)			
5,000	33.60	44.28	70.00
10,000	16.80	22.14	35.00
15,000	12.71	16.93	26.98
20,000	9.53	12.70	20.23
25,000	8.43	11.76	19.55
30,000	7.86	10.64	17.12
Running costs per mile (in pence)			
Diesel*	5.25	6.22	7.88
Oil	0.39	0.63	0.63
Tyres	0.95	1.05	2.01
Servicing	0.82	0.82	1.08
Repairs and replacements	2.99	3.26	5.00
Pence	10.40	11.98	16.60
* at 0.52 p per litre. For every penny more or less add or subtract	0.10	0.12	0.15
Total of standing and running costs based on annual mileages of (in pence)			
5,000	44.00	56.26	86.60
10,000	27.20	34.12	51.60
15,000	23.11	28.91	43.58
20,000	19.93	24.68	36.83
25,000	18.83	23.74	36.15
30,000	18.26	22.62	33.72

It is felt that engine size does not properly reflect the class of car due to the use of turbo chargers. New purchase price is now used for classification.

1995 – Petrol cars

Engine capacity (cc)

	Up to 1100	1101 to 1400	1401 to 2000	2001 to 3000	3001 to 4500
Standing charges per annum (£)					
(a) Road Fund	135.00	135.00	135.00	135.00	135.00
(b) Insurance	247.67	319.28	385.15	594.87	614.53
(c) Depreciation (based on 10,000 miles per annum)	892.88	1,315.18	1,859.64	3,427.11	4,613.53
(d) Subscription	64.00	64.00	64.00	64.00	64.00
£	1,339.55	1,833.46	2,443.79	4,220.98	5,427.06
Cost per mile (in pence)					
5,000	26.79	36.66	48.87	84.41	108.54
10,000	13.39	18.33	24.43	42.21	54.27
15,000	10.12	13.98	18.77	32.71	42.33
20,000	9.38	13.11	17.80	31.38	40.97
25,000	8.93	12.59	17.21	30.59	40.16
30,000	7.44	10.49	14.34	25.49	33.47
Running costs per mile (in pence)					
Petrol*	6.07	6.94	8.10	11.04	12.15
Oil	0.30	0.31	0.32	0.39	0.63
Tyres	0.66	0.86	1.05	2.01	2.59
Servicing	0.79	0.79	0.79	1.23	1.74
Repairs and replacements	2.90	3.29	3.37	5.17	5.32
Pence	10.72	12.19	13.63	19.84	22.43
*unleaded at 0.53 p per litre. For every penny more or less add or subtract	0.11	0.13	0.15	0.21	0.23
Total of standing and running costs based on annual mileages of (in pence)					
5,000	37.51	48.85	62.50	104.25	130.97
10,000	24.11	30.52	38.07	62.05	76.70
15,000	20.84	26.17	32.40	52.55	64.76
20,000	20.10	25.30	31.43	51.22	63.40
25,000	19.65	24.78	30.84	50.43	62.59
30,000	18.16	22.68	27.97	45.33	55.90

1995 – Diesel cars

New purchase price (£)

	Up to £10,000	£10,001 to £15,000	Over £15,001
Standing charges per annum (£)			
(a) Road Fund	135.00	135.00	135.00
(b) Insurance	352.21	385.15	594.87
(c) Depreciation (based on 10,000 miles per annum)	1,163.03	1,677.64	2,812.51
(d) Subscription	64.00	64.00	64.00
£	1,714.24	2,261.79	3,606.38
Cost per mile (in pence)			
5,000	34.28	45.24	72.12
10,000	17.14	22.62	36.06
15,000	12.98	17.31	27.79
20,000	9.73	12.99	20.84
25,000	8.65	12.07	20.17
30,000	8.04	10.89	17.65
Running costs per mile (in pence)			
Diesel*	5.39	6.39	8.09
Oil	0.45	0.72	0.72
Tyres	0.95	1.05	2.01
Servicing	0.85	0.85	1.12
Repairs and replacements	3.09	3.37	5.17
Pence	10.73	12.38	17.11
* at 0.534 p per litre. For every penny more or less add or subtract	0.10	0.12	0.15
Total of standing and running costs based on annual mileages of (in pence)			
5,000	45.01	57.62	89.23
10,000	27.87	35.00	53.17
15,000	23.71	29.69	44.90
20,000	20.46	25.37	37.95
25,000	19.38	24.45	37.28
30,000	18.77	23.27	34.76

It is felt that engine size does not properly reflect the class of car due to the use of turbo chargers. New purchase price is now used for classification.

1996 – Petrol cars

Engine capacity (cc)

	Up to 1100	1101 to 1400	1401 to 2000	2001 to 3000	3001 to 4500
Standing charges per annum (£)					
(a) Road Fund	140.00	140.00	140.00	140.00	140.00
(b) Insurance	235.44	302.99	365.50	564.52	583.18
(c) Depreciation (based on 10,000 miles per annum)	937.52	1,380.94	1,952.62	3,598.46	4,844.21
(d) Subscription	66.00	66.00	66.00	66.00	66.00
£	1,378.96	1,889.93	2,524.12	4,368.98	5,633.39
Cost per mile (in pence)					
5,000	27.58	37.80	50.48	87.38	112.66
10,000	13.79	18.90	25.24	43.69	56.33
15,000	10.44	14.44	19.43	33.92	44.01
20,000	9.71	13.59	18.48	32.64	42.70
25,000	9.26	13.08	17.91	31.87	41.91
30,000	7.72	10.90	14.92	26.56	34.92
Running costs per mile (in pence)					
Petrol*	6.38	7.29	8.50	11.60	12.76
Oil	0.30	0.31	0.32	0.39	0.63
Tyres	0.68	0.88	1.08	2.07	2.67
Servicing	0.82	0.82	0.82	1.28	1.81
Repairs and replacements	2.99	3.42	3.47	5.32	5.48
Pence	11.17	12.72	14.19	20.66	23.35
*unleaded at 56.2 p per litre. For every penny more or less add or subtract	0.11	0.13	0.15	0.21	0.23
Total of standing and running costs based on annual mileages of (in pence)					
5,000	38.75	50.52	64.67	108.04	136.01
10,000	24.96	31.62	39.43	64.35	79.68
15,000	21.61	27.16	33.62	54.58	67.36
20,000	20.88	26.31	32.67	53.30	66.05
25,000	20.43	25.80	32.10	52.53	65.26
30,000	18.89	23.62	29.11	47.22	58.27

1996 – Diesel cars

	New purchase price (£)		
	Up to £10,000	£10,001 to £15,000	Over £15,001
Standing charges per annum (£)			
(a) Road Fund	140.00	140.00	140.00
(b) Insurance	334.24	365.50	564.52
(c) Depreciation (based on 10,000 miles per annum)	1,221.18	1,761.52	2,953.13
(d) Subscription	66.00	66.00	66.00
£	1,761.42	2,333.02	3,723.65
Cost per mile (in pence)			
5,000	35.22	46.66	74.48
10,000	17.61	23.33	37.24
15,000	13.37	17.90	28.76
20,000	10.03	13.43	21.57
25,000	8.98	12.56	20.98
30,000	8.31	11.30	18.32
Running costs per mile (in pence)			
Diesel*	5.73	6.78	8.59
Oil	0.45	0.72	0.72
Tyres	0.98	1.08	2.07
Servicing	0.88	0.88	1.16
Repairs and replacements	3.18	3.47	5.32
Pence	11.22	12.93	17.86
* at 56.8 p per litre. For every penny more or less add or subtract	0.10	0.12	0.15
Total of standing and running costs based on annual mileages of (in pence)			
5,000	46.44	59.59	92.34
10,000	28.83	36.26	55.10
15,000	24.59	30.83	46.62
20,000	21.25	26.36	39.43
25,000	20.20	25.49	38.84
30,000	19.53	24.23	36.18

It is felt that engine size does not properly reflect the class of car due to the use of turbo chargers. New purchase price is now used for classification.

1997 – Petrol cars

Engine capacity (cc)

	Up to 1100	1101 to 1400	1401 to 2000	2001 to 3000	3001 to 4500
Standing charges per annum (£)					
(a) Road Fund	145.00	145.00	145.00	145.00	145.00
(b) Insurance	249.57	322.68	389.26	601.21	621.09
(c) Depreciation (based on 10,000 miles per annum)	984.40	1,449.99	2,050.25	3,778.38	5,086.42
(d) Subscription	70.00	70.00	70.00	70.00	70.00
£	1,448.97	1,987.67	2,654.51	4,594.59	5,922.51
Cost per mile (in pence)					
5,000	28.98	39.76	53.08	91.88	118.44
10,000	14.49	19.88	26.54	45.94	59.22
15,000	10.97	15.18	20.43	35.67	46.27
20,000	10.20	14.29	19.42	34.31	44.87
25,000	9.73	13.75	18.82	33.49	44.04
30,000	8.11	11.46	15.68	27.91	36.70
Running costs per mile (in pence)					
Petrol*	6.90	7.89	9.21	12.55	13.81
Oil	0.30	0.31	0.32	0.39	0.63
Tyres	0.69	0.90	1.10	2.11	2.72
Servicing	0.85	0.85	0.85	1.33	1.88
Repairs and replacements	3.02	3.45	3.50	5.37	5.53
Pence	11.76	13.40	14.98	21.75	24.57
*unleaded at 60.8 p per litre. For every penny more or less add or subtract	0.11	0.13	0.15	0.21	0.23
Total of standing and running costs based on annual mileages of (in pence)					
5,000	40.74	53.16	68.06	113.63	143.01
10,000	26.25	33.28	41.52	67.69	83.79
15,000	22.73	28.58	35.41	57.42	70.84
20,000	21.96	27.69	34.40	56.06	69.44
25,000	21.49	27.15	33.80	55.24	68.61
30,000	19.87	24.86	30.66	49.66	61.27

1997 – Diesel Cars

	New purchase price (£)			
	Up to £10,000	£10,001 to £15,000	£15,001 £20,000	Over £20,000
Standing charges per annum (£)				
(a) Road Fund	145.00	145.00	145.00	145.00
(b) Insurance	249.57	322.68	389.26	601.21
(c) Depreciation (based on 10,000 miles per annum)	1,121.85	1,608.39	2,154.25	3,128.38
(d) Subscription	70.00	70.00	70.00	70.00
£	1,586.42	2,146.07	2,758.51	3,944.59
Cost per mile (in pence)				
5,000	31.72	42.92	55.16	78.88
10,000	15.86	21.46	27.58	39.44
15,000	12.07	16.45	21.26	30.47
20,000	9.05	12.34	15.95	22.85
25,000	8.04	11.44	15.20	22.28
30,000	7.53	10.37	13.50	19.41
Running costs per mile (in pence)				
Diesel*	6.23	7.01	7.38	9.34
Oil	0.45	0.45	0.58	0.72
Tyres	0.69	0.90	1.10	2.11
Servicing	0.92	0.92	1.15	1.39
Repairs and replacements	3.02	3.45	3.50	5.37
Pence	11.31	12.73	13.71	18.93
* at 61.7 p per litre. For every penny more or less add or subtract	0.10	0.11	0.12	0.15
Total of standing and running costs based on annual mileages of (in pence)				
5,000	43.03	55.65	68.87	97.81
10,000	27.17	34.19	41.29	58.37
15,000	23.38	29.18	34.97	49.40
20,000	20.36	25.07	29.66	41.78
25,000	19.35	24.17	28.91	41.21
30,000	18.84	23.10	27.21	38.34

It is felt that engine size does not properly reflect the class of car due to the use of turbo chargers. New purchase price is now used for classification.

1998 – Petrol cars

Engine capacity (cc)

	Up to 1100	1101 to 1400	1401 to 2000	2001 to 3000	3001 to 4500
Standing charges per annum (£)					
(a) Road Fund	150.00	150.00	150.00	150.00	150.00
(b) Insurance	264.29	342.37	414.56	640.29	661.46
(c) Depreciation (based on 10,000 miles per annum)	1,023.78	1,672.72	2,132.26	3,853.95	5,289.88
(d) Subscription	72.00	72.00	72.00	72.00	72.00
£	1,510.07	2,237.09	2,768.82	4,716.24	6,173.34
Cost per mile (in pence)					
5,000	30.20	44.74	55.38	94.32	123.46
10,000	15.10	22.37	27.69	47.16	61.73
15,000	11.43	17.14	21.30	36.58	48.21
20,000	10.62	16.20	20.24	35.14	46.74
25,000	10.13	15.64	19.60	34.28	45.85
30,000	8.45	13.03	16.34	28.57	38.21
Running costs per mile (in pence)					
Petrol*	7.60	8.69	10.14	13.83	15.21
Oil	0.33	0.34	0.35	0.43	0.69
Tyres	0.72	0.94	1.15	2.21	2.86
Servicing	0.89	0.89	0.89	1.40	1.97
Repairs and replacements	3.05	3.48	3.53	5.42	5.58
Pence	12.59	14.34	16.06	23.29	26.31
*unleaded at 67 p per litre. For every penny more or less add or subtract	0.11	0.13	0.15	0.21	0.23
Total of standing and running costs based on annual mileages of (in pence)					
5,000	42.79	59.08	71.44	117.61	149.77
10,000	27.69	36.71	43.75	70.45	88.04
15,000	24.02	31.48	37.36	59.87	74.52
20,000	23.21	30.54	36.30	58.43	73.05
25,000	22.72	29.98	35.66	57.57	72.16
30,000	21.04	27.37	32.40	51.86	64.52

1998 – Diesel cars

New purchase price (£)

	Up to £10,000	£10,001 to £15,000	£15,001 £20,000	Over £20,000
Standing charges per annum (£)				
(a) Road Fund	150.00	150.00	150.00	150.00
(b) Insurance	264.29	342.37	414.56	640.29
(c) Depreciation (based on 10,000 miles per annum)	1,166.72	1,672.72	2,240.42	3,253.51
(d) Subscription	72.00	72.00	72.00	72.00
£	1,653.01	2,237.09	2,876.98	4,115.80
Cost per mile (in pence)				
5,000	33.06	44.74	57.54	82.32
10,000	16.53	22.37	28.77	41.46
15,000	12.57	17.14	22.17	27.44
20,000	9.43	12.86	16.62	23.83
25,000	8.41	11.96	15.88	23.27
30,000	7.84	10.80	14.07	20.23
Running costs per mile (in pence)				
Diesel*	6.86	7.72	8.12	10.29
Oil	0.49	0.49	0.64	0.79
Tyres	0.72	0.94	1.15	2.21
Servicing	0.97	0.97	1.21	1.46
Repairs and replacements	3.05	3.48	3.53	5.42
Pence	12.09	13.60	14.65	20.17
* at 68 p per litre. For every penny more or less add or subtract	0.10	0.11	0.12	0.15
Total of standing and running costs based on annual mileages of (in pence)				
5,000	45.15	58.34	72.19	102.49
10,000	28.62	35.97	43.42	61.33
15,000	24.66	30.74	36.82	47.61
20,000	21.52	26.46	31.27	44.00
25,000	20.50	25.56	30.53	43.44
30,000	19.93	24.40	28.72	40.40

It is felt that engine size does not properly reflect the class of car due to the use of turbo chargers. New purchase price is now used for classification.

1999 – Petrol cars

Engine capacity (cc)

	Up to 1100	1101 to 1400	1401 to 2000	2001 to 3000	3001 to 4500
Standing charges per annum (£)					
(a) Road Fund	100.00	155.00	155.00	155.00	155.00
(b) Insurance	281.37	376.36	452.10	698.27	721.35
(c) Depreciation (based on 10,000 miles per annum)	1,064.73	1,568.31	2,217.55	4,008.10	5,501.47
(d) Subscription	74.00	74.00	74.00	74.00	74.00
£	1,520.10	2,173.67	2,898.65	4,935.37	6,451.82
Cost per mile (in pence)					
5,000	30.40	43.47	57.97	98.71	129.04
10,000	15.20	21.74	28.99	49.35	64.52
15,000	11.55	16.58	22.28	38.25	50.35
20,000	10.79	15.57	21.15	36.70	48.76
25,000	10.34	14.97	20.46	35.77	47.81
30,000	8.62	12.47	17.05	29.81	39.84
Running costs per mile (in pence)					
Petrol*	7.83	8.95	10.44	14.24	15.66
Oil	0.34	0.35	0.36	0.44	0.70
Tyres	0.74	0.96	1.17	2.25	2.92
Servicing	0.94	0.94	0.94	1.47	2.07
Repairs and replacements	3.08	3.51	3.57	5.47	5.63
Pence	12.93	14.71	16.48	23.87	26.98
*unleaded at 68.9 p per litre. For every penny more or less add or subtract	0.11	0.13	0.15	0.21	0.23
Total of standing and running costs based on annual mileages of (in pence)					
5,000	43.33	58.18	74.45	122.58	156.02
10,000	28.13	36.45	45.47	73.22	91.50
15,000	24.48	31.29	38.76	62.12	77.33
20,000	23.72	30.28	37.69	60.57	75.74
25,000	23.27	29.68	36.94	59.64	74.79
30,000	21.55	27.18	33.53	53.68	66.82

1999 – Diesel cars

New purchase price (£)

	Up to £11,000	£11,001 to £15,000	£15,001 £20,000	Over £20,000
Standing charges per annum (£)				
(a) Road Fund	155.00	155.00	155.00	155.00
(b) Insurance	281.37	376.36	452.10	698.27
(c) Depreciation (based on 10,000 miles per annum)	1,213.39	1,739.63	2,330.04	3,383.65
(d) Subscription	74.00	74.00	74.00	74.00
£	1,723.76	2,344.99	3,011.14	4,310.92
Cost per mile (in pence)				
5,000	34.48	46.90	60.22	86.22
10,000	17.24	23.45	30.11	43.11
15,000	13.11	17.95	23.18	33.25
20,000	9.83	13.46	17.39	24.94
25,000	8.81	12.56	16.64	24.36
30,000	8.17	11.30	14.70	21.14
Running costs per mile (in pence)				
Diesel*	7.26	8.17	8.60	10.90
Oil	0.50	0.50	0.65	0.80
Tyres	0.74	0.96	1.17	2.25
Servicing	1.02	1.02	1.27	1.53
Repairs and replacements	3.08	3.51	3.57	5.47
Pence	12.60	14.16	15.26	20.95
* at 71.9 p per litre. For every penny more or less add or subtract	0.10	0.11	0.12	0.15
Total of standing and running costs based on annual mileages of (in pence)				
5,000	47.08	61.06	75.48	107.17
10,000	29.84	37.61	45.37	64.06
15,000	25.71	32.11	38.44	54.20
20,000	22.43	27.62	32.65	45.89
25,000	21.41	26.72	31.90	45.31
30,000	20.77	25.46	29.96	42.09

It is felt that engine size does not properly reflect the class of car due to the use of turbo chargers. New purchase price is now used for classification.

2000 – Petrol cars

Engine capacity (cc)

	Up to 1100	1101 to 1400	1401 to 2000	2001 to 3000	3001 to 4500
Standing charges per annum (£)					
(a) Road Fund	100.00	155.00	155.00	155.00	155.00
(b) Insurance	330.77	440.65	517.51	799.30	825.72
(c) Depreciation (based on 10,000 miles per annum)	1,117.97	1,646.73	2,328.43	4,208.50	5,776.54
(d) Subscription	75.00	75.00	75.00	75.00	75.00
£	1,623.74	2,317.38	3,075.94	5,237.80	6,832.26
Cost per mile (in pence)					
5,000	32.47	46.35	61.52	104.76	136.65
10,000	16.24	23.17	30.76	52.38	68.32
15,000	12.32	17.64	23.61	40.53	53.25
20,000	11.47	16.53	22.36	38.81	51.49
25,000	10.97	15.86	21.62	37.79	50.44
30,000	9.14	13.21	18.01	31.49	42.03
Running costs per mile (in pence)					
Petrol*	9.19	10.51	12.26	16.72	18.39
Oil	0.35	0.36	0.37	0.45	0.71
Tyres	0.76	0.98	1.19	2.29	2.98
Servicing	0.99	0.99	0.99	1.54	2.17
Repairs and replacements	3.11	3.55	3.61	5.52	5.69
Pence	14.40	16.39	18.42	26.52	29.94
*unleaded at 80.9 p per litre. For every penny more or less add or subtract	0.11	0.13	0.15	0.21	0.23
Total of standing and running costs based on annual mileages of (in pence)					
5,000	46.87	62.74	79.94	131.28	166.59
10,000	30.64	39.56	49.18	78.90	98.26
15,000	26.72	34.03	42.03	67.05	83.19
20,000	25.87	32.92	40.78	65.33	81.43
25,000	25.37	32.25	40.04	64.31	80.38
30,000	23.54	29.60	36.43	58.01	71.97

2000 – Diesel cars

New purchase price (£)

	Up to £11,000	£11,001 to £15,000	£15,001 £20,000	Over £20,000
Standing charges per annum (£)				
(a) Road Fund	155.00	155.00	155.00	155.00
(b) Insurance	330.77	440.65	517.51	799.30
(c) Depreciation (based on 10,000 miles per annum)	1,274.06	1,826.61	2,446.54	3,552.83
(d) Subscription	75.00	75.00	75.00	75.00
£	1,834.83	2,497.26	3,194.05	4,582.13
Cost per mile (in pence)				
5,000	36.70	49.95	63.88	91.64
10,000	18.35	24.97	31.94	45.82
15,000	13.98	19.08	24.56	35.28
20,000	10.45	14.31	18.42	26.46
25,000	9.40	13.37	17.65	25.86
30,000	8.66	11.98	15.54	22.38
Running costs per mile (in pence)				
Diesel*	8.27	9.31	9.80	12.41
Oil	0.51	0.51	0.66	0.82
Tyres	0.76	0.98	1.19	2.29
Servicing	1.07	1.07	1.33	1.61
Repairs and replacements	3.11	3.55	3.61	5.52
Pence	13.72	15.42	16.59	22.65
* at 81.9 p per litre. For every penny more or less add or subtract	0.10	0.11	0.12	0.15
Total of standing and running costs based on annual mileages of (in pence)				
5,000	50.42	65.37	80.47	114.29
10,000	32.07	40.39	48.53	68.47
15,000	27.65	34.50	41.15	57.93
20,000	24.17	29.73	35.01	49.11
25,000	23.12	28.79	34.24	48.51
30,000	22.38	27.40	32.13	45.03

It is felt that engine size does not properly reflect the class of car due to the use of turbo chargers. New purchase price is now used for classification.

2001 – Petrol cars

Engine capacity (cc)

	Up to 1100	1101 to 1500	1501 to 2000	2001 to 3000	3001 to 4500
Standing charges per annum					
(a) Road tax	105.00	105.00	160.00	160.00	160.00
(b) Insurance	379.54	507.60	595.21	938.80	969.84
(c) Depreciation (based on 10,000 miles per annum)	1,207.35	1,778.40	2,514.60	4,545.15	6,238.65
(d) Subscription	77.00	77.00	77.00	77.00	77.00
£	1,768.89	2,468.00	3,346.81	5,720.95	7,445.49
Standing charge per mile (in pence)					
5,000	31.35	43.43	58.55	99.27	128.11
10,000	17.69	24.68	33.47	57.21	74.45
15,000	13.13	21.20	29.02	50.26	66.27
20,000	10.86	15.30	20.93	36.18	47.63
25,000	10.30	14.61	20.09	35.00	46.42
30,000	9.92	14.15	19.54	34.22	45.61
Running costs per mile (in pence)					
(e) petrol*	8.75	10.00	11.67	15.91	17.50
(f) oil	0.35	0.36	0.37	0.45	0.71
(g) tyres	0.79	1.02	1.24	2.40	3.12
(h) servicing	1.03	1.03	1.03	1.61	2.27
(i) repairs and replacements	3.14	3.58	3.64	5.57	5.74
	14.06	15.99	17.95	25.94	29.34
*unleaded at 77.0p per litre. For every penny more or less add or subtract:	0.11	0.13	0.15	0.21	0.23
Total of standing and running costs based on annual mileages of (in pence);					
5,000	45.41	59.42	76.50	125.21	157.45
10,000	31.75	40.67	51.42	83.15	103.79
15,000	27.19	37.19	46.97	76.20	95.61
20,000	24.92	31.29	38.88	62.12	76.97
25,000	24.36	30.60	38.04	60.94	75.76
30,000	23.98	30.14	37.49	60.16	74.95

2001 – Diesel cars

New purchase price (£)

	Up to £11,000	£11,001 to £15,000	£15,001 £20,000	Over £20,001
Standing charges per annum				
(a) Road tax	160.00	160.00	160.00	160.00
(b) Insurance	379.54	507.60	595.21	938.80
(c) Depreciation (based on 10,000 miles per annum)	1,375.95	2,016.45	2,730.30	3,263.30
(d) Subscription	77.00	77.00	77.00	77.00
£	1,992.49	2,761.05	3,562.51	5,439.10
Standing charge per mile (in pence)				
5,000	35.26	48.50	62.15	94.57
10,000	19.92	27.61	35.63	54.39
15,000	14.81	20.65	26.78	41.00
20,000	12.26	17.17	22.36	34.30
25,000	10.72	15.08	19.71	30.28
30,000	9.7	13.68	17.94	27.60
Running costs per mile (in pence)				
(e) diesel*	7.88	8.86	9.33	11.82
(f) oil	0.51	0.51	0.66	0.82
(g) tyres	0.79	1.02	1.24	2.40
(h) servicing	1.12	1.12	1.39	1.69
(i) repairs and replacements	3.14	3.58	3.64	5.57
	13.44	15.09	16.26	22.30
* diesel at 78.0p per litre. For every penny more or less add or subtract:	0.10	0.11	0.12	0.15
Total of standing and running costs based on annual mileages of (in pence);				
5,000	48.70	63.59	78.41	116.87
10,000	33.36	42.70	51.89	76.69
15,000	28.25	35.74	43.04	63.30
20,000	25.70	32.26	38.62	56.60
25,000	24.16	30.17	35.97	52.58
30,000	23.14	28.77	34.20	49.90

It is felt that engine size does not properly reflect the class of car. New purchase price has therefore been used for classification.

Appendix K

VAT Rates 1973 to 2001

Standard rate	*%*	*VAT fraction*
1 April 1991 to current	17.5	7/47
18 June 1979 to 31 March 1991	15	3/23
29 July 1974 to 17 June 1979	8	2/27
1 April 1973 to 28 July 1974	10	1/11

Appendix L

VAT Registration Limits

VAT registration limits	£
1 April 2001 – current	54,000
1 April 2000 – 31 March 2000	52,000
1 April 1999 – 31 March 2000	51,000
1 April 1998 – 31 March 1999	50,000
1 December 1997 – 31 March 1998	49,000
27 November 1996 – 30 November 1997	48,000
29 November 1995 – 26 November 1996	47,000
30 November 1994 – 28 November 1995	46,000
1 December 1993 – 29 November 1994	45,000
17 March 1993 – 30 November 1993	37,600
11 March 1992 – 16 March 1993	36,600
20 March 1991 – 10 March 1992	35,000
21 March 1990 – 19 March 1991	25,400
15 March 1989 – 20 March 1990	23,600
16 March 1988 – 14 March 1989	22,100
18 March 1987 – 15 March 1988	21,300
19 March 1986 – 17 March 1987	20,500
20 March 1985 – 18 March 1986	19,500
14 March 1984 – 19 March 1985	18,700
16 March 1983 – 13 March 1984	18,000
10 March 1982 – 15 March 1983	17,000
11 March 1981 – 9 March 1982	15,000

Appendix M

VAT Offences and Penalties

Criminal offence	*Penalty*
Fraudulent evasion (VATA 1994, s 72(1))	On summary conviction a fine of £5,000 or three times the VAT (whichever is the greatest) or up to six months in prison or both. On indictment an unlimited fine or up to seven years in prison or both.
False documents (VATA 1994, s 72(3))	On summary conviction a fine of £5,000 or three times the VAT (whichever is the greatest) or up to six months in prison or both. On indictment an unlimited fine or up to seven years in prison or both.
Knowledge that evasion intended (VATA 1994, s 72(10))	£5,000 or three times the amount of VAT involved.

Civil offences	*Penalty*
Conduct involving dishonesty (VATA 1994, s 60)	100% of tax involved (subject to mitigation for co-operation).
Misdeclaration of VAT due (VATA, s 63)	15% of VAT due.
Persistent misdeclarations (VATA 1994, s 64)	15% of VAT due on second and subsequent occasion of error.
Failure to register (VATA, s 67)	Under 9 months late = 5% of VAT From 9 to 18 months = 10% of VAT over 18 months late = 15% of VAT.

Late payment (VATA 1994, s 59)	First time	2%
	Second time	5%
	Third time	10%
	Fourth time et seq	15%

Accounting Adjustments Following an Investigation Settlement

The extract below is taken from *Tolley's Accounting Principles for Tax Purposes* by Mike Cochrane with some slight amendments to reflect changes in legislation since publication of that book.

'If it were discovered that for the previous ten years, a director of a company had been diverting, say £10,000 p.a. of cash takings into his own back pocket, so that the accounts had shown a fundamentally incorrect position, then that circumstance would need rectification by means of a prior year adjustment. An example will best illustrate this.

Example 21

A company began trading on 1 April 1988. It has just prepared its draft accounts for the year to 31 March 1998 which in summary form are as below:

	31/03/98		*31/03/97*	
	£	£	£	£
Fixed assets		100,000		80,000
Current assets				
Stock:	170,000			
Debtors:	30,000			
Cash:	10,000			
Current liabilities				
Creditors:	(30,000)			
Directors' Loans:	(120,000)			
Net current assets		60,000	20,000	
Net assets		160,000		100,000
Share capital		10,000		10,000
Profit and loss b/f	90,000		70,000	
Profit for year	60,000		20,000	
Profit and loss c/f		150,000		90,000
		160,000		100,000

	31/03/98	*31/03/97*
	£	£
TURNOVER	1,000,000	850,000
Gross profit	200,000	120,000
PROFIT BEFORE TAX	80,000	25,000
Taxation	(20,000)	(5,000)
RETAINED PROFIT FOR YEAR	60,000	20,000

Now suppose that it is discovered before the 1998 accounts are finalised, that a director (who is also a controlling shareholder) has for each of the past ten years, under-declared turnover and profits by £10,000 p.a. This has been discovered by the Inland Revenue and a quick settlement is agreed with them, the terms of which will be:

	£
Additional profits taxable 01/04/88–31/03/97	90,000
Additional corporation tax at 25%, say	22,500
Interest and penalties thereon	22,500
Total settlement	45,000
Additional profits taxable 01/04/97–31/03/98 (to be included on finalising the current accounts)	10,000

Reproduced below are the finalised accounts reflecting the above settlement.

	31/03/98		*31/03/97*	
	£	£	£	£
Fixed assets		100,000		80,000
Current assets				
Stock:	170,000			
Debtors:	30,000			
Cash:	10,000			
Current liabilities				
Creditors:	(77,500)			
Directors' Loans:	(20,000)			
Net current assets		112,500 (x)		87,500 (i)
Net assets		212,500		167,500
Share capital		10,000		10,000
Profit and loss b/f	90,000		70,000	
Prior year adjustment	67,500 (vi)		60,000 (ii)	
Profit and loss as restated b/f	157,500 (vii)		130,000	
Profit for year	45,000		27,500	
Profit and loss c/f		202,500		157,500 (v)
		212,500		167,500

	31/03/98	*31/03/97*
	£	£
TURNOVER	1,010,000 (viii)	860,000 (iii)
Gross profit	210,000	130,000
PROFIT BEFORE TAX	67,500 (ix)	35,000
Taxation	(22,500)	(7,500)
PROFIT ON ORDINARY ACTIVITIES AFTER TAX	45,000	27,500
EXTRAORDINARY ITEM	–	–
RETAINED PROFIT FOR YEAR	45,000	27,500 (iv)

At first sight this may appear very confusing. The following notes may assist.

In finalising the 1998 accounts, it is first necessary to restate the comparative 1997 figures:

(i) See attached explanation at (x) below.

(ii) There is a prior year adjustment in the 1997 accounts representing the errors of the eight preceding years.

The additional profits of these eight years were £80,000.

The extra tax on these profits was £20,000.

Therefore the additional after tax retained profits are £60,000.

(iii) The extra £10,000 turnover for 1997 (which is year nine of the misappropriation) carries down in the restated profit and loss account.

(iv) The additional £10,000 profit leads to additional tax of £2,500. The restated profit for the year is therefore £27,500.

(v) The restated retained profits b/f (£130,000), plus restated profit for the year (£27,500) gives restated profit c/f of £157,500.

The next step is to adjust the figures for 1998.

(vi) The prior year adjustment for this year reflects nine previous years of misappropriations. This is £90,000 of additional profits less £22,500 of tax yielding a net £67,500 prior year adjustment.

(vii) The restated retained profit b/f is therefore £157,500 (£90,000 + £67,500). As a check, it can be seen that this is consistent with the closing restated retained profit of the 1997 period (as computed in (v) above).

(viii) The current year adjustment is to increase turnover (and profit) by £10,000, the consequential increase of £2,500 to the tax charge, leaving a net £7,500 increase in current year's profits (before exceptional items).

(ix) In 1998 there arises a payment of interest and penalties of £22,500.

In SSAP 6 days this might – and probably would – have been treated as extraordinary. This is not so under FRS 3. The £22,500 is an exceptional item and is therefore deducted in arriving at the profits for the year of £67,500 (£90,000 –£22,500).

Probably, the £22,500 would be broken down into constituent parts – interest on the one hand, penalties on the other – with the interest element included in the interest charge for the year and the penalty part included in the administration costs or other non-specific overhead. If the amounts are material, these will be disclosed in the notes. (It is possible though that the interest charge is factored into the prior year adjustment.)

As the question of materiality is subjective, and the natural temptation of companies will be not to advertise the fact of their wrongdoing, it is possible that separate disclosure will not be made. Preparers of tax computations for companies recently subject to investigation should be aware that the interest and penalties may be incorporated in the accounts in a less than immediately obvious manner.

(x) The net current assets in the final accounts (£112,500) differ from the draft account (£60,000) by £52,500.

In the first place, the director has improperly withdrawn £100,000 of company funds over ten years. He must be "charged" with this. The amount owing to him by the company (apparently £120,000) needs reducing to £20,000.

On the other hand, the company had additional liabilities compared to the draft accounts of:

Extra tax for 1998	£2,500
Extra tax, interest and penalties for earlier years	£45,000
	£47,500

Therefore, an addition to creditors of £47,500 is required.

The total adjustment to net current assets is £52,500 (£100,000–£47,500). Had the detailed figures for 1997 been available, the equivlent figures for 1997 (see (i) above) could have been derived.'

Appendix O

Business Economics

The Revenue monitor business ratios within industry sectors both locally and nationally and so are in an excellent position to spot those that differ from the 'norm'. It is this 'norm' that worries most people because no two businesses are the same. As a guide the following are typical gross profit margins but it must be realised that these are averages so they can only be used as a trigger to make further enquiries. Detailed information on many businesses can be found in Butterworths Investigation Service.

Bakers	Gross profit	40%–45%
Boarding Kennels	Gross profit	60%–65%
Butchers	Gross profit	28%–32%
Delicatessan	Gross profit	30%
Driving Instructors	Fuel/Takings ratio	1/8
Fish and chip shop	Gross profit	40%–50% [no café]
Fish and chip shop	Gross profit	60% [with café]
Fishmongers	Gross profit	28%–30%
Florists	Gross profit	38%
Greengrocers	Gross profit	28%–30%
General Store	Gross profit	16%–18%
Hairdressers	Purchases/Takings ratio	1/10
Jewellers	Gross profit	30%–40%
Off licence	Gross profit	15%–18%
Pharmacy	Gross profit	20%
Restaurants	Gross profit	75%
Shoe repairer	Gross profit	75%–80%
Taxi drivers	Fuel/takings ratio	1/8 [Hackney] 1/6 [Private Hire]

Appendix P

Checklist for letters of offer [see Chapter 8 para 8.21]

1. Does the offer letter make sense?
2. Is it clear and unambiguous and set out the terms that have been agreed?
3. Does it contain the consideration to be paid by the client?
4. Are all the various taxes, and NIC, set out in the letter?
5. Does it contain a reference to default?
6 Is interest mentioned?
7. Are penalties mentioned?
8. Does it set out the gross offer before deductions?
9. Are the deductions set out clearly?
10. Is payment date precisely defined?
11. Does it specifically exclude duties not included?
12. Is it correctly worded by reference to the intended signatory?

Index